Blackstone

CRIMINAL PROCEDUR. ACT 1

This book is dedicated to the memory of our fathers:

Ronnie Leng and William Joseph Taylor

Blackstone's Guide to the

CRIMINAL PROCEDURE AND INVESTIGATIONS ACT 1996

Roger Leng, LLB
Reader in Law, University of Warwick

and

Richard D. Taylor, MA, LLM, Barrister
Forbes Professor of English Law and Head of Department of Legal Studies, University of Central Lancashire

BLACKSTONE
PRESS LIMITED

First published in Great Britain 1996 by Blackstone Press Limited,
9–15 Aldine Street, London W12 8AW. Telephone 0181-740 2277

ISBN: 1 85431 588 9

British Library Cataloguing in Publication Data
A CIP catalogue record for this book is available from the British Library.

Typeset by Style Photosetting Ltd, Mayfield, East Sussex and
Montage Studios Limited, Tonbridge, Kent
Printed by Livesey Ltd, Shrewsbury, Shropshire

Contents

The Code in Operation
The investigation — The division of police functions — Recording of information — Retention of material — Material which must be retained — Earlier versions of witness statements — Draft statements by expert witnesses — Periods of retention — The schedule of unused material — The influence of the disclosure officer — Sensitive material — Super-sensitive material — Revelation of material to the prosecutor — The mechanics of disclosure to the accused

The Reform of Pre-Trial Proceedings

Preparatory Hearings for Complex Cases
Power to order preparatory hearings — The start of the trial — Orders before the preparatory hearing — Disclosure and clarification of issues — Sanctions for non-disclosure — Rulings at the preparatory hearing

Interlocutory Appeals

Reporting Restrictions
The restrictions on reporting preparatory hearings and appeals — Lifting of restrictions — Breach of reporting restrictions

Introduction — Pre-trial hearings — Rulings — Restrictions on reporting pre-trial rulings — Lifting of restrictions — Breach of reporting restrictions

Indication of Intention as to Plea Before Mode of Trial Decision
Background — The new procedure

Committal Proceedings
Background — The repeal of the transfer for trial provisions — The new modified form of committal proceedings — Forms of evidence admissible at committal proceedings — Committals with and without consideration of the evidence — Changing from summary trial to committal proceedings and vice versa — Other amendments to the Magistrates' Courts Act 1980 — Amendments to other statutes — Admissibility of written statements and depositions at trial — Amendments to notice of transfer procedures — Conclusions

Issue of warrant on non-appearance of accused — Enforcement of payment of fines by justices' clerk without reference to magistrates — Summons to witness and warrant for his arrest — Periods of remand in custody for accused aged under 17 — Attachment of earnings

7 Tainted acquittals   91

Acquittal of D for the original offence — Conviction of a person for an administration of justice offence — The tainting of the acquittal (1): the certification by the court convicting of the administration of justice offence — The tainting of the acquittal (2): the four conditions for an order quashing the acquittal — New proceedings against D for the initial offence — Conclusions

8 Derogatory assertions   107

The power to make an order under s. 58 — Interim orders and full orders — The effect under s. 59 of orders made under s. 58 — The offence of contravening an order — Commencement and supplementary

9 Evidence and miscellaneous provisions   114

Television links and video recordings — Provision of blood and urine specimens: road traffic and transport offences — Checks against fingerprints or samples, etc. — Abolition of witness orders — Summons to (reluctant) witness to attend Crown Court — Indemnification of justices and justices' clerks — Meaning of preliminary stage of criminal proceedings

10 Serious fraud   122

Introduction — Pre-trial disclosure — Power to make orders in advance of preparatory hearings — Failure to disclose and departures from cases disclosed — Reporting restrictions — Lifting restrictions — Breach of reporting restrictions

Preface

Legislation affecting the criminal justice system seems to occur at roughly the same interval as a car service — once every twelve months. Regrettably, in terms of frequency, the two seem to be passing each other in opposite directions. Just as technical advances tend to make service intervals longer for motor cars, the criminal justice system seems to get ever more frequent attention but does not seem to run any more smoothly as a result. The Criminal Procedure and Investigations Act 1996 is another major piece of legislation for the criminal justice system to digest. We hope that our explanation and analysis of it will help those whose work or lives are affected by it, to at least understand it (even if they do not come to love it) and to adjust to it with more confidence and less bewilderment than might otherwise have been the case.

Our thanks are due to all at Blackstone Press for their usual, but nonetheless exceptional, efficiency and support and to Laurence Eastham for his patient and skilful editing above and beyond the call of duty even at the last moment as he departed for his holidays. We have also been fortunate in the support and understanding of our families at a time of the year when they could legitimately have expected to be seeing more not less of us. One could say, just as with the Act itself, that it is all a question of balance and we hope that, in each respect, we have got the balance somewhere near right as, perhaps appropriately, on the autumn equinox, we conclude this preface.

Roger Leng
Richard Taylor
22 September 1996

Introduction

The Criminal Procedure and Investigations Act 1996 is the latest major instalment of criminal justice legislation introduced by the present Conservative Government. As such it represents a determined attempt to finish the package of reforms foreshadowed by the Home Secretary's twenty-seven point plan set out in his speech to the Conservative Party Conference in October 1993. It also embodies the Government's response to a number of proposals contained in the Report of the Royal Commission on Criminal Justice (1993, Cmnd 2263). More immediately the Government's legislative plans were set out in a trio of Consultation Papers on *Disclosure* (Cmnd 2864), *Mode of trial* (Cmnd 2908) and *Improving the effectiveness of pre-trial hearings in the Crown Court* (Cmnd 2924).

In introducing the Bill at second reading, the Home Secretary (Michael Howard) spoke of the responsibility of any government to ensure that the criminal justice system is:

fair, efficient and effective — fair towards all those affected by it, efficient in focusing on the issues that really matter at trial, and effective in bringing about the acquittal of the innocent and the conviction of the guilty. The Bill is intended to meet those aims . . . it is designed to restore the balance in our criminal justice system — to make life tougher for the criminal and to improve the protection of the public.

Not everyone would agree that the Act is calculated to achieve such a proper balance and the emphasis of the Act might be thought to have more to do with efficiency and effectiveness than with fairness. Even though the Act was not as controversial as the Criminal Justice and Public Order Act 1994, the varied and contrasting views of participants in the criminal justice system on the right balance to be struck ensure that argument and debate about the various changes introduced by the Act is inevitable, proper and healthy.

The provisions of the Act

The most controversial provisions of the Act are found in Part I which creates a radical new scheme for compulsory pre-trial disclosure. This is an area which has already seen dramatic developments in recent years. The judges, increasingly aware of the link between miscarriages of justice and unused material lurking in police files, have acted decisively, in the best common law traditions, to create a prosecution duty to disclose under the firm supervision of the courts (e.g., *Ward* [1993] 1 WLR 619).

The Government's interest in this area was however stimulated by factors additional to the prevention of miscarriages of justice. The major concern was that allowing defendants to withhold their defences, whilst having full access to prosecution files, tipped the balance too far in favour of the criminal and away from the public interest in punishing offenders. This argument was based upon largely anecdotal evidence of unmerited acquittals following defence ambushes in court; horror stories about the massive burdens placed upon police forces by the duty to supply evidence to accused persons; and claims that prosecutions had been dropped following court orders which if implemented would have disclosed sensitive material such as the identities of informants or details of investigation techniques.

In response to these concerns, the Act cuts down the prosecution duty to disclose relevant material and places the defendant under a duty to disclose his defence pre-trial. If this is done secondary disclosure of material which might assist that defence should follow. Although the court's power to order the disclosure of sensitive material is retained, the chances of this occurring will be reduced because it is no longer a requirement to disclose the existence of sensitive material which the prosecutor considers is irrelevant to the defence. For the accused, the sanction for non-disclosure will be the risk of adverse inferences being drawn at trial. In this respect the 1996 Act follows the Criminal Justice and Public Order Act 1994 in treating omissions by the accused or his legal representatives as potential sources of evidence against him. For the police and prosecutor, failing to disclose material which might be vital to the accused's defence, attracts no obvious sanction. In this respect the Government have clearly been successful in tipping the balance between the interests of the prosecution and the accused.

Among the claims made for the disclosure scheme are that it will clarify issues pre-trial, lead to earlier pleas and reduce the time spent on argument in court. A consideration of how the procedure will work in practice suggests a different picture. The procedure may well generate disputes about whether disclosure has been properly made, which will be dealt with in pre-trial hearings. The trial itself is likely to become bogged down in arguments about whether the defence in court is different from the defence disclosed and if so whether or not there is some acceptable explanation. Directions to juries will tend to become more complicated since they must cover not only the direct evidence but also possible inferences. In the early years numerous extra appeals can be expected in order to clarify some of the questions left open by the legislation. It must be queried whether the extra work for the courts in dealing with issues which are essentially collateral to guilt, will be either economic or productive of justice.

The disclosure scheme will be complemented by Part II which authorises the Home Secretary to promulgate a Code of Practice which for the first time seeks to regulate the police in collecting evidence and in retaining, documenting and disclosing it. At the time of writing, a draft Code has been published for consultation purposes and it is intended that the final version will be laid before Parliament for approval in autumn 1996.

Parts III and IV provide for new pre-trial procedures which are designed to improve efficiency, reduce complexity in trials and to encourage guilty pleas earlier rather than later in the process. Part IV which applies in relation to all Crown Court trials, enhances the effectiveness of pre-trial proceedings by empowering the judge to make binding rulings relating to admissibility of evidence and questions of law. Part III allows judges to order more elaborate preparatory hearings, similar to those used for serious fraud, for cases which are complex or where the trial is likely to be lengthy.

Part V of the Act represents a spectacular about turn by the Government in relation to its initial decision to abolish committal proceedings and replace them with transfer for trial as provided for in s. 44 and sch. 4 of the Criminal Justice and Public Order Act 1994. Implementation of these provisions had been postponed three times because of technical problems and widespread opposition to the changes from lawyers and others working in the magistrates' courts. Amendments to the 1994 provisions were added to the Bill at an early stage in an attempt to resolve the problems and meet the criticisms but in the face of continuing criticism by the Law Society and others these amendments were abandoned when the Bill reached the Commons Committee stage. Instead, the transfer for trial provisions in the 1994 Act have been repealed without ever having been brought into effect. In their place, Part V of the Act streamlines the existing system of committals by limiting them to the consideration of documentary evidence tendered by the prosecution (and none by the defence) with no calling of witnesses to give oral evidence.

A number of other changes to procedures in the magistrates' courts are made by Part VI of the Act, the most significant of which is the requirement for the accused to give an indication of his intention as to plea before determination of mode of trial in either way cases. This change is designed to reduce the number of cases unnecessarily committed to the Crown Court for trial where the accused intends to plead guilty anyway. It is intended to reduce the pressure on the Crown Court but is also likely to produce corresponding increases in the number of defendants sentenced by magistrates and in the number of committals for sentence to the Crown Court.

As part of the increased emphasis on ensuring the conviction of the guilty as well as the acquittal of the innocent, Part VII of the Act contains a new procedure for enabling an acquitted person to be retried where the acquittal is 'tainted' in the sense that it subsequently appears likely to have resulted from criminal intimidation or interference with a juror or witness. The procedure is a lengthy and cumbersome one which is unlikely to be invoked in very many instances but it is nevertheless a significant exception to the normal fundamental rule against double jeopardy.

Part VII also seeks to protect witnesses, victims and others who are the subject of unjustified derogatory assertions in pleas in mitigation and other similar submissions. The protection is afforded by enabling the court to prohibit the reporting of such assertions. Part VII also contains a number of other miscellaneous provisions. Some of these deal with the law of evidence in relation to television links and video recordings for child witnesses, in relation to the taking of blood or urine samples at police stations in respect of alcohol-related driving offences, and in relation to speculative searches of records of fingerprints and samples. Other provisions deal with inter alia the indemnification of Justices and Justices' Clerks against costs orders in criminal proceedings, and the meaning of the 'preliminary stage of criminal proceedings' is modified so as to clarify and tighten the period during which an accused person may be kept in custody before trial.

Drafting and presentation

Quite apart from the changes outlined above, the merits or otherwise of the Act are worthy of debate in terms of the style of drafting and presentation which has been adopted. This manifests itself in a number of ways.

First, there is the lack of a general commencement section with instead a number of appointed day provisions dispersed throughout the Act. The lack of a commencement section means that in principle the whole of the Act came into force on Royal Assent (4 July 1996). However, it is only true in a weak sense to say that the Act 'came into force' on this date because in the majority of instances, the Act only applies to acts done (or omitted to be done) on or after the various days to be appointed by the Secretary of State under numerous sections of the Act for numerous different purposes.

For example, ss. 54 to 57 dealing with tainted acquittals do not have a commencement date nor is there any power given to make a commencement order as such in relation to those sections. It follows that they came into force on Royal Assent. However, s. 54, which contains the crucial power to quash a tainted acquittal, provides in s. 54(7) that 'this section applies in relation to acquittals in respect of offences alleged to be committed on or after the appointed day' which under s. 54(8) is 'such day as is appointed for the purposes of this section by the Secretary of State by order'. Thus although the section is technically in force (as it has to be to give the Secretary of State power to make the appointed day order) it can have no practical application until the appointed day order is made.

Although the absence of a general commencement section may at first cause some surprise and even disorientation for anyone expecting to find it at the end of the Act, the method actually adopted is in some ways an improvement in that it is more evidently precise. If there had merely been a section stating that s. 54 shall come into force on a day to be appointed that might have left open the question of whether, once it is in force, it makes quashing orders available if:

(a)   the conviction for an administration of justice offence was obtained on or after that date, or if

(b)   the original acquittal had to come on or after that date, or whether

(c)   the original offence had to come on or after this date.

As is discussed in Chapter Seven, s. 54(7) makes it clear that the third option is the one chosen and that maximum non-retrospectivity is thereby ensured. Of course, such clarity and precision can be, and often is, obtained by a commencement section coupled with a subsection similar to s. 54(7) which refers to commencement rather than to the appointed day (e.g., see s. 34 CJPO 1994 together with s. 172(2)). The virtue, if there is one, of the new practice is that the question of commencement of a particular provision is effectively dealt with in just one place, where the relevant substantive provisions are located, rather than in two. The defect, if it is one, is that effective commencement provisions are to be found scattered throughout the Act and a person coming to the Act for the first time may spend and waste time looking for a commencement provision in its normal position at the end of the Act. The new arrangement may well be more logical and convenient but its very novelty may cause some inconvenience and yet no publicity seems to have been given to it either by discussion in *Hansard* or elsewhere.

The appointed day mechanism is used repeatedly throughout the Act and at the appropriate point in this guide we indicate when the appointed day for each provision is expected to be. It should also be noted that occasionally there is indeed a reference to 'commencement' rather than to an appointed day. Thus, para. 39 of sch. 1 is headed

'Commencement' and states that the rest of the Schedule 'shall have effect in accordance with provision made by the Secretary of State by Order'. This much less specific provision has to be read in conjunction with s. 77(3) which authorises such an order to include 'such supplementary, incidental, consequential or transitional provisions as appear to be necessary or expedient'. Schedule 1 is concerned to make the necessary amendments to the Magistrates' Courts Act 1980 and to other statutes to enable the changes to committal proceedings to be introduced. The less specific formula used in para. 39 means that the precise details of commencement and the related transitional issues are left to the order itself rather than being spelled out in the Act. Again there is nothing really new in this except that one would normally expect to find a simple commencement provision such as sch. 1, para. 39 at the end of the Act, collected together with other similar provisions rather than seeing them dispersed throughout. (See also, e.g., sch. 2, para. 7, s. 67(2) and s. 65(4)).

A second interesting feature of the drafting of the Act is the use of examples. In so far as this makes clearer the legislative intent, this can again be welcomed. Thus s. 56(2) gives some examples in an attempt to make clear the effect of s. 56(1) (see Chapter Seven for a discussion of the extent to which it succeeds). Section 24 is wholly concerned to give examples but this is somewhat more problematic (see the discussion in Chapter Two) since the examples are, unlike those in s. 56(2), not illustrations of the *actual* effect of a substantive provision but rather examples of the *kind* of thing which *may* be included in a Code of Practice but which equally, presumably, may be left out. It also begs all sorts of questions about whether *other* kinds of things may be included and indeed as to whether a particular provision is of the same kind as an example or is a different kind of thing and if so whether it may legitimately be included.

A third aspect of the drafting of the Act worthy of comment comes in s. 44(6) which provides that the Criminal Justice and Public Order Act 1994 'shall be treated as having been enacted with the amendments made by subsections (2) and (5)'. The amendments referred to are those which repeal s. 44 and sch. 4 of the 1994 Act which were originally intended to abolish committal proceedings and replace them with a new transfer for trial procedure. To do this they would have made substantial changes to ss. 4 to 8 of the Magistrates' Courts Act 1980 but these changes were never brought into force. Given that s. 44 and sch. 4 of the 1994 Act were never brought into force and the changes foreshadowed by them were never implemented, it would have been sufficient merely to repeal s. 44 and sch. 4 prospectively in the normal way and quite unnecessary to have the unusual retrospective repeal contained in s. 44(6) of the 1996 Act. The point is further discussed in Chapter Five but perhaps the best explanation to add to that discussion is the fact that the commencement of s. 44 and sch. 4 had been promised so many times that in some quarters, e.g., *Stone's Justices Manual* for 1995, the Magistrates' Courts Act 1980 had actually been printed as though already amended by s. 44 and sch. 4! In these circumstances, the retrospective repeal, whilst not necessary in law, may have some point if it emphasises, to anyone inadvertently misled, that the transfer for trial amendments have *never* been in force.

In view of the fact that this Act represents the culmination of a reform agenda set some years ago, it might have been expected that its provisions would have been thoroughly prepared in advance and that the Bill would have completed its Parliamentary stages without very substantial amendment. In fact the Bill was subject to numerous changes and additions throughout its Parliamentary passage which more than doubled its size. The result, paradoxically, was ambush of Parliament. Time which would normally be devoted to considering opposition amendments was spent introducing hundreds of Government amendments. Because of last-minute changes in the Bill many carefully prepared Opposition amendments simply had to be torn up and because of time constraints, large sections of the Bill were hardly considered at all.

Implementation and extent

The Act generally extends to Northern Ireland with the exceptions of the provisions on preparatory hearings in Part III and the provisions relating to magistrates' courts' procedure in Part VI (s. 79(3)). Those provisions which apply to Northern Ireland are modified as necessary by sch. 4 (s. 79(4)). The Act does not generally apply to Scotland (s. 79(1)) except for s. 63 which amends the law concerning the provision of samples for drink-driving offences, and s. 73 which makes three minor amendments to the Criminal Procedure (Scotland) Act 1995. Various reporting restrictions, relating to preparatory hearings (ss. 37 and 38), pre-trial rulings (ss. 41 and 42), derogatory assertions (ss. 59–61) and preparatory hearings for serious fraud offences (s. 72 and sch. 3), also extend to Scotland.

Generally the Act does not apply to proceedings relating to Courts Martial or Standing Civilian Courts (s. 78(1)). However, the Act confers a power on the Secretary of State to make provisions corresponding to Parts I (disclosure) and II (investigations) in relation to Courts Martial (s. 78(2)).

As mentioned earlier, the Act contains no commencement section and therefore came into force on Royal Assent on 4 July 1996. However, individual sections do not generally have any real operational effect until such day as is appointed by order of the Home Secretary under the power applicable to the relevant section. (Section 64 is one of the few which not only comes into force on Royal Assent but also applies to events occurring after Royal Assent rather than after an appointed day; see s. 64(2).) Appointed day orders are to be made by statutory instrument (s. 77(4)) and are not subject to prior Parliamentary scrutiny (s. 77(5)) except in the case of an order under s. 25. Unusually, the Act specifically reserves to the Home Secretary the power to make such orders differently in relation to different classes of case or different parts of the country (s. 77(2)). Thus, the Act accommodates the possibility of piloting a new procedure in one area prior to its general introduction. Orders under the Act may also include 'such supplementary, consequential or transitional provisions' as appear necessary or expedient (s. 77(3)). This important tidying-up facility may prove invaluable in view of the hasty preparation and limited Parliamentary scrutiny enjoyed by many of the provisions. For our part, conscious that we cannot subsequently amend this Guide by statutory instrument, we have given the Act as much careful scrutiny as time would allow and have tried to avoid any errors which might be attributable to hasty preparation. We hope that our efforts will enable the reader not only to understand the Act's provisions but to evaluate them as well.

Chapter One
Disclosure in Criminal Proceedings

Part I of the Criminal Procedure and Investigations Act 1996 contains radical new procedures for compulsory reciprocal pre-trial disclosure for all cases to be tried on indictment. A similar scheme, which is voluntary for the accused, applies to contested summary cases. These provisions are complemented by Part II which regulates the retention and disclosure of material collected by the police in the course of criminal investigations.

The first stage of the procedure involves disclosure by the prosecutor of material which might undermine the prosecution case (s. 3). Where this has been done in a Crown Court case, the accused is placed under a duty to provide a defence statement and supporting information (s. 5). Where a case is to be tried summarily, the accused may choose to provide this information (s. 6). Following receipt of the defence statement, the prosecutor must make secondary disclosure of material which might assist the accused's defence (s. 7). Failure by the accused to provide a defence statement or departure from it in court may lead to adverse comment or the jury drawing adverse inferences (s. 11). The power of the court to order that material should not be disclosed in the public interest is confirmed, subject to a duty of the court to keep the issue under review and a right of the accused to request a review (s. 15).

BACKGROUND TO THE REFORM

The new scheme may be seen as a natural and perhaps inevitable product of the development of both the philosophy and practice of criminal justice over recent years. Thus, pre-trial disclosure had been piloted (although not with conspicuous success) in the field of serious fraud, and its general adoption had been recommended by the Royal Commission on Criminal Justice (1993, Cm 2263, 91–100). Prior to this, proposals for disclosure had been made by the Home Office Working Group on the Right to Silence in 1989; by the Law Society and the Crown Prosecution Service in their evidence to the Royal Commission; and by the Civil Liberty Panel on Criminal Justice (P. Thornton et al *Justice on Trial*, 1993) whose deliberations shadowed those of the Royal Commission.

The introduction of a disclosure scheme, which gives courts coercive powers for eliciting evidence and which for defendants substitutes duties for freedom of action, also reflects current debate about adopting a more inquisitorial style of procedure (e.g., Field, 'Judicial supervision of the pre-trial process' (1994) 21 JLS 119). Although a wholesale shift to an inquisitorial system was rejected by the Royal Commission, there is no doubt that the inquisitorial model influenced its thinking.

In practical terms, the introduction of disclosure fits the current trend in both criminal and civil justice to take judicial administration seriously and to wrest control of proceedings from the hands of the parties in the interests of efficiency and value for money. In the criminal context, this trend is already reflected in non-statutory pre-trial plea and directions hearings, which have institutionalised the notion of preparation for trial (or trial avoidance) as a common and cooperative, rather than adversarial, enterprise. That development of court practice is now adopted and enhanced in a coherent structure of proceedings before the empanelment of the jury, which includes not only the disclosure procedures discussed here but also a new power for judges to make pre-trial rulings (see Chapter Four) and a new preparatory stage for long or complex cases (Chapter Three).

The provisions on disclosure were also foreshadowed by the Criminal Justice and Public Order Act 1994, which effectively placed a duty on the accused to disclose aspects of his defence to the police and therefore paved the way for the acceptance of a fuller system of compulsory pre-trial defence disclosure. The 1994 Act was also significant in overcoming the law's traditional reluctance to penalise the silent or uncooperative defendant by drawing adverse evidential inferences against him.

In view of the trends described above, and the political appeal at a time when an election is imminent of measures which are presented as getting tough on crime, it is not surprising that compulsory disclosure was broadly supported in Parliament even by the opposition parties. It would be wrong however to assume that these measures are uncontroversial. Indeed, doubts may be expressed about the credibility of the Government's arguments concerning the need for reform, about the particular balance between prosecution and defence which the legislation achieves, about whether it will deliver the promised benefits in terms of efficiency and savings in time, and about the morality and logic of treating non-compliance with administrative duties as evidence relevant to the issue of guilt on a criminal charge.

The Government's case for reform

The Government's main arguments for reform were expressed both in the Home Office Consultation Document *Disclosure* (1995, Cm 2864) and in debate in Parliament. On the second reading in the Commons, the Home Secretary suggested that the disclosure provisions would restore the balance of the criminal justice system by making life tougher for criminals whilst improving the protection of the public. The arrangements for disclosure then existing were described as requiring too much of the prosecution and too little of the defence.

Three particular problems were identified. First, it was argued that the accused could place heavy and unnecessary burdens on the police by requesting reams of material whether or not it had any relevance to the defence he proposed to run at trial. Secondly, it was argued that there was inadequate protection for sensitive material, such as the identity of informants, because the courts tended to require disclosure in cases where the relevance of such material was marginal at best. It was further suggested that because of the willingness of courts to order disclosure, all too often the prosecution were forced to abandon cases, however strong the prosecution evidence, in order to protect sensitive material. Thirdly, it was suggested that the present arrangements facilitated ambush defences and consequent unmerited acquittals. Contrasting the burdens on the prosecution, the Home Secretary claimed that, with a few specified exceptions, the accused need not disclose anything about his defence until trial. This, it was argued, did not contribute to the efficiency of the trial because it encouraged defendants to come forward with plausible, but false, defences at a very late stage (*Hansard*, Commons, 27 February 1996, cols 738–740).

Burdens of disclosure   The Home Secretary's claims concerning the burdens of disclosure and the abandonment of strong cases in order to avoid disclosing sensitive material have been criticised as misrepresenting the law and lacking supporting evidence (Justice *Disclosure: a consultation paper. The Justice response,* 1995; Liberty *Disclosure: a consultation document,* 1995). The test for what must be disclosed is materiality, defined by Lord Taylor CJ in *Keane* [1994] 1 WLR 746 as:

> ... that which can be seen on a sensible appraisal by the prosecution: (a) to be relevant or possibly relevant to an issue in the case; (b) to raise or possibly raise a new issue whose existence is not apparent from the evidence the prosecution proposes to use; (c) to hold out a real, as opposed to fanciful, prospect of providing a lead on evidence which goes to (a) or (b).

This test is clearly stricter than marginal relevance, as claimed by the Home Secretary, and is applied by the prosecutor. The task of inspecting investigative material to determine whether the test applies would inevitably place a burden on the police or prosecutor, but it must be borne in mind that this will be in proportion to the weight of the case. Thus, for major investigations for which a lot of material is collected, the burden of considering whether any of it might be material to the defence would be significant. On the other hand, for the great bulk of cases for which all the evidence collected is found in the prosecution file and disclosed to the accused, the burden is nil.

Inadequate protection for sensitive material   The claim that many strong cases have been dropped following court orders to disclose sensitive material is also doubtful. Although the Association of Chief Police Officers have publicised the existence of a dossier of 73 cases which have been dropped to protect sensitive information, this dossier has yet to be made available for external scrutiny (Pollard, C., 'A case for disclosure' [1994] Crim LR 42; 'Police fury as legal system lets off 1 in 3', *Sunday Times* 9 July 1995).

The implication that the relevant legal test is too liberal in permitting the disclosure of sensitive material is also misleading. This issue of disclosure should arise only where the prosecutor identifies the material in question as potentially relevant. The prosecutor should then place the material before the court for a decision on disclosure. In cases where the very existence of the material is sensitive information, the application may be made in the absence of the defence (*Davis, Johnson and Rowe* [1993] 1 WLR 613). Where the material falls within a well-established sensitive category, such as the identity of an informant, the presumption is against disclosure. The court may however order disclosure if the public interest in confidentiality is outweighed by the competing public interest in enabling a defendant to put forward a tenable defence (*Agar* [1990] 2 All ER 442). As was made clear in *Keane*, this test will be difficult for the accused to satisfy, unless he is prepared to disclose and substantiate his intended line of defence. As described, the law would not appear to offer the easy means of sabotaging the prosecution which the Home Secretary implies.

Ambush defences and unmerited acquittals   The ambush defence argument is now familiar, having already underpinned the encroachments on the right to silence in the Criminal Justice and Public Order Act 1994. The argument however remains unsubstantiated by those who propose it: the available research evidence suggests that, prior to 1994, ambush defences were very rare and succeeded even more rarely (see R. Leng *The right to silence in police interrogation*, 1993, Royal Commission on Criminal Justice Research Study No. 10. Chap. 5). There has been no research to indicate what the position is since the 1994 Act came into force. However, it seems unlikely that any ambush problem has worsened in view of ss. 36 and 37 of the 1994 Act, which encourage suspects to give an early explanation for incriminating objects, substances and marks and for their presence near the scene of a crime, and s. 34, which provides for adverse inferences to be drawn when a defence is raised at court which had not been mentioned by the accused when interviewed or charged. The Home Secretary's statement that 'with a few specified exceptions, the accused need not disclose anything about his defence until trial' (*Hansard*, Commons, 27 February 1996, col. 738) is remarkable in view of the fact that s. 34 applies in every case in which the suspect in the police station contemplates raising a defence in court.

The carrot and stick principle

The new statutory scheme of extensive prosecution disclosure can be presented as a direct linear descendant of prosecution disclosure as developed at common law and by the Attorney-General's Guidelines. But this is to misunderstand the nature and purpose of the new legislation and the extent of departure from the common law position. The motivations for the common law rules were natural justice for the accused, tempered by the constitutional principle that a prosecutor on behalf of the Crown should not seek a conviction at all costs but should function as a minister of justice. From these principles it followed that the accused was entitled to know of any weakness in the Crown's case, and also that the fruits of investigations by the police as a state agency should be available even-handedly to both sides.

Although natural justice has not been completely banished, the new scheme has other motivations. In particular it aims for efficiency by clarifying and narrowing issues at the earliest opportunity, and seeks the conviction of the guilty by preventing ambush defences. These aims are pursued by rationing the defendant's access to the fruits of state investigations and by a carrot and stick approach to encouraging early disclosure of the defence. The carrot is dangled by restricting initial access to prosecution material but with the promise of further disclosure of relevant material once a defence has been disclosed. The stick is the threat of adverse inferences to be drawn against a defendant who raises a defence in court which has not been previously disclosed.

THE DISCLOSURE PROCEDURE

Cases to which the procedure applies

The disclosure procedure applies in relation to two categories of case which are set out in s. 1(1) and (2). Primary prosecution disclosure under s. 3 must be made for both categories. Once this has been completed, disclosure by the accused is compulsory under s. 5 for cases to be tried on indictment (s. 1(2)) whereas for contested summary cases (s. 1(1)) the accused has an option to make disclosure under s. 6.

The cases to which the compulsory procedure applies under s. 1(2) comprise:

(a)   indictable offences which are committed for trial;
(b)   indictable cases of serious or complex fraud which are transferred to the Crown Court for trial under the Criminal Justice Act 1987;
(c)   indictable child abuse cases which are transferred to the Crown Court under s. 53 of the Criminal Justice Act 1991;
(d)   summary offences which are included in indictments by virtue of being based on the same facts as indictable offences, under s. 40 of the Criminal Justice Act 1988;
(e)   cases for which a voluntary bill of indictment is preferred.

The voluntary procedure applies to all not guilty pleas tried summarily, including cases involving young persons under the age of 18 which are tried summarily in the youth court (s. 1(1)).

Throughout, the Act refers to the accused only and it is not provided that that which may be done by the accused may be done also by his legal representative. The Government argued that such a provision would be unnecessary since it is implicit that what may be done by the accused may be done by his legal representative (*Hansard*, Commons Standing Committee B, 14 May 1996, col. 30). Presumably, the courts will interpret the disclosure provisions in this way.

Disclosure of the prosecution evidence

At the time when the issue of primary prosecution disclosure arises, the defence will normally have received some notice of the prosecution case. For cases to be tried on indictment this will involve copies of the evidence on which the prosecution intend to rely of the following types:

(a)   evidence required to be tendered at committal proceedings (under s. 4(3) of the Magistrates' Courts Act 1980, as substituted by sch. 1 to the 1996 Act);
(b)   evidence supplied in relation to transferred child abuse cases, under para. 4 of sch. 6 to the Criminal Justice Act 1991;
(c)   evidence supplied in relation to transferred serious fraud cases under s. 5(9) of the Criminal Justice Act 1987; or
(d)   in relation to voluntary bills of indictment, evidence supplied under r. 9(1)(a) of the Indictments (Procedure) Rules 1971 (SI 1971 No. 2084).

For cases which are triable either way but which are actually tried summarily, the defence may currently obtain advance disclosure of either (at the discretion of the

Crown Prosecution Service) copies of the prosecution evidence or a summary of the prosecution case, under the Magistrates' Courts (Advance Information) Rules 1985 (SI 1985 No. 601). In view of research evidence as to the poor quality of police summaries it is doubtful whether as a matter of practice providing case summaries only should be considered acceptable, although such summaries remain acceptable as a matter of law (see J. Baldwin *Preparing the record of taped interview*, 1993, Royal Commission on Criminal Justice Research Study No. 2). For purely summary cases the defence presently have no right to advance disclosure. However, since disclosure is in the interests of both parties in disposing of the case efficiently, it will often be granted routinely if requested by the defence, on the same basis as for either way offences.

It should be noted that in all of the above circumstances the prosecution duty is to supply evidence or a summary of evidence rather than the prosecution case. Thus, the accused may have to rely upon her lawyers to guess at what inferences the prosecution would draw from the factual evidence disclosed.

Primary prosecution disclosure

The prosecutor's duty of primary disclosure under the Act is to disclose to the accused any prosecution material which has not previously been disclosed and which in the prosecutor's opinion might undermine the case for the prosecution (s. 3(1)). The schedule of non-sensitive unused prosecution material must also be disclosed if at that stage it has been received from the police officer responsible for disclosing material to the prosecutor (disclosure officer) (s. 4(1)). The implication is that if the prosecutor makes primary disclosure before the non-sensitive schedule is received, the duty to release the schedule to the accused is abrogated. This does not make sense and is unsatisfactory. It does not make sense because the prosecutor cannot exercise the necessary judgment about whether there is undisclosed undermining material, until after he has considered the schedule and copies of potentially undermining material supplied by the disclosure officer. It is also unsatisfactory in that it suggests that the duty to release the schedule may depend upon the time at which disclosure is made.

This state of affairs is not corrected by the prosecutor's continuing duty to disclose under s. 9 which relates only to material which might undermine the prosecution or assist the defence. It is to be hoped that prosecutors will follow the spirit of the Act rather than its letter and disclose the non-sensitive schedule when available as a matter of course where this has not been done at primary disclosure.

It is intended that the duty of primary disclosure, and the further stages of disclosure, should be subject to time limits (s. 3(8)) to be set by regulations to be made by the Secretary of State (s. 12). No time limits will be set until the Government have had an opportunity to monitor the Act in operation. Until limits are set, the prosecutor's duty is to act as soon as is reasonably practicable after the accused pleads not guilty (for cases tried summarily) or after the time when the case falls within the jurisdiction of the Crown Court (s. 13(1)).

Rather oddly, for summary cases the accused has a right to disclosure of material undermining the prosecution case, but not to the evidence on which the prosecution case is based. At committee stage in the Lords, Baroness Mallalieu proposed an amendment which would have required full disclosure of the prosecution evidence for all cases, thereby assimilating summary and indictable procedure in this respect (*Hansard*, Lords, 19 December 1995, cols 1448–9). It is unfortunate that the Government chose not to accept this sensible amendment which would have both removed the anomaly relating to disclosure in summary cases and avoided problems associated with reliance on police summaries.

The duty to disclose relates to prosecution material which is defined by s. 3(2) as:

(a)   material which came into the prosecutor's possession in connection with the case against the accused; or

(b)   material which the prosecutor has inspected under the Code of Practice governing investigations made under Part II.

Exemptions are made for material which a court decides it is not in the public interest to disclose (s. 3(6)) and for material obtained under the Interception of Communications Act 1985 (s. 3(7)). Where there is no material which in the prosecutor's opinion might undermine the prosecution case, the prosecutor must provide the accused with a written statement to this effect (s. 3(1)(b)).

Material undermining the prosecution case

The test for primary prosecution disclosure is whether in the prosecutor's opinion the material might undermine the case for the prosecution (s. 3(1)). This is a subjective test (based on the prosecutor's opinion) which contrasts with an objective test (might reasonably be expected) for secondary prosecution disclosure in s. 7(2). The explanation given for the disparity is that the subjective test for primary disclosure is designed to rule out the possibility of judicial review, whereas challenge in the courts is contemplated in relation to alleged failures of secondary disclosure (*Hansard*, Lords, 18 December 1995, cols 1441–2). This reasoning is consistent with the accused's right to challenge prosecution disclosure (or lack of it) after secondary disclosure (s. 8).

Although the Act does not prescribe a means of challenging the scope of primary disclosure, the accused, armed with the schedule of unused material, may request disclosure of further identified items. Any such request should be considered by the prosecutor in pursuance of the continuing duty to keep under review the question whether there is prosecution material which has not been disclosed and which might undermine the prosecution case (s. 9(2)).

Certain matters for which a duty to disclose has been developed at common law will fall squarely within the category of that which might undermine the prosecution case. These include previous inconsistent statements or criminal records of prosecution witnesses, and any request for a reward by a prosecution witness (*Taylor*, 11 June 1993 (unreported); *Rasheed* (1994) *The Times*, 20 May 1994). As was made clear by the Court of Appeal in *Winston Brown* [1994] 1 WLR 1599, this list is not closed and disclosure would be required also for other collateral material which could affect the credibility of a prosecution witness.

It is apparent that the Government considers that the undermining test is considerably narrower than the test of relevance which was developed at common law. Thus, attempts to reinstate the relevance test were resisted on the basis that it would do nothing to narrow the issues and would leave the police with a considerable burden of disclosure. Similarly, a proposed amendment which would have extended the duty of primary disclosure to material which might assist the defence was rejected on the ground that it might require the prosecutor to hand over material which was not ultimately used and that this would be inefficient and unnecessary (*Hansard*, Lords, 18 December 1995, cols 1436–47). The implication is that the prosecution case would be undermined by material such as a prior inconsistent statement by a witness, which affects the credibility of a particular item of prosecution evidence, but would not be undermined by evidence supporting a discrete defence.

Under the doctrine of *Pepper* v *Hart* [1993] AC 593, the courts may refer to *Hansard* and thus may accept the Government's narrow view of the undermine test as representing the law. That the undermine test is narrower than common law tests is also implicit in the abolition of common law disclosure rules by s. 21. However, the concept of undermining is ambiguous and there are arguments relating to the normal meaning of the word, the statutory context and policy which might suggest a broader definition.

A consideration of the ordinary meaning of undermine suggests a wider test than that favoured by the Government. If something is undermined it is likely to fall or fail. A prosecution case is likely to fail if found to have some internal inconsistency or flaw. Equally the prosecution case is likely to fail if the accused is successful in establishing an alternative hypothesis to explain the events in question, or the accused establishes a discrete defence such as self-defence or duress, in either case without directly challenging a single piece of prosecution evidence. In both circumstances it would be natural to describe the prosecution case as undermined.

It is also important to note that the test is whether the prosecution case *might* be undermined. This suggests that evidence should be disclosed even if its undermining potential depends upon some contingency, such as whether or not the defendant chooses to run a particular line of defence. It also suggests that it is sufficient if the material in question has a mere tendency to undermine the prosecution, rather than necessarily doing so on its own. On this basis material might undermine the prosecution, and therefore should be disclosed, if it either directly compromises the weight of some prosecution evidence or if it might support one of a number of possible cases which the accused might hypothetically raise.

A strong argument in policy may also be raised for interpreting the undermine test widely. The Government appear to consider that a case is undermined only where there is material which weakens a specific piece of prosecution evidence. If this is correct, it would be permissible to keep from the defence material which might if true might support a defence. The only argument for exempting such material from primary disclosure is that an accused who has a genuine defence will suffer no prejudice since he will have an opportunity to raise his defence and, if he does so, the relevant material can be released to him on secondary disclosure. This argument works only if it is assumed that all true defences will be known to the accused. This proposition will be true in relation to many simple incidents. Thus, a man charged with occasioning actual bodily harm should not require disclosure in order to work out whether he was acting in self-defence or not. The proposition is clearly not true in relation to more complex crimes such as large-scale frauds. Where a business person is implicated in serious fraud by a mass of circumstantial rather than direct evidence, there will clearly be a possibility that she is innocent. If she is innocent it may be necessary for her lawyers to argue a hypothesis which explains the evidence in a way which is consistent with her innocence. Her very ignorance of the events in question may make it almost impossible to do this without the assistance of material which has been collected in the course of the investigation, but which does not favour the prosecution case.

Who decides what is disclosed?

In the course of the Bill's passage there was considerable debate about precisely who would determine what would undermine the prosecution case and therefore what would be disclosed to the defence. The Government stoutly and repeatedly claimed that the decision would rest with the prosecutor (*Hansard*, Commons Standing Committee B, 30 April 1996, col. 4). In fact a consideration of the material which must be disclosed in the light of the Code (in its present draft form) suggests that the police will exercise considerable influence over what is ultimately seen by the defence.

The first head of disclosable material, that which is in the prosecutor's possession, will include a number of categories of material which are intrinsically likely to undermine the prosecution case, and which accordingly the police must supply to the prosecutor under para. 7.3 of the draft Code. These categories are:

(a)   records of the first description of a suspect given to the police by a potential witness;

(b)   any information provided by the accused which indicates an explanation for the offence in question;

(c)   material casting doubt on the reliability of a confession or of a witness; and

(d)   any other material which the investigator believes may fall within the test for primary prosecution disclosure.

It is also the duty of the disclosure officer to alert the prosecutor to material which is retained by the investigator but which may fall within the test for primary disclosure (draft Code, para. 7.1).

In making primary prosecution disclosure under s. 3, the prosecutor will be assisted by the efforts of the police in identifying material which might undermine the prosecution case. Although the prosecutor will have been provided with a schedule of unused material, it is unlikely that this will provide sufficient information to indicate the relevance or otherwise of the material. This suggests that in most cases the issue of what material is to be disclosed to the accused will be made by the police.

The mechanics of prosecution disclosure

The prosecutor's duty to disclose information is satisfied by securing that a copy of it, in whatever form the prosecutor thinks fit, is supplied to the defence, or where in the prosecutor's opinion this is not desirable or practicable, by allowing the material to be inspected at a reasonable time and place (s. 3(3) and (4)). Thus, the prosecutor may supply copies in the form of a transcript of a tape recording, or photocopies, or on computer disk. If the prosecutor has not been provided with a copy of the material in question, the prosecutor may direct the police disclosure officer, as designated under the Code, to supply it (draft Code, para. 10.1). This applies only to material which there is a duty to provide and the disclosure officer could refuse a request to hand over material at primary disclosure which the prosecutor did not consider might undermine the prosecution case. Where information of which the prosecutor does not have a copy is to be disclosed, the issue of who must disclose it must be determined by agreement between the prosecutor and the disclosure officer (para. 10.2), although the ultimate responsibility to secure disclosure remains with the prosecutor.

The decision that it is not desirable or practicable to provide a copy of material is determined on the basis of the prosecutor's subjective opinion. An example of undesirability given by the draft Code is of a child's evidence in a sexual abuse case, where it is feared that a copy might be circulated to persons unconnected with the case. Even where the prosecutor has allowed the accused to inspect material rather than have a copy of it, on grounds of impracticability or undesirability, it appears that the accused may nevertheless request a copy from the disclosure officer, who must provide a copy unless he is also of the opinion that it would be impracticable or undesirable to supply it (para. 10.3). The implication is that the disclosure officer can override the prosecutor's prohibition on supplying a copy of particular material. Although this would be unlikely to occur in practice it would be more satisfactory if the prosecutor's judgment on the issue was final.

For material which does not consist of information, the duty to disclose is discharged by allowing it to be inspected at a reasonable time and place (s. 3(5)). The disclosure officer is under a corresponding duty to allow the accused to inspect the material (draft Code, para. 10.3).

Compulsory disclosure by the accused

For cases to be tried by the Crown Court, once the accused has been served with the necessary documents and primary prosecution disclosure has taken place (s. 5(1)), the accused is required to give a defence statement to the court and the prosecutor (s. 5(5)). The necessary documents which must have been given to the accused vary according to the route by which the case reached the Crown Court. Thus, for serious fraud and child abuse cases which are transferred to the Crown Court, the accused must have been given a copy of the notice of transfer and copies of documents containing the evidence (s. 5(2) and (3)). Where the case has reached the Crown Court by means of a voluntary bill of indictment, the accused must have been served with a copy of the indictment and copies of the documents containing the evidence (s. 5(4)).

It is sufficient to trigger the accused's duty to disclose that the prosecutor has either complied with the duty of primary disclosure or purported to do so (s. 5(1)(b)). The justification for this provision appears to be that it prevents interruption of the pre-trial process where there has been some inadvertent non-disclosure by the prosecutor (per Baroness Blatch, *Hansard*, Lords, 18 December 1995, col. 1456) and avoids tactical time-wasting challenges. This is unsatisfactory. The provision undermines the system of incentives on which the reciprocal disclosure scheme is based. Thus, the prosecution gain the benefit of defence disclosure however shoddy the primary disclosure, whereas the accused will not be entitled to secondary disclosure without first clearly indicating his own case.

The defence statement must be in writing and must:

(a) set out in general terms the nature of the accused's defence (s. 5(6)(a));

(b) indicate the matters on which he takes issue with the prosecution case (s. 5(6)(c));

(c) indicate the reasons why he takes issue with the prosecution case (s. 5(6)(c)); and

(d) give certain further particulars if the defence involves an alibi (s. 5(7)).

In debate it was argued by Lord Ackner that the duty imposed on the accused is a logical impossibility. As he pointed out, there is a difference between the prosecution evidence and the prosecution case, since that case involves a statement of the particular inferences and conclusions drawn from the prosecution evidence. Thus, without knowing what the prosecution case is, since primary disclosure will be of the evidence rather than the case, it may be impossible for the accused to indicate in what respects he takes issue with it, and why (*Hansard*, Lords, 18 December 1995, cols 1458–9).

In any event, s. 5 imposes a heavy responsibility on the accused's legal advisors at an early stage of the case. Whereas it may be important to disclose enough to stimulate the release of further prosecution material, and it will be vital to avoid inferences from non-disclosure, committing the defence to too much detail may itself carry risks because of the possibility of adverse inferences being drawn if the defence ultimately put forward at trial can be shown to differ from any defence set out in the statement (s. 11(2)(c)).

Although the accused is required to supply copies of the defence statement only to the court and the prosecutor, it is implicit in the draft Code that the statement must also be passed to the officer in charge of the investigation or the disclosure officer. Under para. 8.1 of the draft Code, after the defence statement has been received the disclosure officer must look again at material relating to the investigation which has been retained, and must draw the attention of the prosecutor to any material which might reasonably be expected to assist the accused's defence.

Alibis

Formerly, where an accused wished to rely upon an alibi defence it was necessary to issue an alibi notice to the prosecution under s. 11 of the Criminal Justice Act 1967. The 1996 Act incorporates similar provisions relating to alibis into the general disclosure scheme. The special alibi procedure under the 1967 Act is accordingly abolished by s. 74, except in so far as it applies to courts martial. Consequential amendments are also made to other legislation which refers to the alibi procedures, by substituting references to s. 5(7) of the 1996 Act for s. 11 of the 1967 Act.

The further particulars which must be included where an alibi is disclosed are the name and address, or other information to aid tracing, of any witness whom it is believed is able to give evidence in support of the alibi (s. 5(7)). For this purpose alibi evidence is evidence tending to show that, by reason of the presence of the accused at a particular place or in a particular area at a particular time, he was not or was unlikely to have been at the place where the offence is alleged to have been committed at the relevant time (s. 5(8)). It is now established that evidence to show that the accused was not at the scene of the crime, without suggesting that he was at some other particular place, does not amount to an alibi and will not therefore require the disclosure of the extra particulars required by s. 5(7) (*Aldin Johnson* [1995] 2 Cr App R 1). Thus, if D's defence is that he was not at a club where the offence took place but cannot recall where he was on the night in question, disclosure under s. 5(7) will not be required.

Time limits for defence disclosure

Ultimately, the requirement to give a defence statement will be subject to a time limit under s. 5(9) and late disclosure may be subject to the sanctions of adverse comment and adverse inferences under s. 11(1)(b). However, it appears that the Government do not intend to set time limits until after a period of monitoring the scheme in operation. Until that is done it would seem that the accused's duty to disclose is open-ended. While that remains the case it would seem impossible to invoke the sanctions prescribed under s. 11(1)(a) and (1)(b) for non-disclosure or late disclosure.

Voluntary defence disclosure

The provision of a procedure for voluntary defence disclosure under s. 6 for cases tried summarily reflects the Government's view that reciprocal disclosure is designed to bring benefits as well as risks to the accused. Whatever the category of case, the prosecution must make primary disclosure if a not guilty plea is entered. After that for cases tried summarily the accused may choose to make defence disclosure under s. 6, and if he chooses to do so is then subject to the same supplementary provisions in s. 5(6) to (8) as apply to compulsory disclosure under s. 5.

It remains to be seen whether accused persons will make great use of this facility. In view of the risks and burdens associated with the statutory procedure it is difficult to see why any defendant would choose to use it as opposed to informal cooperative mutual disclosure (see e.g., J. Baldwin *Pre-trial criminal justice*, 1985, Blackwell) which will remain an option.

The particular burdens and risks which might discourage use of the statutory voluntary disclosure scheme are:

(a)   the requirement not only to outline the defence but also to indicate, with reasons, points of issue with the prosecution case;

(b)   the requirement to disclose details of any alibi witnesses, and the risk, or perceived risk, of police tampering which this brings;

(c)   the application of time limits (s. 6(4)); and

(d)   the risk of adverse inferences being drawn for lateness, inconsistency of disclosed defences, departure from the disclosed defence, undisclosed alibi or undisclosed details of an alibi witness (s. 11(2)).

The only circumstance where it might be considered advantageous to participate voluntarily in the statutory scheme would be where the accused wishes to obtain access to material relevant to his defence which he knows or believes to be held by the prosecution. Whether it really is necessary to participate in the statutory scheme to obtain this material depends upon whether the prosecution could lawfully withhold it from a defendant who exercised his right not to participate. At common law the courts had effectively created a duty of disclosure in relation to summary proceedings, by holding that failure to reveal material which undermines the prosecution case amounts to a breach of natural justice and therefore a ground for quashing a conviction (see *Blackstone's Criminal Practice*, D18.3).

Normally, the duty of disclosure in relation to summary proceedings as developed at common law would be satisfied in the course of primary prosecution disclosure under s. 3. However, by extrapolation from the decided cases it seems likely that at common law the courts would also hold that there is a duty on the prosecution to disclose material which supports a particular defence as notified to the prosecutor. If s. 3 is interpreted narrowly as requiring only disclosure of material which undermines particular elements of the prosecution case, then fulfilling the duty of primary disclosure under s. 3 would not be equivalent to satisfying the common law rule. If that is right, and if s. 21 is effective in abolishing the relevant common law duties, then an accused who wishes to get hold of prosecution material supporting his proposed defence must participate in the statutory scheme.

The potential flaw in the argument set out above is the assumption that the purported abolition of the applicable common law rules by s. 21 will be effective. Although it is clearly possible to abolish particular rules of common law, the principles from which those particular rules developed will remain intact. If the effect of statutory change coupled with the abolition of particular common law rules is to create a vacuum, then the common law will begin to operate afresh to fill it. When this occurs, it should be no surprise if the new rule, emanating from the same principles as the old, looks remarkably like the rule recently abolished.

In relation to contested summary cases, s. 21 applies by virtue of s. 1(1) and therefore applicable common law rules are abolished. However, after primary prosecution disclosure under s. 3, whether or not the statutory scheme applies is at the option of the accused. If the accused opts out, then there is an apparent vacuum, since neither the old common law rules nor the new statutory rules apply. In this circumstance a court might well hold, applying principles of natural justice, that where the accused has disclosed a line of defence the prosecutor would be under a duty to release any material in his possession which would support the notified defence.

The argument above suggests that the accused might be entitled to the equivalent of secondary prosecution disclosure without voluntary participation in the statutory scheme. This in turn raises the issue of what should be taken as participation in that scheme. In view of the considerable burdens which attach to participation it might have been expected that the Act would provide a means of determining precisely whether or not a particular accused was participating. Unfortunately, this is not the case, and accordingly there is scope for argument about whether an accused who has disclosed something about a defence is doing so under s. 6 or not. The simple way to resolve the issue is to ask the accused. The marginal heading for s. 6 is voluntary disclosure — suggesting that the choice is that of the accused. It is surely in the interests of both parties and the system as a whole that the accused should not be inhibited from making some limited informal disclosure by the fear that in doing so he is bringing upon himself the bureaucracy and hazards of the statutory scheme.

Secondary prosecution disclosure

After the accused has supplied a defence statement, whether under the compulsory or voluntary procedure, the prosecutor must make secondary disclosure (s. 7). This must be completed within time limits to be prescribed by regulations under s. 12 or, until such limits are set, as soon as reasonably practicable after defence disclosure (s. 13(7)). The provisions about how disclosure is to be made in s. 3(3)–(5) apply equally to secondary disclosure (s. 7(4)).

The prosecutor must disclose any prosecution material which has not been previously disclosed and which might be reasonably expected to assist the accused's defence as disclosed in the defence statement (s. 7(2)(a)). Exemptions are made for material which a court orders should not be disclosed in the public interest (s. 7(5)) and material intercepted under the Interception of Communications Act 1985 (s. 7(6)). Where the prosecutor believes that there is no material which satisfies the test for disclosure, he must give the accused a written statement to this effect (s. 7(2)(b)).

Unlike the test for primary disclosure, the test for secondary disclosure is objective and may therefore be challenged more easily in court (i.e., under s. 8). The duty to disclose applies only in relation to material held by the prosecutor in connection with the case or which he has inspected under provisions of the Code in connection with the case (s. 7(3)). Thus, there is no requirement that the prosecutor should personally consider all material retained in relation to the investigation. Rather the prosecutor must rely upon the disclosure officer who, having received the defence statement, is required to look again at retained material and draw the prosecutor's attention to anything which might assist the accused's defence (draft Code, para. 8.1). Where the prosecutor's attention is drawn to such material, he will have a discretion whether to inspect it or not. If he chooses not to do so there will be no further duty to disclose.

The effectiveness of secondary disclosure will depend upon the disclosure officer. This can be criticised. It remains to be seen what priority disclosure officers and their supervisors will place on reviewing case files long after the end of the investigation and the passing of the case to the CPS. It also may be doubted whether a police officer (or civilian employed by the police) will have adequate legal skills to assess whether or not particular material might assist the accused's defence.

Applications by the accused for disclosure

Section 8 provides for the accused to apply to the court for an order that the prosecutor should disclose material which might be reasonably expected to assist the accused's defence as disclosed in the defence statement made under s. 5 or s. 6. An application may be made only after the prosecutor has made secondary disclosure, has purported to do so or has failed to do so within the prescribed time limit (s. 8(1)). Until time limits are prescribed under s. 12, failure to comply with the duty of secondary disclosure will mean failure to do so within a reasonable time (s. 13(2)).

The time at which the application may be made reflects the carrot principle. The accused earns the right to secondary disclosure and to apply to court for further disclosure only by supplying a defence statement. It is also significant that the right to apply relates only to material which might assist the disclosed defence. This deliberately attempts to exclude the possibility of the accused seeking material to support a range of possible defences, having first made only a token defence disclosure.

As noted above, for the purpose of secondary disclosure the prosecutor need not consider all material collected in the course of the investigation but only that which has been supplied to him and that which he has inspected. The defect is partially rectified by the accused's right to apply for any material collected in the course of the investigation which satisfies the relevant test. Thus, the accused may apply for any material held by or inspected by the prosecutor (s. 8(3)), but also any material which the disclosure officer must either supply to the prosecutor, or allow the prosecutor to inspect, if so requested (s. 8(4)). This covers the remainder of the material collected in the course of the investigation (draft Code, para. 7.4).

Although s. 8 refers only to a court application, presumably in many cases the prosecutor will agree to further disclosure as a means of avoiding the expense of a court action. Indeed the threat of court action may be a means for the accused to obtain greater disclosure than would be strictly justified by s. 8. Should the police disapprove of material being handed over without a court hearing or court order it would be possible for the disclosure officer to refuse to release the material to the accused since, under para. 10.1 of the draft Code, disclosure to the accused is obligatory only where either of the tests for primary or secondary disclosure are satisfied or disclosure is by court order. However, the prosecutor can overcome any police resistance to agreed disclosure to the accused by requiring a copy of the relevant documents for herself, and then copying these to the accused.

To succeed in an application, the accused must have reasonable cause to believe that the prosecution material requested might be reasonably expected to assist his defence. The usefulness of such an application may depend upon how scrupulous disclosure officers are in scheduling unused material. The requirement under the draft Code is that the description of each item should contain sufficient detail to enable the prosecutor to form a judgment on whether the material needs to be disclosed (para. 6.5). The problem with this instruction is that, where a disclosure officer has decided that a particular item need not be disclosed, he is likely to apply a description which tends to confirm this conclusion. This factor, combined with the apparent rigour of the 'reasonable cause to believe' test may make it difficult to mount a credible argument for disclosure.

In an adversarial system in which the accused is disadvantaged in terms of resources, a more appropriate test would be that material should be disclosed if there is a reasonable possibility that it might assist the defence. In view of the historical willingness of courts to order disclosure to achieve fairness between the parties, it may well be that courts adopt a more flexible approach in interpreting the statutory test.

Continuing duty of the prosecutor to disclose

Section 9 provides that the duties to review prosecution material for the purposes of primary and secondary disclosure continue until either the case is dropped or the accused is acquitted or convicted. Thus, following primary disclosure, the prosecutor must keep under review the question whether there is any prosecution material which undermines the prosecution case (s. 9(1) and (2)). The issue should be considered in the light of the current state of affairs including any developments in the case for the prosecution (s. 9(3)). Similarly, following secondary disclosure, the prosecutor must keep under review the issue whether there is any prosecution material which might reasonably be expected to assist the defence as disclosed in the accused's defence statement (s. 9(4) and (5)). In either event, if the prosecutor's review suggests that there is material which satisfies the relevant test, this must be disclosed.

Public interest immunity

Although the topical issue of public interest immunity (PII) was much debated in the course of the Bill's progress through Parliament, the Act expressly preserves the existing law, without seeking to either define or reform it. This was prudent in view of the doubts about the scope of the present law which have been stirred by Sir Richard Scott's report into the Matrix Churchill affair, and by the appointment by the Attorney-General of a consultation group to consider the proper scope of the law on behalf of the Government.

The Act does however create procedures for reviewing court orders to withhold material in the public interest (ss. 14 and 15) and provides for interventions by interested third parties when a court is considering the issue of public interest immunity (s. 16).

The rule established in *Ward* [1993] 1 WLR 619, that relevant material can be withheld on public interest grounds only if so ordered by a court, is adopted in relation to all sections which provide for disclosure to the accused (ss. 3(6), 7(5), 8(5) and 9(8)). The procedures laid down in *Davis, Johnson and Rowe* [1993] 1 WLR 613 for informing the defence that an application for non-disclosure is to be made, unless the degree of sensitivity precludes this, will continue to apply. However, because of restrictions on the duties of disclosure under ss. 3 and 7, courts will be requested to consider the public interest issue on fewer occasions. Thus, no application need be made at the stage of primary disclosure, unless the prosecutor considers that the material in question might undermine the prosecution case. Similarly, at the stage of secondary disclosure, no application need be made unless the prosecutor is of the opinion that the material in question might assist any defence disclosed. Although the accused is given a specific power to apply for further disclosure under s. 8, his ability to do so will be limited by the exclusion of the schedule of sensitive material from the matters which must be disclosed to him.

Sections 14 and 15 create procedures for the review of public interest immunity orders in summary and Crown Court cases respectively. At any time after a court has made an order exempting material from disclosure on public interest grounds, but before the final verdict or a decision not to proceed, the accused can apply for a review of an order that particular material should not be disclosed (ss. 14(2) and 15(4)).

Additionally, for cases tried in the Crown Court, the court must keep the issue constantly under review of its own motion (s. 15(4)). If, having reviewed the issue, a court decides that it is in the public interest to disclose material to some extent, it must so order and inform the prosecutor (ss. 14(3) and 15(5)). The prosecutor then has the option of either disclosing the material or not proceeding with the case in question (ss. 14(4) and 15(6)).

Particular concern has focused on material emanating from third party agencies such as social services departments, welfare charities and hospitals. Section 16 provides that such third parties may be heard by the court in considering applications from prosecutors to withhold material. To qualify, the applicant must claim to have an interest in the material and show that he was involved, directly or indirectly, in the prosecutor's attention being brought to the material. Where a person who fulfils these criteria applies to be heard, the court must not make an order until that person has been heard.

Material intercepted under the Interception of Communications Act 1985

Material obtained by the prosecution under s. 2 of the Interception of Communications Act 1985 is exempted from disclosure by the prosecution at all stages of the process. The exemption extends to information which has been intercepted in obedience to a warrant issued under s. 2 of that Act, as well as to other material which indicates that such a warrant has been issued or such interceptions have taken place. The exemption relating to primary disclosure is found in s. 3(7), and is repeated, in relation to secondary prosecution disclosure, in s. 7(6) and, in relation to the prosecutor's continuing duties of disclosure, in s. 9(9). Intercepted material is also exempted from the draft Code of Practice under para. 1.2.

This major exception to the disclosure rules was not foreshadowed in the Consultation Document on Disclosure; accordingly, the issues raised were generally not addressed by the organisations and individuals who participated in the consultation process. The exemption was raised once only during the parliamentary stages of the Bill when a Government amendment to make the exemption mandatory rather than discretionary was accepted without debate or division (*Hansard*, Lords, 18 December 1995, cols 1450–1).

Under s. 2 of the Interception of Communications Act 1985, messages sent by post and via any public telecommunications system may be intercepted under warrant issued personally by the Home Secretary. A warrant may be obtained where this is necessary for the protection of national security, for preventing or detecting serious crime, or for the purpose of safeguarding the economic well-being of the United Kingdom. Normally a warrant must relate to an address linked to a named individual. Exceptionally warrants may specify an address only, where the purpose is to prevent terrorism. Under s. 9 of the 1985 Act, no evidence may be elicited to show that a warrant has been or is to be issued under the Act. Furthermore s. 6 requires the Home Secretary to make arrangements to ensure that dissemination of intercepted material is kept to a minimum and that the material is destroyed as soon as it is no longer required for the purpose for which the warrant was issued. On a strict reading of the 1985 Act, if a warrant has been issued for the purpose of detecting serious crime it cannot be used for another purpose, i.e., as evidence in court to prove such a charge. Thus, investigators may see a warrant under the Act as a source of information or intelligence, but not as a source of evidence which may be used in a subsequent prosecution.

The function of the Act has been explained by the House of Lords (in *Preston* [1994] 2 AC 130) as balancing the need for information against the need to keep secret the methods and sources of information available to the investigating authorities. The limited purposes for which information obtained under warrant may be used is underlined by the decision in *Preston* that such information must be destroyed when no longer necessary for the prevention or detection of the serious crime in question.

The Government presented the exemption of intercepted material from the scope of the disclosure scheme as flowing inexorably from the terms of the Interception of Communications Act 1985. This may be challenged on both legal and policy grounds. First, the distinction between detection and prosecution which is drawn by the 1985 Act and confirmed by *Preston* is a false one. The mere fact that the prosecuting authorities have a suspect and have constructed a case against him should not be treated as conclusive 'detection'. The function of determining that an offence has been committed by a particular person is properly that of the courts. If this is right, an offence should be considered to be detected only when a conviction has been obtained. It should therefore be proper to retain intercepted material until this point.

Secondly, to exempt intercepted material from the disclosure scheme may expose the accused to risk of wrongful conviction. In *Preston* the House of Lords held that, whilst the defence should be denied access to intercepted material, the interests of the accused could be protected by the prosecutor who had an overall duty to ensure that the defendant did not suffer injustice. As presently drafted, the Code would pre-empt this protective function since the police would be spared any duty to inform the prosecutor of intercepted material (1996 Act, s. 23(6) and draft Code, para. 1.2).

It would be possible for the accused to be afforded some protection if two conditions were fulfilled. First, it would be necessary to adopt the principle that intercepted material should be retained by the investigator until after conviction. Secondly, intercepted material should be included within the terms of the Code so that the prosecutor can fulfil the role prescribed by *Preston* of ensuring that no injustice is done to the accused. This would involve dropping cases in which there was substantial intercepted material favourable to the accused which could not be put before a court.

Sanctions against the prosecutor?

The 1996 Act places prosecutors under a succession of duties to review and disclose material which the prosecution does not intend to use. The purpose of these functions is to enable the accused to muster available resources in his defence and to prevent miscarriages of justice. It is generally accepted that a number of miscarriages of justice might have been averted by responsible prosecution disclosure but, as noted by Chris Mullin MP in committee: 'no prosecutor has suffered the merest inconvenience as a result of having been caught suppressing evidence that is inconvenient to his or her case' (*Hansard*, Commons Standing Committee B, 30 April 1996, col. 12).

The issue of whether the prosecution should be subjected to sanctions for breach of the disclosure rules or departure from the case as disclosed was a recurrent theme during the passage of the Bill. The arguments put in favour of sanctions stressed the historical precedents of wilful non-disclosure and the resulting miscarriages of justice, the sanctions by way of inference which might be imposed on an accused who broke the rules and the need for compliance by both sides if efficiency gains are to be achieved. These arguments were resisted by the Government.

To the suggestion that prosecutors should be subject to disciplinary sanctions for negligent failures, and criminal sanctions for deliberate breaches, Home Office Minister David Maclean argued that the sanction for failure to make primary disclosure would be that the accused would be absolved from a duty to provide a defence statement (*Hansard*, Commons Standing Committee B, 30 April 1996, cols 18–19). This is a poor argument since it is true only where there is a total failure of primary disclosure. Under s. 5(1), the duty to make defence disclosure is triggered by *purported* primary disclosure. Thus, once something described as primary disclosure has been made, however misleading or inadequate, the accused must disclose and fails to do so at his peril.

The Government also rejected an opposition proposal that the prosecution should be required to disclose a case (rather than simply evidence) and that departures thereafter from the case disclosed should be met with adverse inferences similar to those which apply to departures from a disclosed defence. Admittedly, as was pointed out by the Government, should the prosecution depart from the case disclosed, the accused may seek an adjournment to consider the new evidence; if as a result the accused runs a new line of defence, he will almost certainly not have adverse inferences drawn against him (*Hansard*, Commons Standing Committee B, 16 May 1996, cols 75–79). This argument is perfectly good on its merits but does not stand comparison with the justifications offered for drawing adverse inferences against defendants. In particular, it is not clear why an adjournment is a good remedy for a late change of case by the prosecution but not by the defence.

Prosecution delay and abuse of process

The only direct mention of possible sanctions against the prosecutor in the Act is found in s. 10(2), which provides that for the prosecutor to make primary or secondary disclosure outside the prescribed time limits does not on its own constitute grounds for staying the proceedings for abuse of process. It is however conceded that failure to act within the time limits *may* constitute grounds for staying proceedings if it involves such delay that the accused is denied a fair trial (s. 10(3)). It appears that a court will not be *bound* to stay proceedings even if it is found that the accused will be denied a fair trial. However, the criteria to be applied in deciding whether a stay should be granted or not, are not specified. This suggests that the section simply imports the common law notion of abuse of process as developed in *Attorney-General's Reference (No. 1 of 1990)* [1992] QB 630.

In that case, the Court of Appeal established a presumption against staying and set out the factors other than denial of a fair trial which were relevant to the decision. These include fault on the part of the prosecution, whether or not the accused's conduct had contributed to the delay and whether or not the delay was a natural consequence of the complexity of the case. In view of the strictness of this test, the remote threat of the proceedings being stayed is unlikely to provide any real incentive for compliance with the prosecutor's disclosure obligations.

Incentives for the prosecutor?

The only incentive to make primary disclosure within time limits will be that if this is not done the accused will be absolved from supplying a defence statement. This will not guarantee the quality or content of disclosure since 'purported' disclosure will be enough. Once a defence statement has been secured, the prosecution are apparently free to ignore the duty of secondary disclosure with impunity. Should lapses in secondary disclosure occur, it is to be hoped that judges will consider exercising their residual discretion to comment to the jury on any difficulties this might have caused the defence and where appropriate to invite the drawing of inferences adverse to the prosecution.

Adverse comment and inferences against the accused

At common law an accused person was entitled to withhold any defence until court. Accordingly a judge could make no adverse comment and in particular could not invite a jury to draw adverse inferences where a defence was given at trial following silence at police interview. Prior to 1994, that principle had been made subject to two exceptions: for alibi evidence under s. 11 of the Criminal Justice Act 1967 and expert evidence under s. 81 of the Police and Criminal Evidence Act 1984 (PACE). In each case the accused was barred from calling the relevant evidence in aid of a defence without leave of the judge.

The accused's freedom to withhold his defence was considerably curtailed by s. 34 of the Criminal Justice and Public Order Act 1994, which permits a court or jury to draw such inferences as appear proper from the failure of the accused to mention, in the course of police interview under caution or upon being charged, any fact later relied upon in his defence in court. For cases to be tried on indictment, the right to withhold a defence is now further curtailed by s. 5, which requires the accused to provide a defence statement, and s. 11, which provides that adverse comments may be made, and adverse inferences may be drawn, in a variety of circumstances in which the accused has not made adequate advance disclosure of his defence.

There will also be a significant further curtailment of the accused's right to withhold his defence in relation to summary trials. The accused will feel great pressure to provide a voluntary defence statement under s. 6 where to do so is the only means of getting access to material held by the prosecution which might support his defence.

The accused risks inferences in a number of situations in which s. 11 applies where:

(a)   he fails to provide a defence statement when required to do so under s. 11(1)(a);

(b)   either a compulsory or voluntary defence statement is provided but is out of time (s. 11(1)(b) and (2)(a));

(c)   the defence statement sets out inconsistent defences (s. 11(1)(c) and (2)(b));

(d)   a defence is put forward at trial which is different from any defence disclosed in the defence statement (s. 11(1)(d) and (2)(c));

(e)   an alibi defence is run at trial without particulars having been disclosed in a defence statement (s. 11(1)(e) and (2)(d)); and

(f)   an alibi witness is called without the necessary particulars of the witness having been supplied (s. 11(1)(f) and (2)(e)).

These provisions may be expected to generate considerable arguments in court, which must by their very nature be dealt with after evidence has been heard by the jury. This will surely frustrate one of the aims of the Act which is to narrow issues pre-trial and shorten hearings before juries.

It should not be assumed that the issues raised in determining whether s. 11 applies will all be matters of common sense. For instance, many people would consider that on a charge of murder, defences of alibi and absence of *mens rea* would be inconsistent, but in practice they need not be. Thus, there would be no logical inconsistency in arguing that the defendant was not present and that the prosecution evidence is insufficient to prove that the killer acted with intent.

Inconsistency will not be the only concept which will require clarification by the courts. For instance, it is not clear what is meant by a difference between defences. This may refer to differences in legal category or in supporting evidence, or both. For instance, where a father has killed his child and discloses a defence of provocation, citing the child's crying as the provocative event, would it be a different defence if in court he gave additional evidence that his wife had insulted him? If the issue is concerned with legal categories, no inferences could be drawn, since in either event the defence is provocation. Inferences might however be drawn if the notion of difference relates to the factual basis for the defence.

Where s. 11 applies the court or, with leave of the court, any other party may make such comment as appears appropriate (s. 11(3)(a)). Generally the comment should relate to the extent to which it would be proper for the jury to draw inferences under s. 11(3)(b). The scope of comments which may be made appears to be left open, but is almost certain to be subject to guidance from the Court of Appeal soon after the implementation of the Act. In view of this and of the fact that inappropriate comment might lead to a conviction being quashed, it would seem prudent for trial judges to restrict comment to themselves and not to take the opportunity to allow comment by the prosecutor or by a co-accused.

On a literal reading of s. 11(3), the accused would appear to need leave before commenting upon his own alleged faults in disclosure. However, since the issue is whether any inferences can be drawn against the accused, it seems axiomatic as a matter of natural justice that counsel for the accused must be able to comment in the course of the closing speech, and this was probably the intention of Parliament.

The test for what comment may be made is what appears appropriate (s. 11(3)(a)). In the absence of an indication as to whom the comment must appear appropriate, it should be assumed to be the judge (but compare the scope of comments under s. 34 of this Act (see Chapter Three), which permits the party making the comment to be the arbiter of its appropriateness).

In order to determine what is appropriate, it is first necessary to discover what purpose the comment is designed to serve. There are two possibilities: first, that the threat of comment is simply a means of forcing compliance with the disclosure scheme and therefore when comment is made it is a punishment; secondly, that comment is a means of assisting the jury in considering matters which logically affect the weight to be given to the accused's evidence. Although the Government's consultation document strongly suggested the first rationale (Cm 2864, paras 53–56), it is to be hoped that English courts would not consider that an enhanced risk of conviction for a serious offence is a suitable punishment for breach of an administrative duty placed on the accused. If that is correct, the question of what is an appropriate comment relates directly to the probative value of breach of the disclosure requirements.

Some limited assistance in assessing the probative weight of breach is given by s. 11(4), which provides that where the accused puts forward a defence different from any defence set out in a defence statement the court, in deciding what comment is appropriate, must have regard to (a) the extent of the difference in the defences, and (b) whether there was any justification for it. It is doubtful if s. 11(4) will be of much value for two reasons: first, these issues would be considered in determining the appropriate comment in any event; secondly, the courts will have to look beyond these issues. For instance, in relation to any deviation from the defence disclosed, a court would not simply focus on the narrow issue of justification but must also consider whether the fault lay with the accused or rather with her legal advisors, and whether there are explanations or excuses for what occurred.

It should not be assumed that comment will follow automatically from some technical fault in disclosure. The following are examples of situations in which the court may consider no comment should be made:

(a)   disclosure is made out of time, but in sufficient time for the police to investigate the defence raised (cf. *Sullivan* [1971] 1 QB 253);

(b)   the accused claims that he had to vary his defence because the prosecution evidence did not sufficiently disclose the case which was eventually run in court;

(c)   the accused raises a new defence having dispensed with the services of the lawyers who made disclosure on his behalf.

It is implicit from this short list that sooner rather than later the courts will have to face the question of whether they will permit an accused to be prejudiced by the administrative errors or failures of his lawyers.

Multiple inferences

Section 11(5) provides that a person shall not be convicted of an offence solely on an inference drawn under s. 11(3). This follows s. 38(3) of the Criminal Justice and Public Order Act 1994 which similarly bars conviction solely on the basis of an inference from silence under that Act. These provisions properly reflect the limited probative weight of inferences drawn from failures to do something, whether to speak or to fulfil disclosure requirements. Whereas such failures may cast doubt upon any defence raised they generally cannot provide direct proof of an offence.

The 1996 Act provides no guidance on the question of what weight can be attached to multiple inferences from silence and failures of disclosure. Circumstances could arise in which an accused is arrested near the scene of a crime and gives no explanation for his presence there, is later silent in police interview, provides a defence statement, but then, although not giving evidence at trial, adduces evidence at variance with his defence statement. In these circumstances it would be possible to draw inferences under ss. 37, 34 and 35 of the Criminal Justice and Public Order Act 1994 and also under s. 11 of the 1996 Act. Although there is no formal prohibition on treating such inferences as cumulative, in theory their cumulative weight should not be sufficient to found a conviction without substantial evidence of the positive elements of the offence which is accepted by the jury. Where multiple inferences may be drawn, the time devoted to them at trial may mislead the jury into attaching greater evidential significance than they in fact warrant. In such circumstances a judge might sensibly choose to focus on one possible basis for inference to the exclusion of the others, in order to avoid prejudice to the accused and problems for the jury.

Can disclosure negate the effects of silence?

An interesting issue of practical importance which received no attention either in the Government's consultation document or in debate in Parliament is whether disclosure under ss. 5 and 6 can negate the risk of inferences being drawn from silence at interview under s. 34(2) of the Criminal Justice and Public Order Act 1994. The primary issue under s. 34(2) is whether the accused relied upon a fact in his defence in court which he had failed to mention when questioned under caution or charged. However, even when this test is satisfied, it remains to be determined what inferences might properly be drawn. If the working assumption under s. 34 is that delay in disclosing a defence indicates fabrication, then the fact of disclosure pre-trial should not prevent the drawing of inferences. However, it is instructive that this reasoning has been explicitly rejected by the Court of Appeal in relation to alibi in *Sullivan* [1971] 1 QB 253. In that case Salmon LJ held that the key issue for the court in deciding whether to receive evidence of alibi was whether the police had had time to investigate the defence raised. If similar reasoning is applied to inferences from silence, the fact of disclosure under s. 5 (thus giving the police adequate time to check the defence raised) should render it inappropriate to draw inferences from the silence in the police station or at least weaken the inferences which may be drawn (see M. Wasik and R. Taylor, *Blackstone's Guide to the Criminal Justice and Public Order Act 1994*, pp. 57–8).

Application of the disclosure procedure to non-police prosecuting agencies

In the course of the Bill's passage through Parliament there was considerable debate about whether the Code of Practice should apply to investigative agencies other than the police. Ultimately Parliament accepted the Government's rather fudged proposal that there should be a single Code, directly applicable to the police only, but that other investigators should have regard to any relevant provision of the Code which would apply if the investigation were conducted by police officers (s. 26(1)). The issue which did not receive Parliamentary attention was the extent to which the disclosure provisions under Part I could be applied to other investigative agencies if the Code did not so apply. This issue is considered below.

At first glance, Part I clearly applies to prosecutions generally, whatever the prosecuting agency. Thus s. 1 applies to all persons tried on indictment and to all contested summary trials. Indeed, the express reference to transferred serious fraud cases implies that Serious Fraud Office investigations and prosecutions must be covered. The general application of Part I is confirmed by the omission of references to the police or the Crown Prosecution Service in favour of neutral terms such as prosecutor, investigator and disclosure officer.

Problems emerge however, when one considers how provisions which contain references to the Code might apply to non-police investigations and prosecutions by bodies other than the Crown Prosecution Service. For example, under s. 3(1) the prosecutor is required to disclose material falling within two categories:

(a) that which came into his possession in connection with the case; and
(b) that which he has inspected in pursuance of a Code operative under Part II.

Since the Code does not bind non-police investigators, it would be difficult to hold that material held by such an agency and made available to a prosecutor is ever inspected in pursuance of the statutory Code. Thus, under s. 3 a non-police prosecutor would be bound to disclose material falling under (a), but not material falling under (b). Similar considerations apply in relation to the prosecutor's duties of secondary disclosure under s. 7 and continuing disclosure under s. 9.

The purpose of s. 3(1)(b) is to ensure that prosecutors disclose not only relevant material which they hold, but also other relevant material which is held by the investigator. If this duty does not apply to non-police agencies the rigour of the disclosure provisions in protecting the accused and preventing miscarriages of justice will be significantly reduced. The common law might fill this gap. Whether it is able to do so depends upon how the courts approach the purported abolition of the common law rules by s. 21.

Confidentiality of disclosed information

Section 17 provides for the confidentiality of unused material which the accused is allowed to inspect or of which copies are supplied to the accused. The section was inserted at a late stage in the Bill's progress. The mischief at which it is aimed was said to be that unscrupulous defendants might use such material for financial gain or to harass witnesses. The purpose of the provision was to deter those who may be tempted to misuse disclosed material and to reassure those who supply information to the police (*Hansard*, Commons Standing Committee B, 30 April 1996, col. 7).

In the context of this provision, there was much debate in Parliament about the problem of the circulation of evidence from child sex abuse cases. The Government pointed out that very different considerations apply to evidence which is heard in court and accordingly s. 17 does not purport to tackle that problem (*Hansard*, Commons Standing Committee B, 30 April 1996, col. 19).

Under s. 17, confidentiality attaches to any information contained in a document or other object which the accused is given or allowed to inspect under powers in ss. 3, 4, 7, 9, 14 or 15 or under an order made under s. 8. Confidentiality ceases where the information or object enters the public domain by being displayed or communicated to the public in open court (s. 17(3)). The accused has a general liberty to use the relevant material in relation to the proceedings in question or any appeal arising therefrom (s. 17(2)). The accused may also apply to court at any time, including after the end of the proceedings, for permission to use the material for some specified purpose (s. 17(4) and (5)). Such applications will be subject to rules of court to be made under s. 19(2) and also to the possibility of intercession by either the prosecutor or any other person who claims to have an interest in the material (s. 17(6)).

Breaches of confidentiality

Use or disclosure of material which is confidential by virtue of s. 17 is made a contempt of court, punishable in the magistrates' court by imprisonment for six months or a fine of £5,000, or both, and punishable in the Crown Court by two years' imprisonment or a fine, or both (s. 18(1), (2) and (3)). Although the s. 18 offence may be committed by 'a person', it would appear that only an accused who received material as a result of prosecution disclosure can commit the offence because only such persons are referred to in s. 17. This indicates that the protection afforded to confidentiality may be flawed since no offence appears to be committed by disclosure by anybody other than the original accused. It is possible however that a person other than the accused might be held to be 'in contravention of s. 17' if he disclosed material emanating from the accused which fell within the terms of s. 17.

Where a person is found to be in contempt of court under s. 18 for disclosing an object or information recorded in it, he may be ordered to forfeit the object in question or any copy of it in his possession (s. 18(4) and (7)). Forfeited objects may be ordered to be destroyed or to be kept by the prosecutor for a specified period, or dealt with in some other manner (s. 18(5)), but subject to the right of the person found guilty of contempt or any other person claiming to have an interest in the object to apply to be heard by the court on the issue (s. 18(6)).

Section 18(9) also purports to make confidential material disclosed to the accused for the purpose of criminal proceedings inadmissible in civil proceedings, if to adduce the material in such proceedings would in the opinion of the civil court be likely to constitute a contempt under s. 18. It is unusual for an Act dealing with criminal procedure to express rules about admissibility in civil proceedings, particularly where this will turn on a finding by a civil court about whether a person would be likely to commit a criminal contempt.

Commencement: applicability of the disclosure procedures to particular cases

Part I of the Act is to come into force on a day to be appointed by the Home Secretary. It is likely to be in early 1997. The disclosure provisions will apply to any alleged offence for which the investigation has not begun before the appointed day (s. 1(3)). Thus, the new regime will apply to investigations begun on the appointed day or thereafter. For offences alleged to be committed before the appointed day it will be necessary to determine precisely when the investigation began. For this purpose 'criminal investigation' is defined in s. 1(4) as 'an investigation which police officers or other persons have a duty to conduct with a view to it being ascertained . . . whether a person should be charged with an offence, or . . . whether a person charged with an offence is guilty of it'.

Problems may arise in determining when an investigation had begun. For instance, would it be considered that an investigation had begun where the matter had been reported to and recorded by the police but where no substantial investigation has started? The definition of investigation will sit uneasily with proactive CID methods, which, for recurring offences like car theft, may involve targeting investigations on suspected offenders rather than on reported offences. Could it be said that an investigation had begun where the police had a suspected car thief under surveillance but where the particular thefts with which he is later charged have merely been recorded but have not been investigated? This would clearly amount to an investigation under s. 1(4) since the purpose is to ascertain whether a person should be charged with an offence. However, under s. 1(3) the investigation must be 'into' the relevant alleged offence if the disclosure provisions are to apply. It is far from clear that there is an investigation into an offence at a time where the link between the investigated suspect and the particular offence has yet to be made.

The question whether the disclosure provisions are barred by an investigation before the appointed day may turn upon how earlier investigations are characterised. This will turn upon the meaning of 'offence' in s. 1(3) and in particular whether the term relates to a particular incident or legal category. An instance in which the issue would arise is a case of grievous bodily harm which is investigated as such before the appointed day, but later prosecuted as murder after the victim dies. If the murder is treated as a different offence to the grievous bodily harm, then the disclosure provisions would apply. If however the murder can be characterised as the same 'offence' then the disclosure provisions would be barred because the investigation had begun before the appointed day. As a matter of policy, the latter approach is preferable, since it would be unsatisfactory for the disclosure provisions to apply unless the whole investigation had been conducted in accordance with the investigations Code.

Difficulties will also be experienced in relation to 'latent' offences. The notion of latency is borrowed from the civil law of latent damage. An offence is latent where after commission it remains hidden for a period but is then discovered. Examples would include murders where a person goes missing and the body is discovered some years later, or regular pilfering from a company which continues for some years before discovery. Where such an offence is discovered after the appointed day and there was no prior suspicion or investigation, there will be no difficulty and the disclosure provisions will apply. Cases may arise however in which there was some earlier suspicion and investigation. For instance, it is common in relation to latent murders for there to have been some investigation at the time when the victim was first reported missing. In relation to long-term pilfering there may have been suspicion and investigation at an earlier stage which came to nothing. In such cases it would seem that the fact of the earlier investigation will bar the application of the disclosure provisions, and the common law in relation to disclosure will continue to apply.

This may quite arbitrarily exempt from the procedures a handful of serious offences which are dealt with long after the procedures have come into force. For the future this problem might be averted by amending the current legislation to apply the disclosure provisions to any case in which the investigation upon which the prosecution case is founded is conducted after the investigations Code comes into force and subject to that Code.

Challenges to the disclosure scheme in the transitional period

In view of objections to disclosure raised by some defence lawyers it seems likely that challenges to the applicability of the disclosure regime will properly occur during the transitional period and also in relation to latent offences. The basis of the challenge would be that Part I of the Act was inapplicable because an investigation had begun before the appointed day. Such challenges might be made at various stages.

The first stage at which the defence might challenge the procedure is by refusing to provide a defence statement to the court and prosecutor when required to do so under s. 5(5). A challenge at this stage would carry some risks for the accused. Inevitably, the issue of whether the investigation had begun will be determined by reference to two factors: the meaning to be ascribed to this test by the courts and factual information to which the defence may not be privy. Non-disclosure would carry three potential disadvantages. First, the defence would not have the benefit of secondary prosecution disclosure, although this would be no problem in a standard case in which all the material available to the police is subject to primary disclosure. Secondly, the accused would risk adverse comment by the prosecution or judge in court. Thirdly, the accused would risk adverse inferences being drawn by the jury from the failure to disclose any defence under s. 11(3).

The second circumstance in which the applicability of the disclosure scheme might be challenged would be if the defence had made disclosure under s. 5 or 6 but the prosecution argued that adverse comment or inferences were appropriate because the defence disclosure was late, because inconsistent defences were disclosed, or because the defence raised at trial differed from the one disclosed (s. 11(1)(b), (c) and (d), s. 12(1)(b), (c) and (d)).

In any case in which the defence argue that the disclosure scheme is inapplicable, no adverse comments or inferences could be made if the court accepted that the investigation had begun before the appointed day. Even if the court determined that the disclosure scheme was applicable, it could be argued that adverse comment or inference would be inappropriate in view of the defence solicitor's belief that the disclosure scheme was inapplicable and the accused's reliance on the solicitor's advice to this effect. In such a case it would be inappropriate to make adverse comment or to invite the jury to draw adverse inferences under s. 11(3), particularly if the solicitor's advice was based on reasonable or arguable grounds.

Chapter Two
Criminal Investigations

Part II of the Act complements the duties of disclosure in Part I by specifying for the first time the duties of police investigators in relation to information and other material collected in the course of an investigation. Whereas the legislation itself runs to four statute pages, the real meat is found in the detailed Code of Practice to be issued by the Home Secretary under powers in s. 23. The first draft of the Code was published in December 1995, following demands from peers who wished to consider it during the Committee stage of the Bill. At the time of writing, the Home Secretary has published a further draft of the Code for consultation, as required by s. 25(1). The consultation period will end on 20 September 1996. After that time, the Home Secretary must consider whether to modify the Code in the light of representations made to him. The final version must be laid before Parliament (s. 25(2)) and may be brought into force by order subject to the approval of both Houses of Parliament (s. 77(5)). Once promulgated the Code may be revised from time to time by the same procedure (s. 25(4)). The discussion in this chapter will relate to the draft Code issued by the Home Secretary on 4 July 1996.

The impetus for the Code came from the Report of the Royal Commission on Criminal Justice (1993, Cm 2263, 96) and was inspired by the familiar PACE Codes. However, the form of the Code and its relationship with the primary legislation differs markedly from the PACE model. The function of the PACE Codes is to describe best practice and to restate, in a more accessible form, duties and rights established by the primary legislation. The Code under the Criminal Procedure and Investigations Act 1996 will operate in a very different way. The primary legislation sets out the aims of the Code (s. 23) and provides a catalogue of example disclosure provisions (s. 24), but leaves the Code to define precisely the duties and responsibilities of the police. Thus, the Code will not simply be a user-friendly practitioner's manual to the Act, but a normative document in its own right.

Inevitably, the draft Code repeats much of the substance of ss. 23 and 24. It is necessary to consider the statutory provisions separately from the present draft Code, since the latter may be modified before it is brought into operation and may be subject to modification in future.

THE STATUTORY FRAMEWORK

The aims of the Code

The aims of the Code are set out in s. 23(1). The relationship between s. 23 and the Code made under it is a clumsy one, since that section can be understood only by reference to the Code. In particular it is necessary to look to the Code to discover upon whom particular duties are laid. Thus, for instance 'the person who is involved in the prosecution of criminal proceedings . . . and who is identified in accordance with prescribed provisions' (s. 23(1)(e)) is identified in the Code as the prosecutor. '[T]he person who is to allow the accused to inspect information' (s. 23(1)(h)) is identified in the Code as the disclosure officer.

Interestingly, until the final report stage, the Bill contained no provision relating to the scope of investigations or the collection of evidence. However, concern was expressed in debate that investigations should not be confined to proving the guilt of a particular suspect and that investigators should be under a broad duty to consider alternative suspects and to pursue inquiries which might exculpate as well as incriminate. This concern was adopted by the Government who inserted s. 23(1)(a), which requires that all reasonable steps are taken for the purposes of the investigation and that all reasonable lines of inquiry are pursued.

If that subsection is designed to focus the investigation on hypotheses other than a particular suspect's guilt, it is surely right in principle. Neglect of alternative suspects may lead to the true offender escaping and has led to miscarriages of justice in the past. It is accepted in both scientific and forensic theory that the best way to test a proposition is to attempt to refute it. There seems no good reason for reserving such testing until the trial. Thus, it is in the interests of both justice and economy for the police to test the case against a suspect by attempting to refute it. That said, it is not clear to what extent s. 23(1)(a) requires the police to pursue alternative inquiries. The reference to 'all reasonable lines of inquiry' clearly does not mean every conceivable line of inquiry. If commitment to a particular suspect's guilt is strong and investigative resources are scarce, it will be easy to conclude that it would not be reasonable to pursue other lines of inquiry. Ultimately, the subsection attempts to change deeply ingrained police culture. Since there are real doubts about the effectiveness of rules and prohibitions in changing police culture (M. McConville et al. *The Case for the Prosecution*, 1991), it seems unlikely that the exhortatory tone of s. 23(1)(a) will have much effect.

Section 23(1)(b), (c) and (d) prescribes that relevant information obtained in the course of an investigation must be recorded and retained, as must any other material (i.e., a physical object) which is relevant to the investigation. Although the Act does not specify upon whom these duties are to be laid, the Code lays them on the investigator.

Section 23(1)(e) places the disclosure officer under a duty to 'reveal' to the prosecutor all information or other material retained in the course of the investigation. It appears that this statutory duty is satisfied by listing such information and material in a document or schedule (s. 23(g)) and permitting the prosecutor to inspect the relevant material (s. 23(f)). The draft Code places the disclosure officer under a general duty to supply copies if requested (para. 7.4). This is surely the right approach. Although the police are understandably defensive about the resource implications of storing, retaining and supplying unused material, logistical difficulties in gaining access to unused material must not be permitted to undermine the prosecutor's duties to review unused material for the purpose of primary and secondary disclosure.

Where the prosecutor decides for the purpose of either primary or secondary disclosure that particular material should be disclosed to the accused (s. 23(1)(f)), it is for the disclosure officer to determine whether it is appropriate for the accused to be given a copy of it or merely to be allowed to inspect it (s. 23(1)(h)). However, where the accused is allowed to inspect material he should be given a copy of it if he so requests unless the disclosure officer is of the opinion that it is not practicable or desirable to do so (s. 23(1)(i)). This provision does little to enhance the rights of the accused since the test is wholly subjective and therefore completely within the control of the disclosure officer. Thus, if the disclosure officer has decided not to provide copies in the first place, he may simply refuse to do so if requested on the grounds of impracticability or undesirability.

This provision is surely wrong in principle. The question whether it is desirable for the defence to take copies is not an appropriate one for an officer of relatively low rank. The provision also rather undermines Government assertions that power over the scope of disclosure should rest with the prosecution rather than the police.

A controversial issue is the extent to which the defence should have access to the schedule of unused material prepared by the investigator. In the Home Office Consultation Document on *Disclosure* (1995, Cm 2864) it was argued that there should be no scope for 'fishing expeditions' and that accordingly the schedule should be available only to the prosecutor, who would then determine if any unused material would assist defences notified by the accused, and disclose them accordingly (Cm 2864, 13–14). This proposal met with considerable criticism on the basis that this would deny the defence any opportunity to challenge the prosecutor's decision about what material should be disclosed (see Leng [1995] Crim LR 705).

In the light of this criticism the Government announced a change of heart. Thus, in introducing the Bill in the House of Lords, Baroness Blatch said 'As a result of representations we received, we are now persuaded that [the schedule] should be given to the defence' (*Hansard*, Lords, 27 November 1995, col. 464; see also the Home Secretary, Michael Howard, *Hansard*, Commons, 27 February 1996, col. 740). The extent to which this clear promise is embodied in the Act is unclear. Under s. 4, the prosecutor must supply the schedule of unused material to the accused at primary disclosure, but only where the schedule has already been supplied to the prosecutor by the police. If the prosecutor is supplied with the schedule after primary disclosure then, under s. 23(1)(g), where the prosecutor so requests the accused must be allowed to inspect it or be given a copy of it. The combined effect of these provisions appears to be as follows. Whether or not the accused has a right to the schedule of unused material depends arbitrarily upon whether the prosecutor has received the schedule before making primary disclosure. After this stage, the accused may be given access to the schedule, but only if the prosecutor so requests, the prosecutor being under no duty to do so.

Although the Act does not seem to give full effect to Government promises in both Houses of Parliament that the accused will have access to the schedule of unused material, it is to be hoped that the Act will be operated in the spirit of those promises and that the Code will be revised accordingly.

Powers and duties in relation to investigations

Section 24(2) provides, in rather obscure terms, that the Code should require a police officer to be identified as the investigating officer in charge of any investigation (s. 24(2)(a)) and that officer should take steps to ensure that a person (whether or not a police officer) fulfils the duties of disclosure officer (s. 24(2)(b)). In relation to a particular investigation, the Code should provide that either duty may be carried out by different people in succession, for instance when the officer dies or retires (s. 24(2)(c)). It is not made clear whether these duties can pass from person to person where there are less permanent interruptions of service such as illness or holidays. In view of the continuing duties of the officer in charge and of the disclosure officer, it would seem sensible to interpret s. 24(2)(c) to cover such circumstances also.

The Code may include provisions about the manner of recording information, the manner of retaining information and other relevant material, and about the period for which information and material must be kept (s. 23(4)). Where a person is charged, the period of retention may extend beyond the resulting conviction or acquittal. Retention beyond the end of the trial would be necessary to accommodate any necessary appeals and also following acquittal if there were any possibility of the case being retried (under Part VII of the 1996 Act) on the ground that the acquittal was tainted.

The Code may also contain provisions about the timing, manner and extent of disclosure to the prosecutor (s. 23(5)). The Code may also make different provision in relation to different categories of case or contain exceptions in relation to certain categories of case (s. 23(7)).

In line with the general policy of the Act, material obtained by telephone tapping under a warrant issued under s. 2 of the Interception of Communications Act 1985 is to be excluded from the provisions of the Code (s. 23(6)).

Examples of disclosure provisions

Section 24 provides examples of the kinds of provisions which may be included in the Code. The form of s. 24 is novel and it is not clear what effect this section has. The wording of the section suggests that it was not designed to bind the Home Secretary as to the substance of the Code or later revisions of it. Thus, the term 'may' suggests that the Home Secretary retains an ultimate discretion, and the phrase 'examples of the kind of provision' avoids the degree of specificity which would be required if the section were to bind the Home Secretary. If this interpretation of s. 24 is correct then it would provide no basis for judicial review of any future Code, except perhaps if the Code promulgated was so dissimilar to the examples given that it fell foul of the test of unreasonableness in *Associated Provincial Picture Houses* v *Wednesbury Corporation* [1948] 1 KB 223.

An alternative view is that s. 24 may leave the Home Secretary with a discretion but subject to limits. Thus, if s. 24 prescribes the kind of provisions which may be included in the Code, this may suggest that other kinds of provisions may not be so included. On this basis, if the Code were to contain provisions which could be said to be different in kind to those in s. 24, those provisions could be quashed as *ultra vires*.

Apart from the question whether s. 24 binds the Home Secretary, it is not clear what function the section has. It is clearly a guide to drafting the Code, but such briefs to draftsmen are not normally published. It might have been of assistance to Parliamentarians during the passage of the Bill had a draft of the Code itself not been published in time to be debated. The section will be of minimal value to the users of the Act who will look straight to the Code.

The examples of disclosure provisions found in s. 24 deal with duties to produce schedules of sensitive and non-sensitive material (s. 24(2) and (3)), the duties of the police to make both sensitive and non-sensitive material available to the prosecutor (s. 24(4) and (5)), and to make available any other sensitive or non-sensitive scheduled material as requested by the prosecutor (s. 24(6) and (7)). These provisions will not be subjected to detailed analysis in view of the fact that they are given effect by the Code.

Abolition of the common law

Section 27 seeks to abolish the rules of common law relating to the duties of police officers or other persons charged with the conduct of investigations in relation to revealing relevant material to prosecutors. The intention is clear: to replace the disclosure scheme developed by the courts with the one found in the Code. The notion of abolishing the relevant common law is however problematic. Should the new scheme fail to cover all of the ground covered by the common law rules, inevitably the common law will be called upon to fill the gap. Where this is the case it seems likely that the law will be informed by the same principles and policies which underpinned the pre-Act law. Whether this is viewed as the creation of new common law or the reinstatement of the old is of little importance. What is important is that the common law will have a continuing influence in this area.

Perhaps the major lacuna between the scope of the Act and the scope of the pre-existing common law relates to non-police investigations (considered below). Under the Act non-police investigators are charged to have regard to relevant provisions of the Code which would apply if the investigation were conducted by the police (s. 26(1)). The extent to which the phrase 'have regard to' can place a person under a legal duty is debatable, even where the relevant investigative function closely mirrors that of the police. Where the functions and practices of the non-police agency differ markedly from the police it may be even more difficult to deduce what impact the Code should have. Where this is the case, it seems likely that the common law will have an important function in developing the relevant rules and duties.

Application of the Code to non-police investigations

The disclosure provisions in Part I of the Act are reciprocal. Rightly, they will not come into force until the Code governing investigations is in place. It would not be satisfactory to require the defendant to make disclosure unless the prosecution case and any other material which undermined it had first been disclosed to him. Such prosecution disclosure will not be assured until the Code is in operation.

The compulsory disclosure provisions of Part I of the Act will apply to all prosecutions on indictment — whoever conducted the initial investigation. Therefore, in principle, all agencies involved in the investigation of indictable offences should be subject to the Code. This is not in fact the case. Section 22 of the Act restricts the definition of criminal investigations to which the Code applies to those conducted by police officers, as does para. 2.1 of the draft Code. Others who are charged with duties to investigate crime are however enjoined to 'have regard to any relevant provision of a code which would apply if the investigation were conducted by police officers' (s. 26(1)).

The issue of the applicability of the Code to other investigative agencies was raised at a number of stages in the parliamentary progress of the Bill. Amendments were tabled and rejected which would have extended the Code to 'police officers or officers of another investigative agency' (*Hansard*, Lords, 19 December 1995, cols 1526–1529) or persons, such as forensic scientists, who are instructed by a police officer or other investigator to take part in the investigation (*Hansard*, Commons Standing Committee B, 16 May 1996, cols 88–94), which would have required other investigators to observe relevant parts of the Code rather than merely have regard to them (*Hansard*, Commons Standing Committee B, 21 May 1996, cols 95–102), and which would have empowered the Home Secretary to promulgate codes for other investigative agencies (*Hansard*, Commons, 12 June 1996, cols 373–377).

These initiatives were rejected by the Government for a variety of inter-linked reasons. It was argued that a code designed for the police, who act as investigators only, could not be applied to other agencies which might undertake both investigation and prosecution; that it would not be feasible to have a single code covering agencies with different operational practices; that to require other investigators to follow the Code to the letter would deny them necessary flexibility; that it would be difficult to impose the Code on an agency which followed an existing code of practice; that the duties of an investigator should not be imposed upon forensic scientists whose role in the process is that of witness; and that it would not be proper for the Home Secretary to promulgate codes for agencies for which he was not ministerially responsible.

The major reason offered by the Government for not binding other agencies to the Code, was that s. 26(1), which requires other investigators to have regard to the Code, would be sufficient to maintain standards in other agencies. The Government relied upon the precedent of s. 67(9) of PACE, which similarly requires other investigators to have regard to relevant provisions of PACE Codes whilst carrying out their duties. Following the PACE model will be convenient in that it seems likely that agencies which have been held to be bound by the PACE Codes will similarly be bound by the investigations Code. Thus, the Code will probably apply to trading standards officers (*Dudley MBC* v *Debenhams plc* (1994) 154 JP 18; *Tiplady* (1995) 159 JP 548), electricity board officials engaged in collecting evidence with a view to prosecution (*Stewart* [1995] Crim LR 500), company security staff employed to investigate alleged offences (*Twaites* (1990) 92 Cr App R 106), and other private employees specifically engaged to investigate offences (*Halawa* v *Federation Against Copyright Theft* [1995] 1 Cr App R 21).

However, even after a decade of PACE being in force, this list covers only a fraction of those whose work involves criminal investigation. Whereas many of the public investigative agencies play safe by adhering to PACE, there are many public officers and private employees who remain unsure about if and to what extent they are bound. This suggests that s. 67(9) is hardly a good precedent to follow. The Government might have been better advised to accept the opposition's invitation to promulgate a second, perhaps less specific, code, coupled with a list or description of the agencies to which it would apply.

Sanctions for breaches of the Code

Section 26(2) follows s. 67 of PACE in providing that failure to comply with the Code by a police officer or any other investigator who must have regard to it shall not of itself give rise to civil or criminal liability. From one perspective, this appears entirely reasonable. Why should a busy police officer be liable for a mere administrative slip or omission committed in the course of her job? An alternative view is that the Act and the Code embody procedural rights of the accused which are vital for a fair trial. Some sanction for breach of the Code is required if the accused's rights are to be taken seriously and protected. Procedural rights for the accused have a rather hollow ring if they may be infringed with impunity (cf. Sanders 'Rights, remedies and the Police and Criminal Evidence Act' [1988] Crim LR 802). As was pointed out by Chris Mullin MP in the second reading debate: 'It is a feature of all proven miscarriages of justice that no one has ever been held to account for negligent or deliberate failure to disclose, however blatant' (*Hansard*, Commons, 27 February 1996, col. 771).

Not surprisingly, in view of the different perspectives which may be taken on this issue, the absence of sanctions for breach of the Code proved controversial during the passage of the Bill. Suggestions were made that failure to retain and disclose information as required by the Code should lead to adverse inferences against the prosecution case, to match the inferences which might be drawn following a similar failure to disclose by the defendant (per Lord McIntosh, *Hansard*, Lords, 18 December 1995, cols 1457–8). It was also suggested by the opposition that breach of the Code by a police officer or prosecutor should lead to disciplinary or criminal proceedings (per Jack Straw MP, *Hansard*, Commons, 27 February 1996, col. 777).

Calls to provide specific sanctions for non-compliance with the Code were strongly resisted by the Government. It was argued that serious breaches would amount to criminal offences for which prosecutions could be brought and that breaches by police officers would amount to disciplinary offences under the Police and Magistrates' Courts Act 1994 (per David Maclean, Home Office Minister, *Hansard*, Commons, 27 February 1996, cols 776–777).

These arguments are not convincing. The relevant criminal charge is attempting to pervert the course of justice. Liability for this offence would not depend upon the seriousness of any breach of the Code but rather on whether the officer intended to pervert justice. Thus, very serious breaches of the Code which might prejudice the accused's ability to defend herself, but which arose through carelessness rather than malice, would remain without sanction. The reference to disciplinary sanctions was also presumably tongue-in-cheek. It is notorious that breaches of the PACE Codes, even those which attract censure in the courts, are not proceeded against as disciplinary offences. There is no good reason to think that police forces would treat breaches of the investigations Code any more seriously.

The Act contemplates that in some circumstances breach of the Code might lead to civil or criminal proceedings. Thus, by s. 26(3), the Code is specifically made admissible in any such proceedings. This is complemented by s. 26(4), which provides that if it appears to a court or tribunal in any civil or criminal proceedings that either the Code itself or any failure to comply with it are relevant to any question in the proceedings, then it shall be taken into account in deciding the question.

These provisions are modelled on s. 67(11) of PACE. Notwithstanding that pedigree, it is not clear what effect s. 26(4) is designed to have. The phrase 'shall be taken into account' implies admissibility but nothing more, since there is no requirement as to the weight to be given to such evidence. It may also be doubted whether s. 26(4) is designed to go beyond this and override rules of evidence which deny admissibility to otherwise relevant evidence. The best example of such a rule is the general rule against admission of the defendant's previous misconduct, unless the probative value is so great as to outweigh the risk of prejudice (*DPP* v *P* [1991] 2 AC 447). It is reasonable to assume that if the Act (or PACE before it) were intended to create a new exception to such a well-established rule of common law this would have been made explicit.

Remedies for breaches of the Code

Where there has been a breach of the Code, the question arises of what remedies may be available to any defendant prejudiced as a result. In relation to breaches of the PACE Codes the most effective remedy (at least for suspects who are charged) is the exclusion of evidence under s. 78 of PACE. Typically this applies to confessions obtained following breaches of the Code relating to detention and interview or identification evidence obtained following breaches of the Code relating to identification procedures. It seems unlikely however that s. 78 will provide a remedy for defendants who are prejudiced by breaches of the investigation Code in all but the most exceptional cases. The reason for this is that s. 78 gives the trial judge a discretion to exclude where the circumstances in which evidence was obtained make it unfair for that evidence to be admitted in the proceedings. This provides a potential remedy where illegal conduct precedes the obtaining of evidence, but could not generally operate in relation to a breach of rules relating to the retention and disclosure of evidence already obtained.

Although s. 78 may not be applicable, breaches of the Code are likely to lead to adverse consequences for the prosecution, which may or may not be viewed as remedies. In particular, a court may exercise its discretion not to make comment on faults in disclosure by the defence under s. 11(3)(a) and not to invite a jury to draw inferences against the accused under s. 11(3)(b). In many cases this will be justified simply on the basis of the weight of the relevant evidence. Consider a case in which there had been a failure at primary disclosure to disclose evidence undermining the prosecution case, but this was later discovered by the defence. It would be inappropriate to draw adverse inferences against the accused for putting forward a new defence based on this undermining information. Inferences would be improper for the simple reason that the fact that the defence was undisclosed would not logically suggest guilt.

In other situations a court might consider exercising its discretion under s. 11(3) not to make comment or draw inferences, following a breach of the Code, even where the breach did not logically reduce the evidential weight of the fault in disclosure by the accused. The purpose of exercising discretion in this way would not be to assist the jury in correctly attributing evidential weight, but rather to vindicate the accused's procedural rights, to discipline the police or prosecution and encourage future compliance, or to maintain the integrity of the criminal process as a whole (see A. Ashworth, 'Excluding evidence as protecting rights' [1977] Crim LR 723).

Discovering breaches of the Code

In the recent past, developments in the common law duty of disclosure by the prosecution have been a major factor in uncovering procedural breaches and omissions by the police which have led to a number of acquittals. The Act will have the effect of tightening up the duty on the prosecution to disclose and will considerably increase the powers of both police and prosecutors to determine what is disclosed. Ironically, the Act itself will make it very difficult for the defence to learn of breaches of the Code which the prosecution side does not wish to reveal. By choosing a low-visibility, rather than transparent, model, the Government runs the risk that the procedural safeguards for the accused guaranteed in theory by the Act will be routinely disregarded with impunity.

THE CODE IN OPERATION

The investigation

Criminal investigation is defined in para. 2.1 of the draft Code (following s. 22) as an investigation conducted by police officers with a view to it being ascertained whether a person should be charged with an offence, or whether a person charged with an offence is guilty of it. However, for the purposes of the Code, the definition is extended beyond investigations into crimes that have been committed to include investigations to determine whether a crime has been committed as well as surveillance operations conducted in the belief that a crime is about to be committed. This is important because it extends the scope of material which must be retained and may be required to be disclosed to the defence. Thus, where a suspect drug dealer has been arrested following surveillance on particular premises, the prosecution's disclosure duties should cover material collected during the operation but before that individual fell under suspicion.

The extension for surveillance is limited by the requirement of a belief that a crime is about to be committed. This would appear to exclude longer-term surveillance of a suspected criminal group to which the defendant is linked. The effect of this limitation would be to deny the defendant access to the products of such surveillance. This may be criticised because it is exactly this sort of material which may point suspicion away from the defendant and towards another suspect.

It is apparent that investigations into summary offences are included since the reference to ascertaining whether a person should be charged is not confined to the procedure under s. 37(7) of PACE but also includes laying an information and summons.

The division of police functions

Police functions in relation to an investigation are divided between the officer in charge, the investigator and the disclosure officer. Arrangements for allocating these functions are left to each police force and there is no bar to one person performing all three functions (draft Code, para. 3.1). In each police force the Chief Constable must make arrangements to ensure that for every investigation the identities of the officer in charge and the disclosure officer are recorded (para. 3.2). The Code attempts to guard against a hiatus in responsibility by providing that if for any reason an officer in charge or disclosure officer ceases to be responsible for those functions his supervisor or the officer in charge of criminal investigations for that area must assign someone else to assume the relevant responsibility, and their identity must be recorded (para. 3.6).

The officer in charge of the investigation is made responsible for ensuring that proper procedures are in place for recording information, and retaining records of information, in the investigation. In view of the responsibility for procedures, it seems that this officer is unlikely to be the traditional 'officer in the case' but rather an officer of supervisory rank. In view of the caseload of busy police stations it seems likely that cases will be allocated to officers in charge on a bulk basis and that this may dilute the power of that officer to exercise meaningful control over the cases in her charge.

An investigator is any police officer involved in a police investigation. All investigators share responsibility for recording information and retaining records (para. 2.1). It is confirmed that the duty to pursue all reasonable lines of inquiry, as imposed by s. 23(1)(a), attaches to the investigator (rather than the officer in charge) and applies whether such lines of inquiry point towards or away from the suspect (para. 3.4). It is doubtful whether it is sensible to attach these duties to investigators where there may be more than one. In such a case there would be no means of knowing which of two or more officers must fulfil the duty. The better approach would have been to attach the duty to the office in charge, subject to her power to delegate tasks to other investigators under para. 3.3.

The disclosure officer is the person (not necessarily a constable) responsible for examining the records created during the investigation and criminal proceedings and disclosing material as required to the prosecutor or the accused. The disclosure officer is also responsible for certifying that certain actions have been taken in accordance with the Code (para. 2.1), and in particular that material has been revealed to the prosecutor for the purposes of primary and secondary disclosure (para. 9.1).

Recording of information

It is the responsibility of the officer in charge to ensure that relevant information is recorded in writing, on video or audio tape, or on computer disk (para. 4.1). This applies also to relevant parts of larger records or documents where it would not be practicable to keep the whole (para. 4.2). The Code emphasises that 'negative' information, such as the fact that a number of people present said that they saw nothing, must be recorded (para. 4.3). This duty reflects both the requirement to follow up lines of inquiry which point away from a suspect, and the growing recognition that police investigations should be a resource for both sides of the adversarial contest.

Where relevant information is obtained, it must be recorded contemporaneously or as soon as practicable (para. 4.4). Similar rules apply to the recording of interviews with suspects under PACE Code C, para. 11. The reasons for requiring contemporaneity are to minimise errors of recollection and the risk of tampering or fabrication. Although witness statements are generally not admissible as evidence, some information recorded by the police may be prima facie admissible. Where this is the case, failure to observe the Code rules on recording may lead to the evidence being ruled inadmissible under s. 78 of PACE.

Retention of material

The investigator is under a duty to retain material obtained in the course of an investigation which may be relevant to that investigation. This applies both to material coming into the hands of the investigator and material, such as interview records, which is generated by her (draft Code, para. 5.1).

Where material has been seized under powers conferred by PACE, its retention is subject to s. 22 of PACE. That section permits material seized for the purpose of criminal investigation to be retained for use as evidence at a criminal trial, or for forensic examination or investigation in connection with an offence, except where a photograph or copy would be sufficient for that purpose. At the time when PACE was passed, prior to recent developments in the duty of prosecution disclosure at common law, it was probably envisaged that retention for investigation under s. 22 meant for the purposes of the prosecution case. On this interpretation, once a decision had been made that particular material would not be required for the prosecution case, it might be returned to the person from whom it had been seized. The 1996 Act and the draft Code confirm a broader view of investigation, encompassing lines of enquiry pointing away from the suspect (s. 23(1) and para. 3.4). This indicates that material which might assist the defence may be retained lawfully for the purpose of the investigation.

If either the officer in charge or the disclosure officer becomes aware as a result of developments in the case that material previously examined but not retained is relevant, that officer should take steps to obtain it or ensure that it is retained for further inspection or production in court if required (para. 5.3). This requirement would be satisfied by simply seeking an assurance from the holder of material that it would be made available if required. Although there is no mention of disclosure, it is implicit that such material might also be disclosed since the purpose of inspection would be to see if the material should be disclosed.

Material which must be retained

Paragraph 5.4 of the draft Code specifies a number of categories of material which must be retained. The duty it imposes does not extend to items which are ancillary to such material and possess no independent significance, such as duplicate copies of documents (para. 5.5). Most of the categories of material to be retained are unproblematic. These are: crime reports, including crime report forms; relevant parts of incident report books or officer's notebooks; records of telephone messages containing descriptions of an alleged offence or offender; exhibits mentioned in witness statements, unless these have been returned to their owner on the understanding that they will be produced in court if required; interview records, including written records or audio or video recordings of interviews with actual or potential witnesses or suspects; any material casting doubt on the reliability of a confession or of a witness; and any material which may fall within the test for primary disclosure in the Act.

Earlier versions of witness statements

More problematic is the duty to retain final versions of witness statements and draft versions where their content differs in any way from the final version. Whereas it is perfectly proper to retain the final version of a witness statement, the implication that an earlier version or earlier versions may be discarded may be criticised. If there are two or more versions it may be expected that there will be some differences. There is a risk that a police officer will not register the significance of a seemingly minor difference, and will discard an earlier statement which might have conveyed a different shade of meaning. Statements taken by the police are not spontaneous streams of consciousness but rather products of an interaction between police interviewer and witness. The content of such statements may be powerfully influenced by the prior beliefs and aims of the police interviewer. Once a final statement has been produced, it may be extremely difficult to disentangle the relative inputs of interviewer and interviewee, particularly since the process of interview may influence the witness's beliefs thereafter. One way of gaining an insight into the normally invisible process by which a statement is constructed is to compare earlier and later versions. This will be facilitated in cases where there is a difference between draft and final versions, in which case both should be retained.

This suggests that in principle *all* versions of police interviews and witness statements should be retained for future scrutiny. Although this will place an additional burden on the resources of the police this should not be excessive in view of the time limits which police forces may apply to the retention of investigative material (para. 5.10).

Draft statements by expert witnesses

To the extent that there is a duty to retain draft versions of witness statements, an exception is made for draft statements of opinion prepared by expert witnesses (draft Code, para. 5.6). The reason given is that earlier versions tend to be based on incomplete information, and tend to evolve as further information comes to light and additional expert contributions are obtained. This reasoning is not convincing. An expert opinion should make clear on what factual basis the opinion is given. Where the factual basis is incomplete this should be apparent and the value of the opinion assessed accordingly. A generalised and unsupported assertion about first drafts of expert evidence should not be sufficient to exclude them from the retention and disclosure system. Indeed, it may be argued that it is particularly important to scrutinise the process by which expert opinions are created, in view of the importance and persuasiveness of such evidence. As it stands, para. 5.6 would obscure any attempt by the police to tailor or influence expert evidence to fit the police case, as occurred in the notorious *Confait* case (Sir Henry Fisher *Report of an inquiry into the death of Maxwell Confait*, 1977, HMSO).

Periods of retention

The Code prescribes minimum periods for which material must be retained and places each Chief Constable under a duty to develop a policy on the length of time for which material is to be held beyond such minimum periods. The minimum periods for holding material are until a decision is made not to institute criminal proceedings (draft Code, para. 5.7) or until the case is completed by either the prosecutor deciding not to proceed, an acquittal, a conviction followed by the expiry of the time limit for appeal without an appeal being lodged or the determination of any appeal (para. 5.8).

In developing policies for determining how long material should be kept beyond such minimum periods, Chief Constables may, under para. 5.9, take account of the following criteria:

(a)   the seriousness of the offence;
(b)   the plea entered by the accused;
(c)   whether the proceedings resulted in acquittal;
(d)   whether a retrial is likely (i.e., under s. 54(4) where the acquittal is tainted);
(e)   the length of any custodial or community penalty imposed;
(f)   whether an appeal against conviction or sentence is pending or is expected (in principle this should include Attorney-General's references under s. 36 Criminal Justice Act 1972);
(g)   the possibility that a complaint or civil action against the police might follow, particularly if an investigation has not resulted in charges; and
(h)   any statutory requirements for the retention of material imposed other than under the Code.

Chief Constables are given a discretion to set either a fixed period for the retention of all material, or to set different retention periods for different categories of case (para. 5.10).

The extent to which retention policies will be developed locally is debatable. On the one hand, Chief Constables are expressly permitted to take into account the current practices of their forces in relation to the retention of material; on the other hand, they must also consider the retention policies developed or likely to be developed by other forces (para. 5.9). In view of the extent to which forces work together and liaise with the Home Office to create national police policy, it seems inevitable that something akin to a national policy on retention periods will develop.

The schedule of unused material

The effective performance of the prosecutor's disclosure duties will depend upon the schedule of unused retained material prepared by the disclosure officer. Such a schedule must be prepared where the accused is charged with an offence triable only on indictment, or an either way offence where it is considered likely that the case will be tried on indictment, or where it is considered that the accused is likely to plead not guilty at summary trial (para. 6.1). Where a belief that the accused will plead guilty at summary trial proves wrong, the disclosure officer must prepare a schedule as soon as practicable after it is decided to try the case on indictment or the accused pleads not guilty (para. 6.3).

The Code points to two factors which may indicate whether or not the accused is likely to plead guilty at summary trial. These are whether a person has admitted the offence and whether a police officer witnessed it (para. 6.2). Clearly neither factor will determine the question and it would seem that in most cases the disclosure officer will have to acquaint himself with the case file and take advice from investigators.

The disclosure officer must certify that he does not believe that the schedule contains any sensitive material (para. 6.4). Any such sensitive material must be listed in a separate schedule (para. 6.8) or, exceptionally, revealed to the prosecutor separately (para. 6.9).

Generally, each item of material must be listed separately, numbered consecutively, and described in sufficient detail to enable the prosecutor to form a judgment on whether the material should be disclosed (para. 6.5). Where it is impracticable to list items separately, for instance where there are many items of a similar nature, these may be listed in a block or described by quantity and generic title (para. 6.6). Where this is done, it remains the duty of the disclosure officer to list and describe individually any items which might meet the test for disclosure (para. 6.7).

The schedule (together with the schedule of sensitive material discussed below) must be signed and dated and sent to the prosecutor, if possible at the same time as the case file (para. 7.1). Where a schedule is not sent because it is believed that the case will be dealt with summarily by guilty plea, the schedule must be sent as soon as practicable after a plea of not guilty is entered or a decision is taken to try the case on indictment.

The influence of the disclosure officer

A particular concern of a number of those who commented on the Home Office Consultation Document *Disclosure* was that the proposed scheme would give low-ranking police officers *de facto* power over what material was disclosed to the defence (see responses to the Home Office by Liberty and Justice). Despite Government protestations that the critics had misunderstood the proposals and that responsibility would lie with the prosecutor, a close examination of the Code indicates how the manner in which the disclosure officer performs her duty may determine later decisions of the prosecutor about whether such material should be disclosed. Thus, the prosecutor's duty of secondary disclosure can be performed only if the descriptions of material given by the disclosure officer are sufficient to indicate whether an item might assist the accused's defence. Similarly, where a list of similar items contains a single piece of vital evidence, whether or not the prosecutor discloses it will depend upon whether the disclosure officer has the skill and inclination to recognise its significance.

Sensitive material

Perhaps the major criticism of the regime of prosecution disclosure developed at common law was that some cases had to be dropped because of the zeal of the courts in requiring the disclosure of material relevant to the defence which the police considered to be sensitive. The risk of this occurring is now reduced by a number of mechanisms provided in the Act and the draft Code. These are:

(a)   restrictions on the scope of primary prosecution disclosure;

(b)   limitation of secondary prosecution disclosure to matters relevant to any defence raised;

(c)   non-disclosure of the existence of other sensitive material, thereby avoiding the risk of the defence calling for it; and

(d)   the possibility of severing material in order that the part which is of evidential value to the accused may be disclosed whilst keeping secret those parts in which there is a public interest (draft Code, para. 10.5).

At common law the issue of whether allegedly sensitive material should be disclosed could arise in any case in which the defence knew of the existence of some evidence within this category or where the prosecutor held such evidence and sought a court ruling on whether it must be disclosed.

Under the Code the primary determination of sensitivity is made by the police. The disclosure officer or the investigating officer must list in a separate schedule material which she believes it is not in the public interest to disclose.

Paragraph 6.8 lists a number of examples of material which may be considered sensitive. These are: material relating to national security; material received from the intelligence and security agencies; material relating to intelligence from foreign sources which reveals sensitive intelligence-gathering methods; material such as telephone subscriber checks which is supplied to an investigator for intelligence purposes only; material given in confidence; material relating to the identity or activities of informants or undercover police officers, or other persons supplying information to the police who may be in danger if their identities are revealed; material revealing the location of any premises or other place used for police surveillance, or the identity of any person allowing a police officer to use premises for surveillance; material revealing, either directly or indirectly, techniques and methods relied upon by a police officer in the course of a criminal investigation, for example covert surveillance techniques, or other methods of detecting crime; material the disclosure of which might facilitate the commission of other offences or hinder the prevention and detection of crime; internal police communications such as management minutes; communications between the police and the Crown Prosecution Service; material upon the strength of which search warrants were obtained; material containing the details of persons taking part in identification parades; material supplied to an investigator during a criminal investigation which has been generated by an official of a body concerned with the regulation or supervision of bodies corporate or of persons engaged in financial activities, or which has been generated by a person retained by such a body; material supplied to an investigator during a criminal investigation which relates to a child witness and which has been generated by a local authority social services department or other party contacted by an investigator during an investigation.

Super-sensitive material

The Code also allows for exceptionally sensitive material to be excluded from the sensitive schedule and revealed to the prosecutor separately (para. 6.9). Two examples of such super-sensitivity are given; these relate to material which, if disclosed, might lead directly to loss of life or directly threaten national security. The investigator must inform the prosecutor of such sensitive material as soon as practicable after the prosecution file is sent to the prosecutor. The investigator must also ensure that the prosecutor is able to inspect the material in order to determine whether a ruling on disclosure should be sought (para. 6.10).

Revelation of material to the prosecutor

The disclosure officer's duties to reveal material to the prosecutor correspond to the two stages of prosecution disclosure to the defence. The whole edifice of reciprocal disclosure in the Act will depend upon how well this function is performed, since it will be unlikely that prosecutors will recognise the significance of particular material unless prompted by a person directly involved in the investigation. At the time of sending the schedule, the disclosure officer must draw the attention of the prosecutor to any material which may fall within the test for primary disclosure, and should explain why the investigator has formed this view (para. 7.2).

The disclosure officer must also give the prosecutor copies of any material falling within specified categories (para. 7.3), including any material casting doubt on the reliability of a witness or of a confession, and any other material which the prosecutor believes may undermine the case for the prosecution and therefore should be subject to primary disclosure.

The disclosure office must also provide copies of any records of the first description of a suspect given to the police by a witness, whether or not the description differs from that of the alleged offender. This rule reflects the *Turnbull* guidelines (*Turnbull* [1977] QB 224), which require that, where the case against an accused depends wholly or substantially on the correctness of an identification, the jury must be warned of the special need for caution with such evidence and the possibility of mistaken identification. Among the particular issues which the jury must be directed to consider is whether there are any material discrepancies between the description of the alleged offender first given by a witness and the appearance of the accused. Under the *Turnbull* guidelines, where there is a discrepancy the prosecution should supply the defence with particulars of the first description, and in any event must provide such particulars if the accused requests them. Under PACE Code D, para. 2, descriptions must be taken from potential witnesses prior to any identification procedure, and must be provided to the accused or his legal advisor.

It should be noted that the present Code refers to first descriptions given by a potential witness. This is ambiguous since it is not clear whether it refers to those who witnessed or claim to have witnessed the events in question, or those who may be called as witnesses in court. In principle, if the purpose is to enable the defence to test any identification evidence offered by the prosecution, anything which contradicts it should be considered. This suggests that the term 'potential witness' should be interpreted as meaning any witness or purported witness to the event in question, whether or not the prosecution intend to rely upon his evidence in court.

The prosecutor must also be provided with copies of any information provided by the accused which indicates an explanation for the offence with which he was charged (para. 7.3). This would include things said in mitigation for an admitted offence, which might influence the prosecutor's discretion to drop the case on the ground that there would be no public interest in proceeding. It is not clear whether the paragraph also includes denials or other exculpatory remarks made outside the formal interview. In principle such material should be made available to the prosecutor because of its potential significance, for instance in determining whether inferences should be drawn from a failure to mention a fact during formal interview (under s. 34 of the Criminal Justice and Public Order Act 1994) or in generally undermining the prosecution case.

Having received the schedule, the prosecutor may require the disclosure officer to allow him to inspect or be provided with copies of material which has not been copied to him already (para. 7.4). Where the disclosure officer believes that certain material is too sensitive to be copied, it may be inspected only. For material which is recorded other than in writing (e.g., on audio tape), the questions of how it should be revealed and whether it should be revealed in full are matters for agreement between the disclosure officer and prosecutor (para. 7.5).

Having received the schedule and any material which must be disclosed to him, the prosecutor must make primary disclosure to the defence under s. 3. The prosecutor is not bound to disclose material falling within the categories which the disclosure officer is under a duty to reveal to him. This is surprising, in view of the patent potential of material within these categories to undermine the prosecution case. Presumably, it will be in exceptional cases only that such material will not be disclosed as a matter of course.

Following primary prosecution disclosure the defence may submit a defence statement under s. 5 or s. 6. This should set out the general nature of the defence and indicate the matters on which issue is taken with the prosecution case and the reasons for this. It is implicit in the Act and the Code that this defence statement should be communicated to the investigators and the disclosure officer. While the investigators should investigate any defences raised, the disclosure officer is required to review the unused material again and must draw the attention of the prosecutor to any material which might reasonably be expected to assist the accused in asserting the disclosed defence (para. 8.1). The disclosure officer also remains under a continuing duty to consider any new material coming to light and to reveal it if it meets the tests for disclosure (para. 8.2).

The mechanics of disclosure to the accused

Where a prosecutor has possession of copies of material and decides to disclose these to the accused, they may be supplied to the defence by either the prosecutor or the disclosure officer, subject to agreement between them (para. 10.2). However, where the prosecutor requests disclosure of material of which he has not got a copy, the disclosure officer must make that disclosure to the accused, but only in circumstances specified in para. 10.1. These circumstances are:

(a) that in the opinion of the prosecutor, the material might undermine the prosecution case;
(b) that the material might reasonably be expected to assist the defence as disclosed by the accused; or
(c) the court has ordered disclosure of the material under Part I of the Act.

The implication of para. 10.1 is that, except in these clear cases, a disclosure officer may refuse to copy to the accused material of which the prosecutor has not first obtained a copy. There would however be no purpose in blocking disclosure in this way, since the prosecutor may personally disclose material to the accused having first called for material under para. 7.3.

Where material is to be disclosed to the accused, the disclosure officer has a primary discretion either to provide a copy or to allow the accused to inspect the material. However a copy should generally be supplied if specifically requested (para. 10.3). There is a similar discretion to provide recorded material in either its original form or as a transcript which has been certified by the disclosure officer as a true record (para. 10.4).

A copy may be withheld where in the opinion of the disclosure officer it is either not practicable or not desirable to disclose it (para. 10.3). Although examples are given of both impracticability and undesirability, the test is apparently subjective, giving the disclosure officer considerable leeway to refuse. The example given of impracticability is that the material consists of an object which cannot be copied. The example given of undesirability is a written statement of a child witness in relation to a sexual offence.

Chapter Three
Preparatory Hearings

THE REFORM OF PRE-TRIAL PROCEEDINGS

A number of concerns have combined to prompt the rapid development of pre-trial court proceedings and other linked reforms in recent years. These concerns include: wastage of court and prosecution resources when a plea of guilty is unexpectedly tendered on the day of trial; wastage of prosecution resources through over-preparation of cases because of ignorance of the defences to be raised; extensive adjournments after the jury have been empanelled, and in the course of the trial, for legal arguments over admissibility of evidence and other issues; unmerited acquittals arising from unanticipated 'ambush' defences; and, not least, the pressures placed upon the criminal justice system by the increasing crime rate.

Prior to the 1996 Act, the only new statutory procedure was the discretionary preparatory hearing, introduced for serious fraud cases on the recommendation of the Roskill Report (*Fraud Trials Committee*, 1986) by s. 7 of the Criminal Justice Act 1987. This initiative had itself been inspired by the development of pre-trial reviews, which had been introduced informally at some Crown Courts and had first been officially recognised in a Practice Direction in 1977. The explicit purpose of these reviews was to highlight the issues involved in the forthcoming trial and to facilitate listing; the implicit purpose was to advance the stage at which plea bargaining might begin. A study conducted in 1992 indicated that reviews took place in about a quarter of all Crown Court cases, most reviews were primarily concerned with plea and the great majority took less than half a day (Zander and Henderson *The Crown Court Study*, 1993, Royal Commission on Criminal Justice Research Study No. 19).

The desirability of extending court-based pre-trial procedures was reviewed by the Royal Commission on Criminal Justice (1993, Cm 2263, Chap. 7). The Commission rejected the suggestion that plea and directions hearings (PDHs) should be made compulsory in every case, on the basis that this would lead to a waste of resources for simple cases. Instead, the Commission favoured a system of reciprocal pre-trial disclosure to clarify the issues, coupled with new power for judges to make binding rulings before the jury is empanelled. In the Commission's view, the existence of such powers would actually reduce recourse to pre-trial hearings since they would give an incentive to the parties to reach agreement between themselves. The Commission did however recognise the value of pre-trial hearings for more complex cases and recommended that such hearings should be the norm for trials expected to last for more than five days, and also that the parties or the judge should have a right to require a pre-trial hearing for some reason other than the length of the trial. Although the Commission noted the cultural resistance of practitioners to clarifying issues pre-trial, they believed that this could be overcome by requiring inter-party discussions out of court, followed by the deposit at court of certificates of readiness. The certificate would include an estimate of the time required for trial, and any failure to comply with these procedures could be met by costs penalties imposed by the court.

Although adopting much of the reasoning of the Royal Commission, the Government reached different conclusions and opted for a uniform system of plea and directions hearings, which were introduced by Practice Direction in 1994 ([1995] 1 WLR 1318, see *Blackstone's Criminal Practice*, D11.14) with the intention that they would operate in all courts by the end of 1995. The first function of the PDH is to take the defendant's plea. Where there is a plea of guilty, the court moves straight to the sentencing stage, whereas for not guilty pleas the hearing will attempt to identify the issues to be raised at trial. Where appropriate, further issues such as admissibility of evidence or points of law may be resolved and the presiding judge may order a further preliminary hearing to consider pre-trial issues in more detail.

Although a pilot study of the implementation of PDHs indicated that they had had some success in reducing the numbers of cases listed for trial and cracked trials, the Government returned to the issue in its Consultation Document *Improving the effectiveness of pre-trial hearings in the Crown Court* (1995, Cm 2924). The Government identified two factors requiring attention. First, the objective of clarifying the issues prior to trial was inhibited by the lack of a duty on the accused to disclose his defence in advance. Secondly, the effectiveness of the hearings was limited by the unwillingness of the parties to participate in them and by the absence of a power in the judge to make binding rulings.

The Government proposed what it described as a graduated response to these problems. For all contested cases the accused would be required to disclose his case in advance. This proposal is now given effect in Part I of the Act. In relation to all Crown Court cases, the effectiveness of PDHs and subsequent preliminary hearings would be bolstered by a judicial power to make binding rulings on any question of evidence or law. This would permit effective clarification of issues for all cases and would be necessary to enable disputes about the proper scope of required disclosure to be resolved pre-trial. Although the Government recognised the desirability of having the same judge dealing with both pre-trial procedures and the trial, it was considered that any benefits would be outweighed by the problems of listing and judicial administration that this would cause.

For complex or lengthy cases the Government recommended the adoption of more elaborate preparatory hearings, as presently used in serious fraud cases. At such hearings the judge would have a range of additional powers to identify, simplify and narrow the issues in advance of trial. Because of the complexity and probable rarity of cases requiring preparatory hearings, the Government felt that the benefits of judicial continuity would outweigh any problems of judicial administration which this might bring.

The new preparatory hearings for complex cases established under Part III of the Act will be considered in this chapter and the extension of the judge's powers in relation to other pre-trial proceedings under Part IV will be considered in Chapter Four.

PREPARATORY HEARINGS FOR COMPLEX CASES

Power to order preparatory hearings

The new provisions for preparatory hearings in long or complex cases are closely based on the procedure established for serious fraud cases under the Criminal Justice Act 1987. It might be thought that the Government have played safe by adopting an existing model, rather than adopting a brand new one as recommended by the Royal Commission. Unfortunately, as will be discussed below, the process of trying and testing the preparatory procedure for serious fraud has exposed its weaknesses and limitations rather than confirmed its vigour and usefulness. In view of this, early amending legislation may be required unless the courts manage to resolve some of problems of interpretation associated with these provisions.

Part III will come into force in relation to cases which reach the Crown Court after a day to be appointed (s. 28(1)). The appointed day is likely to be in early 1997. The Government has announced that preparatory hearings may be piloted in particular Crown Courts before general introduction. This is made possible by s. 28(3), which provides that an order appointing a commencement date may apply in relation to specified Crown Courts only.

The preparatory hearing does not replace the plea and directions hearing. Indeed, the order to hold a preparatory hearing will normally be made at PDH, although it may be made at any stage before the jury is sworn (s. 29(1)(a)). A preparatory hearing may be ordered on the application of the prosecutor, the accused or one of the accused (if more than one), or on the judge's own motion (s. 29(4)).

A preparatory hearing may be ordered where it appears to the judge that the case is of such complexity, or is likely to be of such length, that substantial benefits would be likely to accrue from a preparatory hearing for one of a number of specified purposes (s. 29(1)). The purposes in question are those of:

(a) identifying issues which are likely to be material to the verdict of the jury;
(b) assisting the comprehension of such issues;
(c) expediting the proceedings before the jury; and
(d) assisting the judge's management of the trial.

The test is subjective, being based upon what appears to the judge, and the power to order a preparatory hearing is discretionary, since even if the test is satisfied the judge is not required to order a hearing.

Although it is not made clear what is meant by 'substantial benefits' in this context, it is probably intended that the judge should weigh any expected benefits against any likely disadvantages such as possible extension of the overall proceedings. There is thus no presumption in favour of preparatory hearings even for very complex cases and no assumption that preparatory hearings are inherently likely to produce a net benefit. This reflects a recent study on judges' attitudes to pre-trial reviews which found that only one in ten reviews was believed to have resulted in a significant saving in time or money (M. Zander and P. Henderson *The Crown Court Study*, 1993, Royal Commission on Criminal Justice Research Study No. 19). One of the purposes of the proposed pilot introduction of preparatory hearings will be to assess their effectiveness and to test the view that only a small proportion of cases will require such hearings (Consultation Document, p. 16).

There is no power to order a preparatory hearing under the 1996 Act where it appears to the judge that the evidence reveals a case of serious fraud which would therefore qualify for a preparatory hearing under s. 7(1) of the Criminal Justice Act 1987. In the absence of a precise definition of fraud there is a risk that courts will become embroiled in expensive demarcation disputes about whether serious and complex cases are of fraud or of something else. Whether it is sensible to maintain two parallel but exclusive systems of preparatory hearing is a moot question, particularly since the combined effect of Part III and sch. 3 (which modifies the 1987 Act) is to assimilate the two procedures.

The start of the trial

An important conceptual difference between pre-trial hearings and preparatory hearings established under Part III is that, whereas the former have as their purpose the clarification of issues for a later trial, the latter are a preparatory stage of the trial itself and may be used to resolve a variety of issues without requiring the attendance of the jury. Section 30 confirms that the trial starts with the preparatory hearing and provides that the arraignment shall take place at the start of that hearing unless it has taken place before then. From that point the trial will be in continuous session until final disposal, subject to the judge's power to adjourn the hearing from time to time under s. 31(2).

The start of the preparatory hearing will also be the start of the trial for the purpose of custody time limits under s. 22 of the Prosecution of Offences Act 1985. This is an exception to the new rule that generally for the purpose of custody time limits the trial starts with the swearing of the jury or guilty plea (s. 71, see Chapter Nine at p. 120). Thus, it is apparently accepted that longer periods of custody are justifiable for cases in which the trial is likely to be complex and lengthy.

It follows from the fact that the trial starts with the preparatory hearing that a single judge must preside throughout, except for exceptional circumstances such as the death or serious illness of the judge (*Southwark Crown Court, ex parte Commissioners for Customs and Excise* [1993] 1 WLR 764). This is in contradistinction to PDHs which may be dealt with by a judge other than the one who presides at the eventual trial. It also follows that the defendant has a right to be present. The Consultation Document had recommended that, after arraignment, the judge should have a discretion to dispense with the defendant's attendance. To have made a defendant's attendance at his own trial subject to the discretion of the judge would have marked a major change in our system of criminal justice. Wisely, this proposal finds no place in the final legislation.

Notwithstanding s. 30, the concept of the preparatory hearing as the start of the trial is partially contradicted by s. 31(3), which provides that the judge may make rulings as to admissibility and other questions of law. If the preparatory hearing is the start of a fully fledged trial one would expect the judge to possess all those powers available at trial, except for those powers which require or imply the presence of the jury. As will be discussed below, a similar provision in the context of serious fraud cases has been interpreted as restricting the power of the judge in preparatory hearings, thereby diluting the effectiveness of the preparatory hearing as the start of trial.

Orders before the preparatory hearing

The preparatory hearing will normally be preceded by, and ordered in the course of, a plea and directions hearing. To enable the preparatory hearing to be an effective procedure, s. 32 provides that the judge who orders a preparatory hearing may order the prosecution and defence to make disclosure for the purpose of the hearing (discussed below) in advance of it.

Disclosure and clarification of issues

The main vehicle for clarifying the issues at a preparatory hearing is the judge's power to order a further round of reciprocal disclosure under s. 31(4) to (6). This may not always be utilised in view of the extent of disclosure before this stage by virtue of:

(a) evidence tendered by the prosecution at committal proceedings under the Magistrates' Courts Act 1980, as amended by sch. 1 to the 1996 Act;

(b) primary disclosure by the prosecutor of material which might undermine the prosecution case under s. 3 of the 1996 Act;

(c) compulsory disclosure by the accused under s. 5; and

(d) secondary prosecution disclosure of material under s. 7 which might assist the defence disclosed by the accused.

Under s. 31(4), the judge may order the prosecutor to give to the court and to the accused a case statement. The order may specify the time within which it must be complied with (s. 31(10)), subject to minimum and maximum periods to be specified by Crown Court Rules (s. 33(2)). The case statement will differ from the bundle of evidence supplied at committal in that it should state the facts as the prosecution believe them to be, including for instance any inferences drawn from the primary evidence, and should also indicate how as a matter of law each count on the indictment is to be proved. However, in making an order under this section, the judge may take account of anything done in pursuance of the disclosure provisions in Part I of the Act (s. 20(2)).

Section 31(5) provides that the case statement should comprise the following:

(a) the principal facts of the case for the prosecution;

(b) the witnesses who will speak to those facts;

(c) any exhibits relevant to those facts;

(d) any proposition of law on which the prosecution proposes to rely;

(e) the consequences in relation to any of the counts in the indictment that appear to the prosecutor to flow from matters falling within (a) to (d).

At this stage the prosecutor is not placed under any fresh duty to review material in police or prosecution hands for the benefit of the accused. However, it should be borne in mind that the prosecutor's duty under s. 9 to consider whether there is prosecution material which either undermines the prosecution case or might assist the defence continues until final disposal of the case.

Once a case statement has been supplied by the prosecutor, the judge may order the accused to provide to the court and the prosecutor:

(a)   a written statement setting out in general terms the nature of his defence and indicating the principal matters on which he takes issue with the prosecution;

(b)   a notice of any objections which he has to the prosecution case statement; and

(c)   written notice of any point of law or of admissibility of evidence which he wishes to take, and to any authority on which he intends to rely for that purpose (s. 31(6)).

The order may specify the time within which it must be complied with (s. 31(10)), subject to maximum and minimum periods to be set by Crown Court Rules (s. 33(2)). When making the order the judge must warn the accused of the risk of adverse comment at trial or of adverse inferences being drawn if the accused should fail to comply (s. 31(8)).

Inconveniently, the Act does not prescribe a name for the bundle of material which the accused may be ordered to disclose under s. 31(6). It should not be described as a defence statement (which is the term applied to disclosure under s. 5), but might be described as a further defence statement for the preparatory hearing. Unlike disclosure under s. 5, for which the content is fixed, the judge ordering disclosure under s. 31(6) may choose what must be disclosed from the menu provided by the subsection. Thus, the judge may omit from a disclosure order any matter which has already been fully disclosed under s. 5(5).

In two respects defence disclosure under s. 31(6) may be fuller than the earlier defence statement. First, the accused may have more to answer since at this stage he should have been presented with a reasoned prosecution case rather than the bundle of evidence which he would have received at committal. Secondly, the accused must disclose points of law on which he relies, including any point as to the admissibility of evidence.

It is clear that at this stage the burden of disclosure on the defence is considerably less than that on the prosecution. It is less clear what degree of specificity will suffice. The experience in relation to serious fraud is that defence disclosure under similar provisions has been insufficiently precise to be of much assistance to the prosecution (M. Levi, *The investigation, prosecution and trial of serious fraud*, 1993, Royal Commission on Criminal Justice Research Study No.14). For instance, would it be sufficient to simply deny committing the offence and to supply a list of those witnesses with whose evidence the accused took issue? In relation to points of admissibility, would it be sufficient to indicate that the admissibility of evidence would be challenged under s. 78 of PACE, without specifying which evidence was to be so challenged and why?

Under Crown Court Rules to be made under s. 33, the accused will not be required to disclose the identity of defence witnesses except in relation to experts whose evidence is required to be disclosed after committal under the Crown Court (Advance Notice of Expert Evidence) Rules 1987 (SI 1987 No. 716), and in relation to alibi witnesses, whose identity must be disclosed under s. 5(7). This limitation on the extent of required defence disclosure was introduced in the course of the Act's parliamentary progress in response to fears that disclosure might hamper the defence because of the risk of police interference with witnesses, or the possibility that witnesses might refuse to give evidence because of anxiety about police attention pre-trial.

In terms of the logic of the Act, this protection for the defence might be considered incoherent. A major aim of the legislation is to defuse ambush defences by pre-emptive police investigation. The possibilities for this will be limited if the prosecution has notice of the defence but not of the witnesses supporting it.

Following an objection by the accused under s. 31(6)(b), the judge has power to make whatever amendments appear appropriate to the prosecution case statement (s. 31(4)(d)). It will be appropriate to use this power where part of the prosecution case statement is affected by a judge's ruling, for instance where particular evidence is ruled inadmissible. However, the power to amend is not limited to such circumstances and, in theory, the judge could make other amendments even against the prosecutor's protests. It may be doubted whether many judges would wish to stray this far from the principles of adversarialism. In any event, should this occur, the prosecution would not be bound in their conduct of the case by the judge's amendment since, under s. 34(2), a jury may be invited to draw inferences against a party who departs from the case he disclosed, but there is no provision for inferences where there is a departure from an amendment made by the judge.

The judge may also order the prosecution to prepare its evidence and any explanatory material in such form as appears to the judge likely to aid comprehension by the jury, and to give it to the accused and the court in that form (s. 31(4)(b)). Provision was first made for presenting evidence in ways which would make it more readily understandable by ss. 30 and 31 of the Criminal Justice Act 1988. At that time this was seen as a resource to be used by the prosecution (or defence) as they saw fit. It now appears that presenting evidence in these ways may, at the discretion of the judge, become a prosecution duty. This is a significant move away from the principle that the adversaries are free to present their cases as they see fit. It will however be advantageous to have such evidence available at the preparatory stage in order that any disputes about its form may be resolved prior to the empanelling of the jury.

In pursuit of narrowing the issues, the judge may order the prosecution to notify the accused of any documents which in the view of the prosecutor ought to be admitted as true and of any other matter which, in the prosecutor's view, ought to be agreed (s. 31(4)(c)). Where such a notification has been made, the judge may order the accused to notify the court and the prosecutor of the extent to which he agrees with the prosecutor, and the reason for any disagreement (s. 31(7)). When making such an order, the judge must warn the accused of the risk of adverse comment at trial or of adverse inferences being drawn if the accused should fail to comply with the order (s. 31(8)).

This duty to notify any disagreement with evidence which the prosecutor believes should be agreed will operate not only to clarify what evidence must be called at trial, but also as a further means of flushing out ambush defences. This is made clear by s. 31(9), which empowers a judge to require better reasons if she feels that reasons given by the accused for not agreeing evidence are inadequate. Exercise of this power will serve a useful function in putting the accused on notice that he risks adverse inferences if he does not give fuller reasons for not agreeing evidence. The provision may however be criticised on the ground that it may be used to force the accused to disclose more detail of his defence than would be required under s. 31(6). Thus, there is nothing to prevent a prosecutor notifying the accused that, in his view, every element of the prosecution case ought to be admitted. Having done so, the prosecutor can expect to be notified of reasons for disagreement and, if not satisfied, may press the judge to order further particulars under s. 31(9) in the hope of obtaining a detailed response to every piece of evidence in the prosecution case.

Sanctions for non-disclosure

Following the model established by the Criminal Justice and Public Order Act 1994 and by Part I of the 1996 Act, s. 34(2) provides that adverse comment and adverse inferences are the sanctions for non-disclosure and also for departure at trial from the case disclosed at preparatory hearing. Adverse comment may be made against either a prosecutor or an accused who fails to comply with a requirement to disclose under s. 31 or who departs from the case disclosed at the later hearing before the jury.

The possibility of inferences against the prosecution is surprising in view of strenuous Government arguments against extending the sanction of inferences to prosecution failures in relation to primary and secondary disclosure under ss. 3 and 7 (*Hansard*, Commons Standing Committee B, 30 April 1996, col. 18). In all cases comment may be made only with leave of the judge, and it remains to be seen to what extent judges will be prepared to allow the prosecution's chances to be prejudiced by adverse comment.

Where no leave has been given, the accused is protected from innuendo or the jury's untutored inferences by a prohibition on any mention of the defence statement before the jury without consent of the accused (s. 34(4)). This follows a common law principle established in *Hutchinson* (1985) 82 Cr App R 51. Where a failure or departure is established, the judge or, with leave of the judge, any other party may comment. This suggests that not only may the defence comment upon prosecution failures but also that one accused may comment on a failure to disclose by her co-accused. Presumably, where a co-accused applies to do this, the judge should consider the extent to which the co-accused's case is affected by the failure or departure, although this is not referred to in s. 34(3), which prescribes what the judge should have regard to in considering whether to give leave.

Remarkably, although s. 34 provides judicial control over whether a party can comment, there is apparently no fetter on the content of such comment once permitted. Thus, the party given leave may make such comment as appears to that party to be appropriate.

In deciding whether to give leave (and presumably in deciding whether to make a comment), the judge must have regard to the extent of any departure or failure and whether there is any justification for it (s. 34(3)). The issue of the extent of the departure from the duty to disclose will be problematic. Although there is no requirement to warn the accused that disclosure is considered inadequate (cf. s. 31(9)), justice would seem to require that the accused is given notice that the judge takes this view. This would allow the defence an opportunity either to address the judge on the issue of the adequacy of the disclosure already made or to make good any deficiency with supplementary disclosure.

As discussed above, requirements to give notice of the general nature of the defence or of any point of law to be relied upon might apparently be satisfied with quite brief (and uninformative) statements. Should the judge disagree and hold that more detail is required, it would nevertheless be unjust to permit adverse comment or inferences in relation to an accused whose lawyers had responsibly taken a different view of the obligations imposed on their client. This would cease to be true when the degree of specificity is established by precedent.

The issue of whether the judge should permit comment on the accused's failure to disclose or on a departure from the defence disclosed, or whether he should prohibit comment on the basis that the failure or departure is justified, will be riddled with difficulty on a number of levels. The issue is likely to arise once the trial of the facts before the jury has begun and must be tried in the absence of the jury. It is not clear what standard of proof should prevail on the issue of justification: must the judge be convinced or would it be sufficient that the accused had raised a prima facie case to support his claim? By the very nature of the procedure some commentable failings will result from poor legal advice or representation. Whereas there are strong procedural arguments for treating the client and his lawyer as one, could it ever be just to translate a lawyer's ineptitude into an evidential inference against a person charged with a serious offence?

Quite apart from the difficult issues of substance, s. 34 is likely to generate considerable argument in court on issues which are wholly collateral to the question of guilt or innocence. Some may doubt whether this will contribute to the joint causes of expedition and efficiency which underpin the new scheme of preparatory hearings.

Rulings at the preparatory hearing

The ultimate impact of preparatory hearings in increasing the efficiency of the trial process will depend upon the extent of the judge's power to make determinations or rulings which do not require the presence of the jury, and on the ability finally to resolve any appeals against such determinations and rulings before the trial of the facts begins. This will be particularly important for complex cases in which there are necessarily a mass of critical pre-trial rulings. Each one of these has the potential to lead to a quashed conviction and retrial, unless any dispute about such rulings can be resolved before the trial of the facts.

By s. 31(3), the judge is empowered to make rulings as to any question as to the admissibility of evidence and any other question of law relating to the case. These issues would normally have been determined on the *voir dire*. Any such order will normally be binding, although it may be varied or discharged on the application of a party if the judge believes that it is in the interests of justice to do so (s. 31(11)).

In the context of similar provisions relating to serious fraud, the Court of Appeal in *Gunawardena* [1990] 1 WLR 703 has held that the power to make binding rulings must be limited by implication to the purposes for which preparatory hearings may be ordered. Thus, applying this principle to the 1996 Act, it would seem that the power to make rulings under s. 31(3) is restricted to the purposes set out in s. 29(2), namely (a) identifying issues likely to be material to the verdict of the jury; (b) assisting their comprehension of any such issues; (c) expediting the proceedings before the jury; and (d) assisting the judge's management of the trial. The principle in *Gunawardena* has proved difficult to apply. After a period of uncertainty, it now appears that whether or not a particular order falls within the purposes of a preparatory hearing must be judged objectively, according to the effect which the ruling would have (*Hunt* [1994] Crim LR 747) or according to the judge's purposes in making the order (*Maxwell* Court of Appeal 94/7352/S2 (unreported)).

The tentative conclusion to the brief discussion above is that the power conferred on the judge under s. 31(3) will be limited to case management issues. Paradoxically, the power of the judge to make rulings at pre-trial hearings under s. 40 is not so fettered, although rulings under that section do not carry the possibility of final determination of the issue by interlocutory appeal prior to trial. Unfortunately, it is not open to a judge at a preparatory hearing to avoid constraints on his power to make rulings under s. 31(3) by making orders under s. 40. The reason for this is that the s. 40 power is exercisable only at hearings which occur before the start of the trial (s. 39(3)) — as noted above, preparatory hearings are the start of the trial and therefore the exercise of any pre-trial powers in ruled out.

The argument above suggests that either the scheme for preparatory hearings under Part III is congenitally flawed or that it has been fatally injured by the well-meaning attentions of the courts. If the scheme is to be effective, early legislative intervention to free the judges's powers under s. 31(3) from the suffocating grip of s. 29(2) will be required.

INTERLOCUTORY APPEALS

Rulings made by the judge under s. 31(3) may be appealed with the leave either of the judge or of the Court of Appeal (s. 35(1)), and from the Court of Appeal to the House of Lords (s. 36(1)). Where leave to appeal has been granted, the preparatory hearing may continue, but the trial of facts before the jury cannot commence until any appeal is finally determined or abandoned (ss. 35(2) and 36(2)). The Court of Appeal is granted powers to confirm, reverse or vary the decision appealed against (s. 35(3)).

For complex cases, the ability to appeal and resolve issues of admissibility and law prior to the jury being sworn will be vital if preparatory hearings are to achieve their objective of shortening and simplifying hearings before juries. As noted above, this ability will be severely compromised if the courts follow decisions under the Criminal Justice Act 1987 and hold that the power to make rulings is restricted to the purposes for which preparatory hearings may be held.

REPORTING RESTRICTIONS

An essential element of a fair trial is a jury who come to their task unprejudiced as to either the character of the accused or the facts of the case. The law seeks to prevent prejudice by the general law of contempt which prohibits publications which create a substantial risk that the course of justice in active criminal proceedings will be seriously impeded or prejudiced (Contempt of Court Act 1981, s. 2(2)). The interest in preventing prejudice must however be balanced against a legitimate public interest in access to information about the current administration of the law. Thus, except where a specific order has been made postponing the reporting of proceedings or banning the reporting of particular information under s. 4(2) or s. 11 of the Contempt of Court Act 1981, a person cannot be guilty of contempt for publishing a fair, accurate and contemporaneous report of legal proceedings held in public (Contempt of Court Act 1981, s. 4(1)).

The right to report legal proceedings has traditionally been suspended in relation to committal proceedings on the basis that the evidence at committal may be prejudicial because it may present only the prosecution case which may not be subject to cross-examination. The prohibition on reporting of committal proceedings is currently found in s. 8 of the Magistrates' Courts Act 1980. (This provision was to have been substituted by new provisions in the Criminal Justice and Public Order Act 1994, but has now been reinstated by Part V of the 1996 Act).

The risk of prejudicing the eventual trial before the jury also attends the reporting of any pre-trial proceedings. However, since these proceedings have been developed by the practice of the courts rather than by statute, there has been no general prohibition on publication, although in particular cases it is open to the judge to suspend publication by order under s. 4(2) of the Contempt of Court Act 1981. Reporting restrictions were however applied to the statutory preparatory hearings for serious fraud cases under s. 4 of the Criminal Justice Act 1987. The 1996 Act extends similar restrictions to both the new-style preparatory hearings for complex cases under Part III and also to other pre-trial hearings under Part IV (discussed in Chapter Four). The opportunity has also been taken to revise the reporting restrictions for serious fraud cases for the purposes of consistency (see Chapter Ten).

The restrictions on reporting preparatory hearings and appeals

Section 37 creates reporting restrictions in relation to preparatory hearings, applications for leave to appeal and appeals in relation to such hearings (s. 37(2)). The restrictions cover written reports of such preparatory hearings, applications and appeals which are published in Great Britain and reports which are included in programmes broadcast for reception in Great Britain (s. 37(1)). The restrictions cease, and reports may be published, after the conclusion of the trial of the accused or, where there is more than one accused, at the conclusion of the trial of the last one to be tried (s. 37(8)).

As is the case for committal proceedings, certain formal details are exempted from the restrictions by s. 37(9):

(a)   the identity of the court and the name of the judge;

(b)   the names, ages, home addresses (either at the time of the events leading to the charge or the time of the publication or programme: s. 37(10)) and occupations of the accused and witnesses;

(c)   the offence or offences, or a summary of them, with which the accused is or are charged;

(d)   the names of counsel and solicitors in the proceedings;

(e)   in the event of adjournment, the date and place to which proceedings are adjourned;

(f)   any arrangements as to bail;

(g)   whether legal aid was granted to the accused or any of the accused.

Lifting of restrictions

Orders to lift the restrictions on reporting may be made under s. 37(3), (4) and (5). Although the issue is similar to that relating to committal proceedings, the 1996 Act does not follow the committal model. The corresponding provision relating to committals treats the bar on reporting as a protection which the accused may waive if he wishes, or which may be waived at the request of one of a number of accused where it is in the interests of justice to do so (Magistrates' Courts Act 1980, s. 8). In relation to committals, either the restrictions apply or they are lifted, there being no half-way house (*Leeds Justices, ex parte Sykes* [1983] 1 WLR 132).

The present provision adopts a different approach in two respects: first, the restrictions may be lifted completely or partially; secondly, the power to lift restrictions is primarily that of the relevant court, subject to a veto by the accused. The power to lift restrictions in relation to preparatory hearings and applications to the judge for leave to appeal is vested in the judge presiding at the hearing (s. 37(3)). The Court of Appeal and House of Lords may lift restrictions relating to appeals and applications for leave to appeal made to the relevant court (s. 37(4) and (5)). Each court may order that the bar on publication shall not apply or shall not apply to a specified extent.

The Act appears to envisage that the relevant court would act on its own motion and there is no express provision for the accused to apply to have the restrictions lifted. Presumably, a court would consider lifting the restrictions when requested to do so by the accused, but he has no right to have them lifted. There is equally nothing to prevent a request by the prosecutor.

Where a court is considering making an order to lift the restrictions and there is only one accused who objects, the relevant court must lift restrictions if (and only if) satisfied after hearing the representations of the accused that it is in the interests of justice to do so (s. 37(6)). Where there are two or more accused and one of them objects, the relevant court must lift the restrictions if (and only if) satisfied after hearing the representations of each of the accused that it is in the interests of justice to do so (s. 37(7)). In any event the court must not lift the restrictions so as to permit publication of any objections or representations by the accused.

Presumably, the interests of justice test relates to the relevant proceedings only. Thus, a court should deny a request to lift restrictions for some collateral purpose such as publicising a dispute with the police or prosecutor. On the other hand it would be proper to lift restrictions in order to assist the course of justice in the instant case, for instance by alerting other potential witnesses who might not otherwise be aware of the proceedings.

Breach of reporting restrictions

It is an offence to publish or broadcast a report of a preparatory hearing, or any appeal or application for leave to appeal relating thereto, in breach of s. 37. In relation to a report in a newspaper or periodical, the offence is committed by any proprietor, editor or publisher (s. 38(1)(a)). In relation to a written report which is published in some other form, the offence is committed by the person who publishes it (s. 38(1)(b)). In the case of a report included in a broadcast programme, the offence is committed by any body corporate providing the service in which the report is included and any person performing the functions corresponding to those of editor of a newspaper (s. 38(1)(c)).

The offence is punishable on summary conviction by a fine not exceeding level 5 on the standard scale (currently £5,000) (s. 38(2)). No *mens rea* or other fault is required for the offence, nor is a defence of innocent publication prescribed (cf. Contempt of Court Act 1981, s. 3). However, proceedings for the offence may be instituted only with the consent of the Attorney-General (s. 38(3)) and presumably fault or lack of it may be taken into consideration in deciding whether a prosecution should be permitted.

Chapter Four
Pre-trial Rulings

Introduction

Part IV of the Act reinforces the pre-trial procedures which have been developed as a matter of practice by the Crown Court by empowering judges to make binding rulings. This reform, coupled with the introduction of preparatory hearings (discussed in Chapter Three) enacts the Government's 'graduated approach' to improving the efficiency of the trial process by introducing procedures to clarify issues and to settle areas of dispute before the empanelling of the jury. These measures will also complement the new scheme of compulsory pre-trial disclosure in Part I by enabling judges to rule on whether the disclosure obligations of the parties have been fulfilled.

Part IV will come into force in relation to pre-trial hearings beginning on or after a day to be appointed by the Secretary of State (s. 43). The appointed day is likely to be in early 1997.

Pre-trial hearings

The new power is exercisable at pre-trial hearings relating to trials on indictment after the accused has been committed to the Crown Court or the case has been transferred to that court (s. 39(1)), or after the preferment of a voluntary bill of indictment under s. 2(2)(b) of the Administration of Justice (Miscellaneous Provisions) Act 1933 (s. 39(2)). The power may be exercised only before the start of a trial. For this purpose, the start of a trial is when the jury is sworn to consider the issue of guilt or fitness to plead, or when a guilty plea is accepted, or the start of a preparatory hearing ordered under either s. 8 of the Criminal Justice Act 1987 (serious fraud) or s. 30 of the 1996 Act (long or complex cases) (s. 39(3)).

The definition of pre-trial hearings will include plea and directions hearings and any subsequent hearing however described. Since these are pre-trial hearings, it is not a requirement that they be conducted by the eventual trial judge. Accordingly, different judges may make orders at different stages of the process and there is no requirement that any judge making an order is also the trial judge (s. 40(6)).

Rulings

Rulings may be made on application by a party to the case or on the judge's own motion (s. 40(2)), and may relate to any question as to the admissibility of evidence or any question of law relating to the case concerned (s. 40(1)). There is no express, and apparently no implied, restriction on the scope of rulings which may be made under s. 40, except that they must relate to issues of admissibility or law in the case in question. This contrasts with the position in relation to rulings in preparatory hearings for long or complex cases under Part III, which appear to be impliedly limited to the statutory purposes for which such preparatory hearings may be ordered (as discussed in Chapter Three). Since, the power to make rulings under s. 40 relates to pre-trial hearings which have been developed by court practice rather than by statute, there are no statutory purposes which may impliedly limit the power.

Any ruling made under s. 40 has binding effect until the verdict of the jury, or until the prosecutor decides not to proceed (s. 40(3)), unless a judge discharges or varies (or further varies) the ruling under s. 40(4). A ruling may be discharged or varied (or further varied) by a judge where it appears in the interests of justice to do so, either on application by a party or on the judge's own motion (s. 40(4)). Where a party makes an application to vary an earlier ruling he must show that there has been a material change of circumstances since the ruling was made, or (where there has been a previous application) since the last application was made (s. 40(5)).

This provision is designed to discourage the wasting of court time and inhibit parties from attempting to overturn earlier rulings when there has been a change of presiding judge. Whether it will be successful in these respects remains to be seen. Experience suggests that it is rarely beyond the wit of counsel to find a material change of circumstance when the client's interests so require.

The provision is wider than that which applies to preparatory hearings in so far as the judge can vary of his own motion. This reflects the fact that different judges may preside at various stages of a case's progress and that a trial judge would not wish to have her options restricted by decisions made earlier by another judge. It may be noted, however, that significant use of the power to vary earlier rulings will lengthen proceedings and remove many of the benefits to be gained by holding pre-trial proceedings.

Restrictions on reporting pre-trial rulings

The restrictions on the reporting of pre-trial rulings created by s. 41 are similar in form to those relating to preparatory hearings created by s. 37. The reader is referred to Chapter Three for a discussion of the recent history and principles underlying restrictions on the reporting of proceedings prior to jury trial.

Reporting restrictions apply in relation to:

(a)   pre-trial rulings;
(b)   proceedings on applications for rulings;
(c)   orders to discharge or vary rulings;
(d)   proceedings on applications to vary or discharge rulings (s. 41(2)).

The restrictions cover written reports of such rulings and proceedings which are published in Great Britain and reports which are included in programmes broadcast for reception in Great Britain (s. 41(1)). The restrictions cease and reports may be published after the conclusion of the trial of the accused or, where there is more than one accused, at the conclusion of the trial of the last of the accused to be tried (s. 41(6)).

Unlike the restrictions on reporting committals and preparatory hearings, there are no exemptions for the publication of the formal details of the accused, such as name, address and occupation.

Lifting of restrictions

Orders to lift or partially lift restrictions on reporting may be made under s. 41(3). This power is vested in the judge presiding at the hearing.

The Act appears to envisage that the court would act on its own motion and there is no express provision for the accused to apply to have the restrictions lifted. Presumably, a court would consider lifting the restrictions when requested to do so by the accused, but he has no right to have them lifted. There is equally nothing to prevent a request by the prosecutor.

Where a court is considering making an order to lift the restrictions and there is only one accused and he objects, s. 41(4) provides that the relevant court shall lift restrictions if (and only if) satisfied after hearing the representations of the accused that it is in the interests of justice to do so. Where there are two or more accused and one of them objects, the relevant court shall lift the restrictions if (and only if) satisfied after hearing the representations of each of the accused that it is in the interests of justice to do so (s. 41(5)). In any event the court shall not lift the restrictions to permit publication of any objections or representations by the accused.

Presumably, the interests of justice test relates to the relevant proceedings only. Thus, a court should deny a request to lift restrictions for some collateral purpose such as publicising a dispute with the police or prosecutor. On the other hand it would be proper to lift restrictions in order to assist the course of justice in the instant case, by for instance alerting other potential witnesses who might not otherwise be aware of the proceedings.

Breach of reporting restrictions

It is an offence to publish or broadcast a report of a preparatory hearing in breach of s. 41. In relation to a report in a newspaper or periodical, the offence is committed by any proprietor, editor or publisher (s. 42(1)(a)). In relation to a written report which is published in some other form, the offence is committed by the person who publishes it (s. 42(1)(b)). In the case of a report included in a broadcast programme, the offence is committed by any body corporate providing the service in which the report is included and any person performing the functions corresponding to those of editor of a newspaper (s. 42(1)(c)).

The offence is punishable on summary conviction by a fine not exceeding level 5 on the standard scale (currently £5,000) (s. 42(2)). No *mens rea* or other fault is required for the offence, nor is a defence of innocent publication prescribed (cf. Contempt of Court Act 1981, s. 3). However, proceedings for the offence may be instituted only with the consent of the Attorney-General (s. 42(3)) and presumably fault or lack of it may be taken into consideration in deciding whether a prosecution should be permitted.

Chapter Five
Mode of Trial and Committal Proceedings

This chapter is concerned with changes to the processes in the magistrates' court whereby a person charged with an indictable offence can be committed or, as the case may be, not committed to the Crown Court for trial. The principal changes are to be found in ss. 44 to 47 of and sch. 1 to the Act (committal proceedings) and in s. 49 of the Act (indication of intention as to plea before mode of trial). Both sets of changes have their origins in the report of the Royal Commission on Criminal Justice (1993, Cmnd 2263), but both have undergone considerable alteration since the report. The changes to committal proceedings represent a second radically different attempt at reform following provisions contained in the Criminal Justice and Public Order Act 1994 on transfer for trial which were never brought into force. Underpinning both limbs of the changes has been the fact that the current procedures have increasingly been shown not to be an effective or efficient filter either in preventing weak cases being committed to the Crown Court or in diverting to summary trial or sentence those less serious cases that can better be dealt with by magistrates. The changes to committal proceedings represent a complete about-turn from the Government's two-year attempt to abolish them, a reversal of direction that came at a very late stage in the passage of the Act and therefore with relatively little discussion in *Hansard*. The changes to committals will be examined after first looking at the changes relating to mode of trial determination, which logically and sequentially comes before committal proceedings.

INDICATION OF INTENTION AS TO PLEA BEFORE MODE OF TRIAL DECISION

Background

Decisions about mode of trial are of course concerned only with indictable offences which are triable either way. The number of these offences (for persons aged 17 and over) which were committed for trial to the Crown Court increased from 59,600 in 1980 to 73,800 in 1992, having reached a peak in 1987 of 93,100. Although these figures represent only 15 per cent, 17 per cent and (at the peak) 23 per cent of offences triable either way, they account for over 80 per cent of cases tried at the Crown Court. Given the much higher costs of trials in the Crown Court (the Royal Commission quoted figures of £13,500 per contested trial as opposed to only £1,500 in the magistrates' court) and the frequent complaints about delays in getting cases heard, the search for ways of eliminating unnecessary committals to the Crown Court has been a constant theme over the past 20 years. The *Report of the Interdepartmental Committee on the Distribution of Business between the Crown Court and the Magistrates' Court* (1975, Cmnd 6323), 'the James Committee', led to changes introduced initially in the Criminal Law Act 1977 (including the special procedure for criminal damage and the reclassification of a number of offences as summary only.) A similarly entitled Home Office Consultation Paper in March 1986 led to the changes introduced in the Criminal Justice Act 1988 which increased significantly the minimum value for criminal damage to be triable either way and again reclassified some offences as summary only (including common assault, driving whilst disqualified and taking motor vehicles without consent). As a result, there was a decline from the peak figures seen in 1987. In 1990, National Mode of Trial Guidelines were published (see [1990] 1 WLR 1439), partly with a view to encouraging magistrates to retain jurisdiction where appropriate, and these were themselves recently modified in 1995 (although not fully reported, see criticism by White, S., 'The antecedents of the mode of trial guidelines' [1996] Crim LR 471 and for the current text, *Blackstone's Criminal Practice*, D3.7). Finally, s. 46 of the Criminal Justice and Public Order Act 1994 again increased the minimum value for criminal damage and aggravated vehicle-taking (involving damage) to be treated as triable either way from £2,000 to £5,000.

The Royal Commission took the view that more radical reform was necessary since mode of trial decisions were being taken on the basis of mistaken assumptions by both magistrates and defendants and large numbers of cases were ending up inappropriately in the Crown Court where the defendant ultimately pleaded guilty and/or the Crown Court ended up imposing a sentence which the magistrates themselves could have imposed. The following extracts from Chapter 6 of the Royal Commission's report give a flavour of its views:

The magistrates send for trial a large number of cases that they could try themselves; while defendants opt for trial on the basis that they are going to plead not guilty but then usually plead guilty [para. 12] ... We believe that the procedure for determining mode of trial should be changed in order to secure a more rational division of either way cases between the magistrates' court and the Crown Court. We do not believe that this decision should be left to the defendant, though he or she should have a voice in the matter. [para. 13] ... Reduction of the pressure on the Crown Court is a desirable objective although it is not in itself the reason for which we recommend the change. To the extent that more cases remain in the magistrates' courts, savings may be made available which would enable more resources to be devoted to ensuring that the more serious cases going to the Crown Court are not only better prepared but more quickly heard. [para. 15] ... Under our proposed scheme the defendant would have the right to urge any considerations supporting jury trial that he or she wished. If the CPS were persuaded, that would be the end of the matter. If the CPS wished nevertheless to propose summary trial, it would be for the bench to weigh up all the factors and determine the mode of trial [para. 18].

A crucial point about the above proposals was that the defendant would lose the right to *insist* on jury trial in respect of offences triable either way, including theft and other crimes of dishonesty, although in such cases the possible loss of reputation would be one of the important factors affecting the bench in deciding on the mode of trial. A Home Office Consultation Document (*Mode of Trial*, Cmnd 2908, July 1995: see comment at [1995] Crim LR 757), noted (at para. 17) that the Royal Commission's proposals in this area had attracted particular criticism, including criticism from the Lord Chief Justice, 'partly on the grounds that they implied two-tier justice; that is, jury trial for those with no record and the most reputation to lose, but magistrates trial for recidivists'.

The Consultation Document went on to say, somewhat pointedly perhaps, that the Government was 'mindful of the Royal Commission's proposals and of the strong arguments against them and would welcome views' whilst at the same time canvassing two alternative courses of action. The first alternative was a further reclassification of certain offences triable either way as summary only, as had been done in both 1977 and 1988. The most significant possible reclassification which was considered was of minor theft, which, if defined as theft of £100 in value or less, could divert about 9,000 cases from the Crown Court each year. However, the Government noted that this sort of proposal had attracted considerable opposition each time it had surfaced since the James Committee in 1975, a particular difficulty being 'that the value of something stolen is not necessarily an accurate reflection of the seriousness of the offence, for example in terms of its effect on the victim or the circumstances in which it was committed'. The Government again markedly commented that it was 'alive to these objections to the reclassification of minor theft as summary only and would welcome views'. The Consultation Document then went on to point out that the other candidates for reclassification, apart from possession of an offensive weapon which itself might lead to problems, would yield very few 'process gains' in terms of the numbers of cases diverted away from the Crown Court.

However, a third opinion canvassed in the Consultation Document, plea before mode of trial, was clearly the favoured one, and has now found substantive form in s. 49 of the 1996 Act. The Consultation Document noted that:

The current arrangements which allow a defendant to choose his venue for trial are intended to protect the defendant's right to have *the case against him tested by a jury*. But a defendant who pleads, or intends to plead, guilty and accepts the case against him is, by exercising the right of election, able to select his *sentencing* forum. These proposals therefore concentrate on reserving Crown Court trial for those who are not admitting the offence with which they are charged and those whose offence is so serious that despite a plea of guilty, the Crown Court is the only appropriate forum for dealing with it. (para. 21)

The Document then went on to point out that there is currently no opportunity for pleas to be entered before the mode of trial decision. If there were such an opportunity, figures in *Home Office Research Study No. 125 Magistrates' Court or Crown Court? Mode of Trial Decisions* (Moxon and Hedderman, HMSO 1992) suggest that around 25,000 defendants per year who are currently committed for trial to the Crown Court for either-way offences might be willing to plead guilty at the magistrates' court and either be sentenced by the magistrates or be committed for sentence rather than for trial to the Crown Court. Furthermore, the highlighting of sentence discount for early guilty pleas in s. 48 of the Criminal Justice and Public

Order Act 1994 should further encourage guilty pleas at an earlier stage; if a discount of about one-third is allowed, as currently advised by the Magistrates' Association Sentencing Guidelines, that could convert some cases where magistrates may think their sentencing powers are inadequate into ones where they do have sufficient powers to impose the reduced sentence justified by the early guilty plea.

In contrast to the other alternatives canvassed, the Government stated that it saw 'attractions in this proposal, [was] considering the detailed implications for other court procedure, and would welcome views' (para. 25).

It should come as no surprise therefore that s. 49, providing for the accused to give an early indication of plea, was in the Bill from the outset and as enacted attempts to achieve the benefits outlined above by inserting three new sections, ss. 17A, 17B and 17C, into the Magistrates' Court Act 1980.

The new procedure

The three sections inserted into the 1980 Act now provide a new initial procedure to be used prior to determining mode of trial, which therefore takes precedence over the existing procedure outlined in ss. 18 to 21, although this nevertheless remains in place to cover the situations where the accused indicates he is going to plead not guilty (see the amendment to s. 18(1) of the 1980 Act by s. 49(3) of the 1996 Act). The new sections are set out somewhat more logically than the existing provisions (which in many respects they mirror) with s. 17A dealing with the normal case where the accused is actually present in court, s. 17B dealing with cases where the accused is not present on account of his disorderly conduct (but is represented) and s. 17C dealing with the court's powers to adjourn and remand.

Taking first the normal case where the accused is actually present in court, the new s. 17A defines the area of operation of the new procedure, in terms identical to the old s. 18(1), as being where 'a person who has attained the age of 18 years appears or is brought before a magistrates' court on an information charging him with an offence triable either way'. Section 17A(2) then makes it clear that, as far as s. 17A is concerned, everything required to be done has to be done with the accused present in court and then, under s. 17A(3), the charge is to be written down and read to the accused.

The key stage in the new procedure is the accused being asked to indicate how he would answer the following hypothetical question: 'whether (if the offence were to proceed to trial) he would plead guilty or not guilty' (s. 17A(5)). Before he can be asked this question, s. 17(4) requires the court to explain to the accused in ordinary language:

that if he indicates that he would plead guilty—

(a)   the court must proceed as mentioned in subsection (6) below; and

(b)   he may be committed for sentence to the Crown Court under section 38 below if the court is of such opinion as is mentioned in subsection (2) of that section.

Under s. 17A(6), the result of an indication that the accused would plead guilty is that:

the court shall proceed as if—

(a)   the proceedings constituted from the beginning the summary trial of the information; and
(b)   section 9(1) above was complied with and he pleaded guilty under it.

Thus, the ordinary language explanation required to be given might be something along the following lines:

You are shortly going to be asked whether you intend to plead guilty or not guilty at your trial for this offence no matter whether it is decided to try you in this court or at the Crown Court. If you answer that it is your intention to plead guilty then this court will no longer need to consider whether to try you here or commit you to the Crown Court for trial but must proceed to deal with you here and will treat you as actually having pleaded guilty and will therefore convict you without hearing any more evidence. This court would then consider whether its sentencing powers are sufficient for you to be sentenced here or whether you should be committed to the Crown Court on the grounds that the magistrates' powers of sentencing are inadequate.

Once such an explanation has been given, the accused must actually be asked the hypothetical question under s. 17A(5) (how he would plead at trial) and of course, if he pleads guilty, the court has to act as indicated in the explanation given to the accused. If the accused pleads not guilty, the court will move on to the normal procedure under s. 18 for determining mode of trial (see s. 17A(7) and the amendment to s. 18(1) of the 1980 Act made by s. 49(3) of the 1996 Act). A failure by the accused to indicate how he would plead is to be treated as an indication that he would plead not guilty (s. 17A(8)).

The effect of the above provisions is that:

(a)   persons accused of offences triable either way will be given an opportunity to plead guilty at an earlier stage than is currently possible;
(b)   consideration of mode of trial and therefore the possibility of committal to Crown Court *for trial* will not apply in cases where the accused has already indicated that he would plead guilty;
(c)   there will be a substantial decrease in the number of cases committed for trial (possibly as many as 25,000 per annum);
(d)   there will be a substantial increase in cases sentenced by magistrates on, in effect, guilty pleas;
(e)   there will also be an increase in the use of committals for sentence since inevitably some of the cases where a guilty plea is indicated will be cases where, even allowing for any appropriate discount for a guilty plea, the magistrates will still consider their powers of sentencing to be inadequate.

The precise scale of the above effects, and in particular the decrease and increase referred to in (c) and (d) above, will depend on the extent to which defendants are prepared to indicate a guilty plea at this early stage. It may be surmised that those whose offences are clearly likely to be regarded as within the sentencing powers of the magistrates will be more willing to indicate an early plea. Those at the more serious end of the scale who fear that the magistrates may in any event commit them for sentence to the Crown Court may choose to indicate an intention to plead not guilty on the basis that, if in any event they are to be subject to the greater sentencing powers of the Crown Court, they wish to preserve their option of trying to obtain an acquittal by a jury (or indeed by the magistrates). In other words, having more to lose (a potentially heavy sentence) and less to gain (no benefits from being dealt with summarily) by indicating a guilty plea, they are likely to reserve their position and indicate a plea of not guilty. They may also be motivated by the hope that the charges against them may be dropped or reduced before they actually come to trial or the hope or expectation that the disclosure of prosecution material that will follow a not guilty plea will provide a viable line of defence. As Redmayne points out ('Process gains and process values' forthcoming (1997) 60 MLR), the person who has grounds for hoping for a later reduction in charge is in a delicate position — having to balance in advance of prosecution disclosure the possibility, which is kept open by a not guilty plea, of a subsequent reduction to a lesser charge carrying a lesser sentence against the opportunity of securing a sentence discount now by indicating a guilty plea which precludes any possibility of a reduction in charge.

By s. 17A(9), it is made clear that a not guilty plea does no more than reserve the accused's position, since it states that an indication of how the accused would plead under s. 17A is not to be taken as constituting the taking of a plea (subject to s. 17A(6) which does deem an indication of intention to plead *guilty* to be a plea of guilty in the summary trial which is thereby treated as having been in process). There is thus nothing to stop an accused who has indicated he would plead not guilty from changing his plea to guilty either at the trial at the Crown Court, if he is committed for trial there, or at the summary trial, if the magistrates retain jurisdiction and he does not insist on Crown Court trial. By doing so, particularly if he is committed to the Crown Court, he will of course lose all or some of the benefit of any sentence discount that he might have gained by indicating an intention to plead guilty under s. 17A before the decision on mode of trial (depending on how late he leaves it to change his plea).

If, after the accused has indicated an intention to plead not guilty, the magistrates decide that they can try him and he is content to be tried by them, he may then immediately wish to change his plea to guilty safe in the knowledge that, whilst the magistrates can then still commit him to the Crown Court for sentence, they will not normally do so except on the basis of factors not already known to them at the time they decided to retain jurisdiction (e.g., on the basis of the accused's previous convictions or of offences which he asks to be taken into consideration). If therefore the accused's decision to indicate a not guilty plea under s. 17A was motivated by a fear that he might in any event be committed to the Crown Court for sentence, the magistrates' decision to try him may lead him to change his intention as to plea, now that the likelihood of committal for sentence is vastly reduced, particularly since he will know whether the most likely reasons for a committal for sentence (previous convictions or offences to be taken in to consideration) are going to apply. There does not however appear to be any formal provision for the accused to change his indication as to how he would plead after the court has decided that the offence is suitable for summary trial but, given that there will normally be an adjournment to the summary trial, perhaps there should be such an opportunity (e.g., as part of the accused's decision under s. 20(3) of the 1980 Act as to whether he consents to be tried summarily). There is nothing however to prevent an accused informally indicating his change of heart and this may be desirable in order to secure the maximum amount of any remaining sentence discount which may be available.

Section 17A says nothing about legal representation but, by analogy with the cases on the accused's election under s. 20(3) of the 1980 Act as to summary trial or committal proceedings, it will be essential that the accused understands the nature and significance of the question asked of him about his intention as to plea (see *Blackstone's Criminal Practice*, D3.8). The explanation by the court in ordinary language may provide some of this understanding but in addition he will need to understand the law applicable to the charge against him in order to decide whether he has any potential defence and whether he should indicate an intention to plead guilty or not guilty. If his indication that he would plead guilty is due to misunderstanding of his legal position when unrepresented, it should be open to him subsequently to change his plea (for it is treated as a guilty plea under s. 17A(6)(b)), although the court's power to allow a change of plea is a matter lying within its discretion (see *South Tameside Magistrates' Court, ex parte Rowland* [1983] 3 All ER 689). It will therefore normally be desirable that the accused is legally represented at the time he is asked to indicate how he would plead if the offence were to proceed to trial.

By way of contrast, the accused being legally represented is one of the preconditions (s. 17B(1)(b)) for the applicability of s. 17B which deals with the case where 'the court considers that by reason of the accused's disorderly conduct before the court it is not practicable for proceedings under section 17A above to be conducted in his presence' (s. 17B(1)(c)). The procedure under s. 17B is then effectively identical with that under s. 17A except that there is no requirement to explain the procedure in ordinary language and the accused's legal representative indicates how the accused would plead on his behalf. There is some debate about whether normally a legal representative can validly plead guilty on behalf of the accused (see *Blackstone's Criminal Practice*, D17.18), but the effect of s. 17B(2)(c) seems clearly to sanction an effective plea of this type.

The new s. 17C provides the court with the same powers to adjourn and remand as are available under s. 18(4) of the Magistrates' Courts Act 1980 in mode of trial proceedings. Some related amendments to s. 128 and s. 130 of the 1980 Act dealing with remands in custody are also made by s. 49(5) of the 1996 Act, which includes s. 17B with the various other powers to adjourn and remand mentioned in ss. 128 and 130.

It has already been mentioned that s. 49(3) of the 1996 Act amends s. 18(1) of the 1980 Act so as to make mode of trial proceedings applicable only where the accused has already indicated an intention to plead not guilty. Section 49(4) similarly amends s. 19(3) of the 1980 Act so as to delete the requirement to cause the charge to be written down and read to the accused since this will already have taken place under the new procedure for intention as to plea in s. 17A or 17B.

The commencement of the new procedure is not dependent on the date of commission of the alleged offence but applies, as a result of s. 49(6), 'where a person appears or is brought before a magistrates' court on or after the appointed day' but not if he has appeared or been brought before such a court 'in respect of the same offence on a previous occasion falling before the day'. It is anticipated that the appointed day will be in Autumn 1996.

COMMITTAL PROCEEDINGS

Background

Whereas the perceived problem with mode of trial decisions has been that they allowed through to the Crown Court too many cases which could have been tried or dealt with by magistrates, the problem with committal proceedings has been that, despite their cost in time, trouble, and complexity, they have allowed through to the Crown Court too many weak cases which do not merit trial by anyone. The problem is not a new one and the Criminal Justice Act 1967 sought to address the problem of disproportionate cost (whilst ignoring the issue of the committal of weak cases) by limiting full committals to cases where the defendant was unrepresented or the defence wished to argue that there was not a case to answer and dealing with other cases on a purely paper basis under what is now s. 6(2) of the Magistrates' Courts Act 1980.

Figures quoted by the Royal Commission on Criminal Justice (Chap. 6, para. 23) suggest that there are around 8,000 full committals per year, about 8 per cent of all committals. Full committals are time-consuming and cumbersome and enable the defence effectively to require key prosecution witnesses to give their evidence in court twice over, once in the committal proceedings and again at the trial. The Fraud Trials Committee in 1986 concluded that committal proceedings were especially inappropriate for cases of complex fraud since they were likely to be particularly lengthy and lay magistrates were not normally well qualified to assess the complex issues of law and evidence which were relevant to whether there was a case of fraud to be tried. The 'notice of transfer procedure', a method of by-passing committal proceedings altogether for serious or complex fraud, was therefore provided in ss. 4 to 6 of the Criminal Justice Act 1987, and a similar procedure was introduced in the Criminal Justice Act 1991 for certain offences involving child victims or witnesses 'for the purposes of avoiding any prejudice to the welfare of the child'.

The Royal Commission on Criminal Justice, having noted the view of most of the witnesses to it that 'committals, whether full or on paper, served little useful purpose, while full committals put vulnerable witnesses to the stress of having to give their evidence in open court twice over' (Chap. 6, para. 24) concluded, in agreement with both the Royal Commission on Criminal Procedure (1981, Cmnd 8092) and the Fraud Trials Committee (Roskill Report 1986), that 'full committal hearings in their present form should be abolished' (para. 26). It was also of the view that 'the present system of paper committals has no useful purpose, apart from any associated time limit by which the committal papers have to be ready and served on the defence. Such time limits, which we regard as essential, can be provided for without the mainly hollow procedure of committal under s. 6(2)' (para. 25).

The Commission also considered abolishing the opportunity of the defence to submit, in advance of trial on indictment, that there is no case to answer but concluded on balance that 'in the interests of stopping a demonstrably inadequate case against a defendant at the earliest possible stage, there should remain some opportunity for the defence to take the initiative' (para. 26). The commission went on (in para. 27):

We accordingly recommend that, where the defendant makes a submission of no case to answer, it be considered on the papers, although the defence should be able to advance oral argument in support of the submission and the prosecution should be able to reply. Witnesses should not be called: the right place to test their evidence is the trial itself. We do not think that they should be required in effect to give their evidence twice over. Quite apart from the time and trouble wasted by unnecessary duplication, we agree that there is a significant risk that some of them will feel so intimidated on the first occasion that they will be unable to give their evidence at the trial satisfactorily or perhaps at all. We believe that a hearing on the papers would be sufficient to enable the court to prevent from proceeding to trial cases too weak to deserve it.

In furtherance of these recommendations the Government added to the Criminal Justice and Public Order Act 1994, at a late stage in its passage, provisions to abolish committal proceedings and to replace them with a new transfer for trial procedure (s. 44 of and sch. 4 to the 1994 Act). The provisions had some similarities to the notice of transfer procedures made available for complex frauds and cases involving children in 1987 and 1991 respectively. There were however significant differences in that the earlier procedures were an alternative to committal which the prosecution could make use of if they so wished (and were in a position to do so, i.e., they had all the papers ready) whereas the transfer for trial provisions would have completely replaced committals and in that sense would have been mandatory. They also differed in terms of the venue for dealing with applications to dismiss which in the case of the earlier procedures is the Crown Court (with the possibility of oral evidence from witnesses) whereas for transfer for trial it was to have been the magistrates (without any evidence being given orally). Although everyone agreed that something needed to be done about committal proceedings, there was considerable scepticism as to whether the new hastily enacted provisions would prove either to be workable or an improvement on the previous situation.

It was initially intended that the transfer for trial provisions should be brought into force in July 1995, but problems that emerged on consultation on the detailed rules of court which would be necessary caused two further postponements. Ultimately it was decided that the difficulties were such that further amendments to the procedure by means of primary legislation were required, the Criminal Procedure and Investigations Bill being a convenient vehicle. These amendments were tabled at the Committee stage of the Bill in the Lords (*Hansard*, Lords, 19 December 1995, cols 1575–1580) but critics of the transfer for trial scheme, including the Law Society and the Justices' Clerks Association, remained unimpressed. As Lord McIntosh of Haringey put it at report stage (*Hansard*, Lords, 5 February 1996):

We agree that the number of committals will be reduced by the government's proposals. However, there are not very many committals at present. Old style committals make up only 7 per cent of all committals and witnesses give evidence only in some of those. The government propose to make a radical change to make all committals unnecessary, in order to produce benefits which will in any event apply only to a small proportion of cases. It is our view that the Royal Commission's recommendations could be achieved [by alternative means].

Particular criticisms of the transfer procedure were that it would be complex, bureaucratic and inflexible and that, for example, because it imposed time limits (an overall time limit of 70 days for service of the prosecution case) which in some cases would not be met, the procedure would result in defendants in some serious cases having to be discharged. Furthermore, it was suggested that, in order to minimise such problems, the time limits were set too generously for the vast majority of cases which nevertheless would make full use of the time available resulting in more delays than under the current system, increases in remand prison populations and in general terms a less efficient system.

Nevertheless, the Government continued to defend the transfer for trial system and the abolition of committal proceedings of which:

> the central aim was ... to move from a mainly court based system to a mainly administrative one. This will bring with it significant savings, both in terms of time and cost, as well as greatly improving the efficiency of the process.... the fundamental point about the new transfer procedure ... is that, in uncontested cases, as soon as the prosecution has served notice of its case, the case will automatically and immediately be transferred to the Crown Court. In 1994, over 94,000 cases — some 93% of the total — fell into that category. In such cases, there will be no need for any court hearing, or for any consideration of the evidence. The procedure will be a simple one without elaborate paperwork. Savings will arise for the courts because of this streamlining and for the legal aid bill because it will not be necessary for the parties' representatives to attend court (per Baroness Blatch, *Hansard*, Lords, 5 February 1996, col. 76).

Despite these assertions, critics such as the Law Society continued to press for the abandonment of the transfer for trial scheme in favour of modifications to the existing system of committals and they were rewarded less than three months later when the Government announced its change of mind:

> ... work on implementing the transfer procedures highlighted difficulties and complexities, which suggest that the transfer scheme may not, in practice, offer the gains in efficiency that were originally envisaged. We have concluded that the objectives of improved efficiency and protection of witnesses can be better achieved by way of a modified form of committals such as that proposed by the Law Society.
>
> Under our proposals, the evidence considered by magistrates at a contested committal will be limited to documentary evidence tendered by the prosecution, together with any exhibits. Provision will be made to prescribe the form of the evidence to ensure its formality and soundness. No witnesses will be called to give oral evidence. But magistrates will be able to consider any representations by the defence or the prosecution, in addition to the prosecution evidence, to help them reach their decision on whether to commit the case for trial at the Crown Court, or discharge the defendant.
>
> Our proposals differ from those of the Law Society in one significant respect. Its proposal envisages streamlining uncontested committals by allowing cases to proceed to the Crown Court for trial without the attendance of any parties at the magistrates' court, at the discretion of the defence. Our proposals make no change to the existing procedures for uncontested committals. Although we agree that avoiding unnecessary hearings is a sensible objective in principle, during the

course of detailed consultation it has become clear that the implementation of such a measure would require the introduction of the same complex procedural arrangements that has caused concern in the context of the transfer for trial scheme. Instead, our proposals focus on the principal objective of excluding oral evidence in contested committals. They will provide a system that will work, that has the confidence of practitioners, and that spares witnesses the distress of giving evidence at contested hearings, as well as making some savings in time and resources. (per David Maclean, Home Office Minister, *Hansard*, Commons, Standing Committee B, 30 April 1996, col. 8).

These proposals were subsequently enacted via s. 47 of and sch. 1 to the 1996 Act. Before examining these new provisions it is necessary to note the repeals of the provisions in the Criminal Justice and Public Order Act 1994 dealing with transfer for trial which were never brought into force.

The repeal of the transfer for trial provisions

By a curious symmetry, s. 44 of the 1996 Act provides for the omission of s. 44 and sch. 1 from the Criminal Justice and Public Order Act 1994, which themselves purported *inter alia* to abolish committal proceedings and substitute new sections into the Magistrates' Courts Act 1980 in place of the previous ss. 4 to 8.

The side note to s. 44 of the 1996 Act reads 'Reinstatement of certain provisions' which seems to be a reference to the fact that the provisions repealed or replaced as a result of the 1994 Act are no longer to be repealed or replaced and are therefore reinstated, but this is an odd way of looking at the matter since the repeals and replacements were never brought into force and therefore there are not yet any repealed provisions in need of reinstatement. Even more curious at first glance is s. 44(6) of the 1996 Act, which provides '[t]he 1994 Act shall be treated as having been enacted with the amendments made by subsections (2) and (5)'. This looks like an attempt to deem the transfer provisions never to have been included in a statute, almost to erase them from the record like a retrospective repeal, but it is difficult to know why since, again, never having been brought into force, it should presumably be sufficient to deprive them of effect for the future. The draftsman clearly takes the view that the repealing provisions, though never brought into force, somehow still had some sort of ghostly effect constituting a shadow repeal of provisions about committals and therefore those provisions were in need of reinstatement; to achieve this the 1994 Act had to be treated as never having included the repealing provisions. Readers who feel that they have entered fantasy land at this stage should not be surprised if they should encounter there either the authors or Parliamentary Counsel!

The wording of s. 44(6) is another example of the novel and distinctive style of draftsmanship of the Act (see Introduction) for which there are presumably good reasons. These reasons unfortunately were not adverted to in Parliament, possibly in this instance because of the very late stage at which the clause was introduced and the consequent lack of any discussion of it in *Hansard*. One can only therefore speculate as to the reasons. Perhaps one other possible reason worth adverting to is that the draftsman had in mind the decision in *Secretary of State for the Home Department, ex parte Fire Brigades Union* [1995] 2 AC 513, where the House of Lords held that the Home Secretary had been wrong to bring in his own non-statutory

Criminal Injuries Scheme rather than bring into force a more generous scheme passed by Parliament in 1988 but never brought into force. One can understand that there may be some sensitivity as a result of this case in not bringing into force provisions previously enacted by Parliament and bringing in another scheme in their place. However the situation here is quite different in that it is Parliament that has authorised the non-activation of the original transfer scheme and also the modifications to committals which are to be implemented in its place.

By way of contrast, s. 44(3) and (4) amends ss. 34, 36 and 37 of the Criminal Justice and Public Order Act 1994 (inferences from silence) merely with effect from Royal Assent of the 1996 Act (4 July 1996). These amendments make no real practical difference since they replace references to applications for dismissal in transfer proceedings with references to a magistrates' court inquiring into the offence as examining justices and they repeal ('omit') corresponding transitional provisions (transitional on the implementation of the never to be implemented transfer for trial provisions) which have in the meantime treated references to grants of dismissal in transfer proceedings as references to committals for trial! Magistrates' courts will now be comforted to know that they can draw inferences in committal proceedings from the accused's silence under ss. 34(2), 36(2) and 37(2) of the 1994 Act rather than under the now repealed transitional provisions in ss. 34(7), 36(8) and 37(7)!

The new modified form of committal proceedings

More important than the technicalities of the repeals is the fact that sch. 1 to the 1996 Act contains significant amendments to the Magistrates' Courts Act 1980 (as it stands — without any of the transfer for trial amendments and in place of the transfer for trial amendments which were never brought into force and which we now have to treat as never having been enacted). It is anticipated that sch. 1 will come into force in Spring 1997. Paragraph 2(2) of sch. 1 substitutes a new s. 4(3) into the 1980 Act. A comparison of the old and the new s. 4(3) underlines the fact that following its implementation witnesses will not be called to give oral evidence at committal proceedings.

The old s. 4(3) read as follows:

Subject to subsection (4) below and section 102 below, evidence given before examining justices shall be given in the presence of the accused, and the defence shall be at liberty to put questions to any witness at the inquiry.

The new s. 4(3) reads:

Subject to subsection (4) below, evidence tendered before examining justices shall be tendered in the presence of the accused.

Thus evidence is no longer 'given' by witnesses, it is simply 'tendered' (in documentary form) and there are no witnesses to whom questions can be put. For similar reasons, by sch. 1, para. 2(3), the word 'given' is replaced by the word 'tendered' throughout s. 4(4) of the 1980 Act (which deals with cases where the evidence may be tendered in the absence of the accused). Other than the special situations to which s. 4(4) applies, the general rule requiring the presence of the accused remains. The Law Society's proposal to dispense with the need for the presence of the accused in uncontested committals was rejected on this point, since to do so would in the Government's view 'result in the same complex procedural arrangements that caused such concern in the context of the transfer scheme' because there would have to be notice periods for the defence to indicate whether it was going to contest the committal, etc:

> Hearings are required in most cases to deal with a number of ancillary matters other than the committal itself — in particular, with the amendment, substitution or addition of charges and bail issues ... Our discussions with practitioners suggest that hearings in uncontested cases act as a useful focal point for a number of other procedural issues, such as changes in defence election, alternative arrangements for sureties and applications for the extension of custody time limits. (per David Maclean, Minister of State, *Hansard*, Commons Standing Committee B, 21 May 1996, cols 119–120).

Forms of evidence admissible at committal proceedings

It will have been noted that the reference to s. 102 of the 1980 Act (admissibility of written statements) in the former s. 4(3) does not appear in the new version of the subsection. This is because s. 102 is repealed ('omitted') by sch. 1, para. 9 and a new s. 5A inserted by para. 3 of sch. 1 to the 1996 Act which comprehensively, logically and exhaustively sets out the conditions under which various types of documentary evidence may be admissible in committal proceedings.

Section 5A(1) commences with the basic point that the *only* evidence admissible in committal proceedings is that falling within s. 5A(2). Section 5A(2)(a) then requires such evidence to be tendered by or on behalf of the prosecutor. This restriction to prosecution evidence is a major change in theory, although not so great in practice since it is very rare for the defence to call evidence at the committal. The change makes it clear that it is no longer regarded as a proper aspect of the functions of examining magistrates to assess the relative strength of the prosecution and defence evidence but merely to assess whether the prosecution have assembled sufficient evidence of their own to amount to a case to answer.

Section 5A(2)(b) requries such evidence to fall within s. 5A(3) which, although it has six sub-paragraphs, essentially covers four classes of evidence:

(a)   written statements complying with s. 5B, plus documents or other exhibits referred to in such statements;
(b)   depositions complying with s. 5C plus documents or exhibits referred to in such depositions;
(c)   statements complying with s. 5D;
(d)   documents falling within s. 5E.

Written statements   Section 5B in effect replaces s. 102(1) to (6) of the 1980 Act, and is in substantially identical language except that there is no equivalent to s. 102(2)(d), which gives other parties (i.e., normally the defence) the right to object to the tendering of the written statement, and there is no equivalent to s. 102(4), which enables the court of its own motion or on the application of any party to require the maker of the statement to attend as a witness to give the evidence orally. These differences follow from the decision to abandon the version of full committals at which witnesses used to give their evidence orally in court.

Depositions   Since the defence can no longer object to the tendering of written statements in the correct form, the vast majority of evidence in committal proceedings will be written statements falling under s. 5B and there will not be any depositions constituting the written record of the oral evidence of witnesses at the committal since there will no longer be such witnesses. Nevertheless, s. 5C deals with depositions but these are depositions taken *in advance of* rather than *at* the committal proceedings. Section 5C is linked to a new s. 97A of the 1980 Act (inserted by para. 8 of sch. 1 to the 1996 Act), which provides powers to a magistrate to summons (or issue a warrant to) a person who is likely to be able to make a written statement on behalf of the prosecutor or produce a document or other exhibit but who will not do so voluntarily. The summons (or warrant for arrest) will require the person to attend before a magistrate to have his evidence taken as a deposition or to produce the document or other exhibit. Section 97A has many similarities to s. 97 of the 1980 Act, the operation of which is now confined to summary trials as a result of amendments to it in para. 7 of sch. 1 to the 1996 Act. This is because s. 97 provides for a summons to give oral evidence in court (where there can be cross examination, etc.) and this clearly can no longer apply to committal proceedings. Section 97A enables the evidence to be taken as a deposition in advance instead and then copied to the prosecutor under s. 97A(9); this makes it eligible to be tendered in evidence under s. 5C provided (*inter alia*) that under s. 5C(2) the prosecutor copies it to each of the other parties *before the magistrates' court begins to enquire into the offence concerned as examining justices.*

Statements believed to be admissible at trial under ss. 23 and 24 of the Criminal Justice Act 1988   Section 5D relates to documentary evidence in relation to which the prosecutor gives notice to the court and the parties in advance of the committal proceedings that he has reasonable grounds for believing might be admissible at the trial solely under s. 23 or 24 of the Criminal Justice Act 1988 and copies of which are provided by the prosecutor along with such notice. Section 23 deals with so-called first hand documentary hearsay, which may be admissible in criminal proceedings in place of oral evidence on the grounds that the maker of the statement is dead, physically or mentally unfit to attend trial, is abroad or of unknown whereabouts or is in fear or being kept out of the way. Section 24 deals with so-called multiple hearsay in relation to certain types of business documents. These documents were formerly admissible in committal proceedings by virtue of ss. 23 and 24 themselves 'as evidence of any fact of which oral evidence would be admissible' and, unlike at the trial itself, there was no discretion to exclude them under s. 25 of the 1988 Act. Since oral evidence is no longer given at committal proceedings, the hypothesis on which admissibility under ss. 23 and 24 depends is no longer applicable. For this reason, paras 28 and 29 of sch. 1 to the 1996 Act insert new subsections (5) into ss. 23 and 24, making it clear that they do not apply to committal proceedings and therefore admissibility is instead provided for under s. 5C if the prosecutor reasonably believes they would be admissible instead of direct oral evidence at the trial under s. 23 or 24.

Other documents   Section 5E is a catchall to cover documents which by virtue of any enactment:

(a)   are evidence or are admissible;
(b)   may be used, admitted, received or considered;
(c)   whose production constitutes proof; or
(d)   by whose production evidence may be given,

in committal proceedings.

Section 5E appears to be an attempt to cover all the various formulae which might appear in particular statutes (including the Magistrates' Courts Act 1980) making documents admissible in committal proceedings. One example apparently would be a DVLA (Driver and Vehicle Licensing Agency) certificate. Perhaps a more significant example would be a video recording of a child's evidence, which under s. 32A(10) of the Criminal Justice Act 1988 may be 'considered' at committal proceedings. The words 'notwithstanding that the child witness is not called at the committal proceedings' in s. 32A(10) are repealed by para. 33 of sch. 1 to the 1996 Act as being otiose and inappropriate given that no witnesses are now to be called in committal proceedings.

In relation to each of the new ss. 5B, 5C and 5E, by virtue of ss. 5B(6), 5C(6) and 5E(4), 'document' means anything in which information of any description is recorded so it could include videos, tapes, computer disks, CD-ROMs or any other thing on which data is stored (s. 5D does not itself refer to documents).

Proof by production of copy   By virtue of s. 5F, anything admissible under s. 5A may be proved by the production of the original statement, deposition or document or by a copy of it, whether the first or subsequent copy and whether or not the original is still in existence.

Committals with and without consideration of the evidence

Paragraph 4 of sch. 1 substitutes s. 6(1) and (2) of the Magistrates' Courts Act 1980 so as to replace the existing subsections which deal with contested and uncontested committals. The new s. 6(1) is of similar effect to the old even though the ordering of the wording is different in that it authorises the court 'on consideration of the evidence' to 'commit the accused for trial if it is of the opinion that there is sufficient evidence to put him on trial by jury for any indictable offence'. Unlike the old s. 6(1), there is no reference to considering 'any statement of the accused' since s. 72(1) of the Criminal Justice Act 1982 abolished the right of the defendant to make an unsworn statement in criminal proceedings. This makes sense where the accused is represented but it has to be remembered that s. 72(1) expressly preserves the right of an accused 'not represented by counsel or a solicitor, to address the court or jury otherwise than on oath on any matter which, if he were so represented, counsel or a solicitor could address the court or jury on his behalf'. The changed wording of s. 6(1) should therefore not be read so as to exclude the right of an accused to address the court in such a situation. Nevertheless, the absence of any reference to 'any statement of the accused' is appropriate in that an unrepresented accused's right is one to make representations rather than a statement and an echo of this can be seen in para. 13 of sch. 1 to the 1996 Act, which substitutes in sch. 3 to the 1980 Act a right to make *representations* on behalf of a corporation instead of a right to make a *statement* on behalf of a corporation.

The really big change in s. 6(1) is of course is the meaning of 'on consideration of the evidence', which is now limited to the consideration of documentary evidence since the new s. 5A discussed above provides that the *only* evidence admissible is that falling within s. 5A(2) (all of which is documentary) and there will therefore be no live witnesses at the committal. That does not mean that there is no oral hearing since each of ss. 5B, 5C, 5D and 5E, which set out the various forms of documentary evidence, contain the following statement as did s. 102(5) of the 1980 Act:

So much of any [statement, deposition, statement in writing or document] as is admitted in evidence by virtue of this section shall, unless the court commits the accused for trial by virtue of section 6(2) below or the court otherwise directs, be read aloud at the hearing; and where the court so directs an account shall be given orally of so much of any document as is not read aloud.

Thus a full committal will now involve the reading out or summarising of the various witness statements and other forms of documentary evidence but without the presence of the actual witnesses. The evidence read out or summarised will all be prosecution evidence (see s. 5A(2)(a)) and there will be a single opportunity to submit no case to answer with no possibility even of the accused testifying himself, calling witnesses or tendering other evidence or making a further submission if the court rejects the submission that the prosecution evidence does not disclose a case to answer. The lack of an opportunity to present defence evidence will make no difference in the vast majority of cases but the absence of prosecution witnesses and the consequent loss of the opportunity to confront and cross-examine them is likely to lead to far fewer contested committals which in the future are likely to be limited to cases where the defence feels that the prosecution case is weak even on paper. If the Crown Prosecution Service does its job properly, there should be relatively few cases where this is even arguable.

A higher proportion of cases are therefore likely to be dealt with 'without consideration of the contents' under the amended s. 6(2), which is little changed from the old s. 6(2) except that it refers now to s. 5A rather than s. 102 of the 1980 Act and to 'all the evidence tendered by or on behalf of the prosecutor' rather than 'all the evidence before the court (whether for the prosecution or the defence)'. The conditions under which such a committal cannot take place under s. 6(2) remain essentially the same, namely:

(a)   the accused or one of the accused has no legal representative acting for him in the case, or

(b)   a legal representative for the accused or one of the accused, as the case may be, has requested the court to consider a submission that there is insufficient evidence to put that accused on trial by jury for the offence.

Changing from summary trial to committal proceedings and vice versa

Under s. 25 of the Magistrates' Courts Act 1980, magistrates can discontinue a summary trial of an offence triable either way if during the course of the prosecution evidence it emerges that the case is more suitable for the Crown Court. Under the current s. 25(2), they '*may* adjourn the proceedings without remanding the accused' (emphasis added) but equally it is open to them to carry on with committal proceedings without adjourning (since all the witnesses will be present for the summary trial anyway). Since committal proceedings will no longer involve witnesses as such but they will require the evidence to be put in the form prescribed by s. 5A discussed above, sch. 1, para. 5(2) amends s. 25(2) (and s. 25(6) which is of similar effect for juveniles) to substitute '*shall* adjourn the hearing' (emphasis added) for the words quoted above. Adjournment thus now becomes mandatory to enable the papers to be prepared but a new s. 25(8) retains the court's discretion to make the adjournment with or without remanding the accused.

The converse case of changing from committal proceedings to summary trial is provided for by s. 25(3) and by s. 28(3): 'any evidence already given before the court shall be deemed to have been given in and for the purposes of the summary trial'. This latter provision is repealed by sch. 1, para. 6 since no oral evidence will have been given at the committal proceedings.

Other amendments to the Magistrates' Courts Act 1980

Paragraphs 7 and 8 of sch. 1 to the 1996 Act deal with summons or warrants for reluctant witnesses and amend s. 97 of the 1980 Act and insert a new s. 97A. These provisions have already been discussed above in connection with the new s. 5C of the 1980 Act as has para. 9 of sch. 1 which repeals s. 102 of the 1980 Act.

Section 103 of the 1980 Act has been amended several times to ensure that child witnesses to certain types of sexual and violent offences do not have to give evidence orally at committal proceedings but that a statement, whether written or, for example in the form of a video recording, can be admitted instead. Paragraph 10 of sch. 1 amends s. 103 so as to remove references in s. 103(1) to not calling the child as a witness, etc., and merely provides for statements made or taken in writing from a child to be admissible in committal proceedings. This seems to be another example of evidence admissible under the catch-all new s. 5E of the 1980 Act, dealing with evidence admissible under any enactment, in this case s. 103 of the 1980 Act itself. Curiously, s. 103 is in one sense narrower than previously since the statement now has to be in writing which was not previously required under s. 103. However, as noted earlier, a video recording may be 'considered' under s. 32A(10) of the Criminal Justice Act 1988 and this too seems to fall under the new s. 5E.

Given that no witnesses will now be allowed to attend court to give evidence (or be cross-examined) in committal proceedings, s. 105 of the 1980 Act, providing for depositions to be taken from dangerously ill witnesses at a convenient place (with an opportunity for the defence to cross-examine), is no longer appropriate and is therefore repealed by sch. 1, para. 11. Such a situation can in any case be dealt with under s. 23 of the Criminal Justice Act 1988, which is discussed above in connection with the new s. 5D (under which, of course, there is no opportunity to cross-examine as is the case with all statements tendered under the amended form of committal procedure).

Amendments to other statutes

All the amendments to the Magistrates' Courts Act 1980 are contained in Part I of sch. 1. Part II deals with amendments, consequent on the new arrangements for committal proceedings, to other statutes. There are 24 paragraphs in Part II and it is not appropriate or necessary to go through each one individually. They fall into a number of classes. First there are those which repeal or replace provisions which refer to sections of the Magistrates' Courts Act 1980 which have been repealed in Part I. Thus para. 14 repeals ss. 6 and 7 of the Criminal Law Amendment Act 1867, which deal with the admissibility of depositions under s. 105 of the 1980 Act which has itself been repealed by para. 11. Similarly para. 21 replaces a reference to s. 102 of the 1980 Act with a reference to s. 5B of the same Act in para. 55 of sch. 5 to the Children and Young Persons Act 1969 (see below for the effect of this). Paragraph 22 makes rather more complex amendments to s. 46 of the Criminal Justice Act 1972 (written statements made outside England and Wales) to allow the new s. 5B of the 1980 Act to apply to written statements outside England and Wales. This applies both to Scotland and Northern Ireland and also to statements made outside the United Kingdom, but in the latter case a new s. 46(1C) of the Criminal Justice Act 1972 disapplies s. 5B(2)(b), s. 5B(3A) of the 1980 Act and sch. 2, para. 1 of the 1996 Act. The effect of s. 46(1C) is that written statements made outside the United Kingdom will be admissible at the committal proceedings by virtue of s. 5B but not at the trial itself. (The reference to subsection (3A) of s. 5B may appear at first sight to be a mistake since no such subsection appears in s. 5B as printed in sch. 1 to the 1996 Act but in fact subsection (3A) will be inserted into s. 5B by para. 55 of sch. 5 to the Children and Young Persons Act 1969 (if it is ever brought into force), which is itself amended by para. 21 of sch. 1 to the 1996 Act referred to above!)

A second type of provision in Part II of sch. 1 is exemplified by para. 19, which amends s. 27 of the Theft Act 1968 (evidence by statutory declaration) in order to remove references to such declarations being admissible to the same extent as oral evidence and to remove the accused's right to require the attendance of the maker of the statement.

A third, possibly less anodyne, type of amendment can be found in paras 25 and 26, which effectively remove any possibility of magistrates considering at committal proceedings whether confessions are inadmissible under s. 76 of PACE (because the absence of oral evidence will make it difficult for the prosecution to disprove oppression) or whether evidence should be excluded as being unfair under s. 78 of PACE. Consideration of factors such as ss. 76 and 78 has not traditionally been something that would occur at committal proceedings but the wording of ss. 76 and 78 (prior to these amendments) did clearly apply to committal proceedings. The courts had confirmed this in *Oxford City Justices, ex parte Berry* [1988] QB 507 and in *King's Lynn Justices, ex parte Holland* [1993] 1 WLR 324, although it was also made clear that justices should exclude under these sections only in clear cases and exceptional circumstances. The amendments now remove such questions from them entirely as part of the overall thrust of the changes to committal proceedings so as to leave them merely as a vehicle to assess whether a prima facie case is established by documentary evidence tendered in the correct form without the magistrates having to, or being able to, go beyond matters which appear on the face of the documents or having to weigh the respective merits of the prosecution evidence against defence evidence.

Admissibility of written statements and depositions at trial

The use of written statements, which have been admitted in evidence at committal proceedings under the new s. 5B of the 1980 Act, and of depositions which have been admitted under the new s. 97A as evidence in the subsequent trial is dealt with now by s. 68 of and sch. 2 to the 1996 Act. These provisions replace s. 13(3) of the Criminal Justice Act 1925 (see also the repealed s. 102(10) of the 1980 Act).

Schedule 2 has some significant differences from the old law, not least that it applies on its face to written statements where the accused by definition has not had an opportunity to cross-examine the maker (this was formerly true only of written statements, as opposed to depositions, such statements being treated as equivalent to depositions for these purposes by s. 103(7)). As under the old law (see *Collins* [1938] 3 All ER 130 and *Neshet* [1990] Crim LR 578), the court has a discretion (see paras 1(3)(b) and 2(3)(b)) not to admit the written evidence and the written statements or depositions will not normally be admissible if the accused objects (see para. 1(3)(c) and para. 2(3)(c)). Much more surprisingly, the court can override an objection if it thinks it is in the interests of justice so to order (paras 1(4) and 2(4)). This latter provision raises the prospect of an accused being convicted on documentary hearsay evidence on which he has never had the opportunity to cross-examine the maker without any of the specific limitations which are built into ss. 23 and 24 of the Criminal Justice Act 1988 and his only protection being the view of the court which is trying him of what is in the interests of justice without having to satisfy tests such as those which are detailed in ss. 25 and 26 of the Criminal Justice Act 1988. It is a potentially controversial provision to insert into a subparagraph of a schedule which itself was added to the Bill only at a very late stage with very little time for effective Parliamentary scrutiny.

Indeed, sch. 2, paras 1(4) and 2(4) were the subject of late tabled manuscript amendments, prompted by the Bar Council and the Criminal Bar Association, on the very last day of Parliamentary consideration of the Bill on 26 June (this was the only stage at which sch. 2 received any discussion) when the Lords were considering and approving Commons amendments. If the Lords had decided to disagree with any of the Commons amendments, the Bill would have had to return to the Commons once more. Lord Williams of Mostyn said of the proposed but ultimately unsuccessful manuscript amendments to sch. 2:

> The purpose of these amendments is to try to redress the balance which will be unfairly tilted against the defendant ... one would have expected some safeguards to have been included: the kind of criteria that one finds in sections 25 and 26 of the Criminal Justice Act 1988. One would expect to find some categories — for instance, where a witness is dead, has been intimidated, is ill, or beyond the seas; that kind of thing. One fully understands that it may be legitimate to have the statement of such a witness given in evidence subject to the usual warning that a trial judge might give to the jury that the statement has not been cross-examined to.
>
> It may be that the noble Baroness the Minister may be able to indicate quite clearly that the criteria in sections 25 and 26 of the Criminal Justice Act 1988 are intended to apply and that one will not simply have a bald discretion. After all it is a fundamental principle of great validity and respectable antecedence that a defendant in a criminal trial is entitled to see his accuser.

These provisions are too draconian. They take away from the defendant the right to cross examine; they take away from the jury the possibility of assessing a witness' demeanour. They may be necessary in some circumstances but the basis of my support for the amendments in the name of my noble friend is that one needs careful safeguards and one ought to limit that to specific and designated circumstances. (*Hansard*, Lords, 26 June 1996, col. 948.)

In response, Baroness Blatch refused to accept the amendments, or delay the passage of the Bill by considering them further, and said:

It is well established that the courts at present have a discretion to exclude evidence admissible under section 13(3) of the Criminal Justice Act 1925. In deciding whether to admit such evidence, case law has stated that the courts should apply the 'interests of justice' test laid down in section 26 of the Criminal Justice Act 1988. . . . It is anticipated that under the new arrangements the courts will as now turn for guidance to section 26 of the 1988 Act for assistance in applying the provisions in the new schedule to the Bill. (*Hansard*, Lords, 26 June 1996, cols. 951–952.)

It is interesting to note that the provisions of the 1988 Act referred to above were, as first presented to Parliament, originally much broader and less specific in terms of the types of statements which could be admitted as documentary hearsay but concerns about the width and unpredictable nature of the discretion involved meant that the provisions as enacted were much more specific and detailed. It is ironic that a much more general discretion, provided that the witness statement was one tendered at the committal proceedings, has now been introduced by a subparagraph of a schedule which only received any discussion on the last morning that the Bill was to complete its Parliamentary scrutiny. It is also surprising in view of the fact that the area is currently under consideration by the Law Commission (Consultation Paper No. 138, especially Part XI where, for a proposed new, but limited exception to the hearsay rule, the interests of justice test is supplemented by a test of the evidence being 'so positively and obviously trustworthy that the opportunity to test it by cross-examination can safely be dispensed with').

Those concerned about the possible implications of paras 1(4) and 2(4) must put their faith in the courts exercising their discretion to override the objections of the accused sparingly, and also in the Minister's statement that:

We are not seeking to introduce any fundamental changes to the interests of justice test and do not believe that the provision does so. Of course, we shall monitor that position in the future to see whether any difficulties arise and take appropriate action if necessary. I do not believe that it will come to that. (*Hansard*, Lords, 26 June 1996, cols 949–950.)

Section 69 of the Act is fortunately much less problematic in that it amends s. 9 of the Criminal Justice Act 1967, which provides for the admissibility of written statements in criminal proceedings other than committal proceedings. One of the conditions is that the age of the maker of the statement is given if he is under 21. Section 69 alters this age to 18 in line with the age specified now in the new s. 5B of the Magistrates' Courts Act 1980 and renders it consistent with the reduced age of majority established in the Family Law Reform Act 1969. Section 9 of the Criminal Justice Act 1967, it may be noted, does not contain any power to override objection by the defence to the admissibility of a written statement and therefore the power in the court so to override under sch. 2, para. 1(4) is only available if the written statement has been admitted in evidence at the committal. One would have thought that the court's discretion should be available in both situations or neither and to have it available in one and not the other seems rather anomalous.

Amendments to notice of transfer procedures

Although the transfer for trial scheme has now been abandoned, the (optional) notice of transfer procedures for serious or complex fraud and for certain cases involving children still remain very much in force and s. 45 of the 1996 Act makes some minor amendments to both the Criminal Justice Act 1987 and the Criminal Justice Act 1991. These amendments will affect notices of transfer given or served on or after the appointed day (s. 45(8) and (9)), which is expected to be in Spring 1997. The principal effect of these amendments is that the prosecution will not have to send, together with the notice of transfer to the court or the accused, copies of documents (containing evidence) which have already been sent. By way of contrast, a notice of transfer scheme that was provided for in Part I of sch. 1 to the War Crimes Act 1991 is now repealed by s. 46 of the 1996 Act. This is in fact the second time that Parliament has tried to repeal Part I of that schedule, the first time being in virtually identical language in sch. 4, para. 72 and sch. 11 to the Criminal Justice and Public Order Act 1994. That repeal was itself repealed by s. 44(2) and (5) of the 1996 Act, and indeed treated as never having been enacted by s. 44(6), but it is then immediately re-enacted by s. 46! The repeal of the notice of transfer scheme for war crimes is definitely now achieved since there is no appointed day for s. 46 which therefore must actually have come into force immediately on Royal Assent (4 July 1996).

Conclusions

The changes to both mode of trial procedure and to committals themselves should produce gains in efficiency for the criminal justice system, which is the main aim from the Government's point of view. There seems little doubt that there was scope for some such gains without causing any unfair prejudice to the interests of the accused and, as far as committals are concerned, there seems little doubt that the changes introduced are far preferable to the much criticised transfer for trial scheme in preference to which they have been enacted. The question is whether some of the details of the changes, which had very little Parliamentary scrutiny, do not potentially go too far in restricting the rights of the accused to challenge prosecution evidence in advance of the trial (see e.g., the discussion of ss. 76 and 78 of PACE above) or in introducing a discretion to allow evidence tendered at the committal to be admissible in written form at the actual trial, despite objection by the defence. As far as mode of trial is concerned, the implications are more difficult to assess until it is seen how many accused who presently are committed for trial are prepared to indicate an intention to plead guilty prior to determination of mode of trial. The more that they do, the greater the efficiency or 'process' gains that are likely to accrue but, concomitantly, the greater the increase in sentencing by magistrates of cases falling in the upper end of their sentencing jurisdiction — a phenomenon which itself could have a number of unpredictable effects. Nevertheless, the reforms introduced in both the areas discussed by this chapter do have the merit of being preferable to some of the alternatives which were either canvassed, such as the removal of the right of the accused to elect for jury trial in either-way offences, or which had been enacted but unimplemented, as in the case of the unlamented transfer for trial scheme.

Chapter Six
Changes to Magistrates' Courts Procedure

Part VI of the Act (ss. 48 to 53) contains a number of minor technical amendments to procedures in the magistrates' courts. Some of the amendments are based on a Review of Procedure established in 1989 by Douglas Hurd as Home Secretary: 'to consider how magistrates' courts' procedure could be made more effective, efficient and economical, consistent with satisfactory provision for due process'. The Review, which was undertaken by a Committee having representatives from the police, the Crown Prosecution Service, the Lord Chancellor's Department, the Justices' Clerks Society, the Magistrates' Association, the Law Society and the Bar Council, resulted in a list of recommendations which were announced by Kenneth Baker as Home Secretary in 1992 (*Hansard*, Commons, Written Answers, 16 March 1992, col. 792). Many of the 73 recommendations were such that primary legislation was not needed to implement them and a small number were not accepted by the Home Secretary (such as the proposal that drivers should be required to carry their driving licences when driving) or have been overtaken by events (e.g., by the proposals on transfer for trial and the changes to committals which have now been preferred). The recommendations which remained relevant and required primary legislation have now found an appropriate legislative home in Part VI of the 1996 Act, now under the sponsorship of Michael Howard as Home Secretary.

The provisions of s. 49, which deals with the accused's indication of his intention as to plea in the case of offences triable either way, are discussed in Chapter Five.

Issue of warrant on non-appearance of accused

Section 48 is based on recommendation 61 of the Review which stated:

> [Section 13 of the Magistrates' Courts Act 1980], governing the issue of a warrant in the absence of the accused, should be amended to clarify the circumstances in which such a warrant could be issued. Warrants should be issued only where the adjournment notice or summons had been served or the defendant had appeared at the *immediately* previous hearing. (emphasis added)

Accordingly s. 48 amends s. 13(2) of the 1980 Act in order to produce this effect. The amendment makes no real change to the wording where it is proved that a 'summons has been served on the accused within what appears to the court to be a reasonable time before the trial or adjourned trial' (new s. 13(2A)). However, where this is not the case, it is no longer sufficient that the accused had appeared on *a* previous occasion; under the new s. 13(2B), the accused must have been 'present on the last (or only occasion) when the trial was adjourned' and it must also have been the case that 'on that occasion the court determined the time for the hearing at which the adjournment is now made'. The effect should be to avoid the issuing of warrants in cases where the accused was not actually aware of the date of the adjourned hearing. The amendment applies where it is proposed to issue a warrant on or after the appointed day, which is likely to be in Autumn 1996.

Where a person fails to appear, the court has the option of proceeding to try him in his absence under s. 11 of the 1980 Act. It is slightly surprising therefore that there is no corresponding amendment to s. 11(2), which is in substantially similar terms to the original s. 13(2). The result seems to be that the court may still proceed in the absence of the accused (but cannot issue a warrant) where it is not proved that the summons was served with reasonable notice and the accused was not present at the immediately previous adjournment and was not given the time for the hearing at which he has failed to appear.

Enforcement of payment of fines by justices' clerk without reference to magistrates

Section 50 amends s. 87 of the 1980 Act in accordance with recommendation 14 of the Review 'to allow justices' clerks to take action in the High Court or county court without reference to magistrates'. There will still have to have been an enquiry into the defendant's means under s. 82 of the 1980 Act where 'he appeared to the court to have sufficient means to pay the sum forthwith', but it will no longer be necessary for the specific mode of enforcement by action in the High Court or county court to be authorised by the magistrates themselves.

Summons to witness and warrant for his arrest

Section 51 makes a minor amendment to s. 97 of the 1980 Act, which deals with the issuing of summonses (and warrants) to witnesses to attend at a magistrates' court or to produce any document or thing likely to be material evidence. It should be noted that s. 97 is also amended by sch. 1, para. 7 to remove any references to committal proceedings (and a new s. 97A is inserted by sch. 1, para. 8 — see Chapter Five) in view of the fact that witnesses no longer give oral evidence at committal proceedings. Section 97 is thus now limited to summary trial.

Section 51 of the 1996 Act inserts a new s. 97(2B) and (2C) which give a magistrate a discretion to refuse to issue a summons under s. 97(1) or a warrant for arrest of the witness under s. 97(2) 'if he is not satisfied that an application for the summons was made by a party to the case as soon as is reasonably practical after the accused pleaded not guilty'. The amendments will come into force on a day to be appointed, which is expected to be in Spring 1997.

Periods of remand in custody for accused aged under 17

The Criminal Justice Act 1982 introduced a new s. 128(3A) into the 1980 Act which allowed for remands in custody (for no more than eight days) in the absence of the accused, in certain conditions, on up to three consecutive occasions. The accused has to consent in advance to this power being applicable but, if he does so, the effect is that he need only be brought to court for a further remand every 28 days. The Criminal Justice Act 1988 introduced a new s. 128A to allow remands (on second and subequent remands) for up to 28 days without the consent of the accused in certain circumstances provided that a date within that 28-day maximum has been set for the next substantive stage in the proceedings. Both of these changes were designed to avoid the necessity of repeatedly bringing remand prisoners to court every seven days merely to be remanded in custody. One of the limitations on both provisions was that the accused must have attained the age of 17 and this limitation is now removed by s. 52 in relation to offences alleged to have been committed on or after the appointed day, which is expected to be in Autumn 1996.

Attachment of earnings

Prior to the 1996 Act, magistrates had no power to make an attachment of earnings order at the time when a fine is imposed or when a compensation order is made. This option becomes available only after the offender has failed to pay within the time allowed and a means enquiry has taken place (see s. 86 of the 1980 Act). Where an offender does have earnings, an attachment of earnings order may be a highly effective way of enforcement and indeed may be of benefit to the offender in that it provides him with the discipline necessary to pay off the fine or compensation order and avoid further proceedings or committal to prison for default. The 1992 Review of Magistrates' Court Procedure therefore recommended that courts should have the power to make an attachment of earnings order with the consent of the offender at the time of imposition of a fine rather than on default. Section 53 accordingly amends the Attachment of Earnings Act 1971 so as to permit the court to make an attachment order at the time of imposing the fine or compensation order providing that the convicted person consents. The amendments apply to fines and compensation orders made in respect of offences committed on or after the appointed day, which is expected to be in Autumn 1996.

Chapter Seven
Tainted Acquittals

A new procedure for re-opening acquittals which are allegedly tainted by a criminal interference with the administration of justice is created by Part VII of the Act, that is by ss. 54 to 57. The purpose is to tackle miscarriages of justice which take the form of wrongful acquittals rather than wrongful convictions and to deter what has come to be known as jury and witness nobbling.

These provisions on tainted acquittals are arguably important more for their symbolic significance rather than for their potential practical impact, which in the short term at least is likely to be small. Their symbolic significance can be seen from a number of perspectives. From a political perspective, the Home Secretary can point (as he did at second reading: *Hansard*, Commons, 27 February 1996, col. 743) to the fact that they give effect to the last of the 27 measures to crack down on crime which he announced in October 1993 at the Conservative Party Conference. From a law reform perspective, they constitute a further enactment of recommendations of the Royal Commission on Criminal Justice — see 1993, Cmnd 2263, Chap. 10, paras 72 to 76 (although they go somewhat wider than the original proposals). Perhaps most importantly, from a constitutional perspective they represent a major inroad into the fundamental rule against double jeopardy and become arguably the only true exception to the availability of the plea in bar of *autrefois acquit*, an exception whereby an accused may now be prosecuted a second time for a crime of which he has already been acquitted at a trial which was not itself ultra vires or otherwise a nullity. The classic statement of the double jeopardy rule is in Hawkins' *Pleas of the Crown*, Chap. 35, s. 1 as cited by Lord Hodson in *Connelly v DPP* [1964] AC 1254 at p. 1330:

That a man shall not be brought into danger of his life for one and the same offence more than once. From whence it is generally taken, by all the books, as an undoubted consequence, that where a man is once found 'not guilty' on an indictment or appeal free from error, and well commenced before any court which hath jurisdiction over the cause, he may, by the common law, in all cases whatsoever plead such acquittal in bar of any subsequent indictment or appeal for the same crime.

The double jeopardy rule is sufficiently fundamental that in the United States it is enshrined in the Fifth Amendment to the Constitution and has there been described in the Supreme Court as a:

guarantee that the State with all its resources and power [shall] not be allowed to make repeated attempts to convict an individual for an alleged offence, thereby subjecting him to embarrassment, expense and ordeal and compelling him to live in a continuing state of anxiety and insecurity [Brennan J in *Ashe* v *Swenson* 397 US 435 at p. 451 (1970) quoting from *Green* v *U.S.* 355 U.S. 184 at p. 187 (1957.)].

Whether the provisions on tainted acquittals in the current statute confer sufficient practical advantages to be worth the derogation from such a fundamental bulwark of civil liberties is a question worth asking. (In this respect a contrast can be made with the safeguards built into the Attorney-General's reference procedure, whereby the reference on a point of law to the Court of Appeal cannot affect the original acquittal and care is taken to avoid even identifying the acquitted person.) This question will be examined later once the details of the procedure for dealing with tainted acquittals has been outlined.

The procedure can be broken down into a number of components each of which will be examined in turn. These are:

(a)   the acquittal of D for the original offence;
(b)   the conviction of X for an administration of justice offence;
(c)   the tainting of the acquittal (1) — the certification by the court convicting of the administration of justice offence;
(d)   the tainting of the acquittal (2) — the four conditions for an order quashing the acquittal;
(e)   the new proceedings against D for the original offence.

Acquittal of D for the original offence

The essence of the tainted acquittals procedure is that, where all the conditions are satisfied, 'proceedings may be taken against the acquitted person for the offence of which he was acquitted' under s. 54(4), and therefore the first precondition is the acquittal of D for an initial offence. There is nothing to limit the types of offences for which D might initially have been acquitted, although if the trigger for re-opening it is interference with or intimidation of a juror it will obviously have to have been an indictable offence which was actually tried on indictment with a jury. The original recommendation of the Royal Commission would in effect have limited the tainted acquittals procedure to such acquittals since it was exclusively concerned with taints resulting from interference with jurors (i.e., jury nobbling). However, the procedure as introduced goes wider in that, ostensibly because of the introduction of the offence of witness intimidation in s. 51(1) of the Criminal Justice and Public Order Act 1994 (*Hansard*, Lords, 27 November 1995, col. 467), it extends to interference etc. with *witnesses* and thus as a result is not necessarily limited to acquittals by a jury. Indeed s. 57(1) specifically makes s. 45 of the Offences Against the Person Act 1861 subject to the new procedure and s. 45 is only itself concerned with initial offences of assault and battery tried summarily (where the complaint was preferred by or on behalf of the person aggrieved). Moreover s. 56(2)(b) clearly envisages the new procedure applying to offences tried summarily. Against this it may be argued that summary trial does not technically result in an acquittal but rather in a dismissal of the charge. However, this objection loses much of its force when one considers that Parliament has previously referred to acquittals following summary trial in s. 73(2)(b) of PACE (proof of convictions and acquittals).

It should also be noted that an acquittal need not immediately result from either summary trial or trial on indictment but may be the result of a successful appeal (see s. 2(3) of the Criminal Appeal Act 1968 and s. 48 of the Supreme Court Act 1981).

Effective commencement The precondition of an acquittal of D for the original offence may seem to be, and indeed is, an obvious one, but it also has an importance in relation to the effective commencement of the new procedure relating to tainted acquittals. By virtue of s. 54(7), the innovation of putting D in jeopardy of being tried a second time is quite rightly not made retrospective. Indeed, it not only cannot apply where the act of intimidating etc. a witness or juror occurred before the date to be appointed by the Secretary of State but it also cannot apply unless the original offence of which D was acquitted is alleged to have been committed on or after the appointed day (s. 54(7)). (See also s. 75(2) for offences alleged to have been committed over a period of more than one day or sometime during a period of more than one day; these are treated as alleged to be committed on the last day in the period in question.) Arguably, if the legitimacy of the new procedure is accepted, it is only necessary, in order to be fair to the accused, to limit its operation to *acts of interference with the course of justice* (as opposed to the *original offence*) on or after the appointed day since the only real prejudice would arise where the *witness or jury nobbling* took place before it had been made clear that this could lead to the re-opening of the original offence. The accused can hardly argue that he would not have committed the *original offence* if he had realised there was a procedure to try him twice if a tainted acquittal was gained on the first trial. On balance, however, given the novelty and constitutional significance of the new procedure, it is perhaps as well that the maximum degree of non-retrospectivity has been ensured. This does however mean that in practice, it will be a long time before the new procedure can be invoked since all the following events must occur:

(a) the appointed day must be appointed by order of the Secretary of State;
(b) subsequently, the initial offence has to be committed;
(c) there has to be a trial and an acquittal;
(d) there has to be a trial and conviction of someone for an administration of justice offence connected with the trial of the initial offence;
(e) there has to be an application to the High Court for an order quashing the initial acquittal;
(f) only then can proceedings be instituted for the second time in relation to the original offence.

It is thus likely to be a number of years before the first retrials can take place.

Conviction of a person for an administration of justice offence

Whereas the first precondition in s. 54(1) was an *acquittal* of a person for the initial offence, the second precondition requries a *conviction* of a person (not necessarily the same person as the one acquitted of the initial offence). Thus it is required in s. 54(1)(b) that:

a person has been convicted of an administration of justice offence involving interference with or intimidation of a juror or a witness (or potential witness) in any proceedings which led to the acquittal.

Administration of justice offences are defined for these purposes in s. 54(6) as:

(a) the offence of perverting the course of justice;
(b) the offence under section 51(1) of the Criminal Justice and Public Order Act 1994 (intimidation etc. of witnesses, jurors and others);
(c) an offence of aiding, abetting, counselling, procuring, suborning or inciting another person to commit an offence under section 1 of the Perjury Act 1911.

It should be noted immediately that the mere conviction of one of these offences listed in s. 54(6) is not of itself enough, even if the administration of justice offence relates in some way to the initial acquittal. The administration of justice offence must also (as it often, but not invariably, will) involve interference with or intimidation of a juror or witness (or potential witness) in any proceedings which led to the acquittal. For example, an attempt (successful or unsuccessful) to destroy, falsify or conceal evidence is no doubt within the offence of perverting the course of justice and is thus an administration of justice offence, but it is not one within s. 54(1)(b) 'involving interference with or intimidation of a juror or a witness'.

The phrase 'any proceedings which led to the acquittal' will normally refer merely to the trial from which the acquittal resulted. It could also refer to proceedings in the Court of Appeal given the Court's power to receive evidence including the evidence of witnesses (under s. 23 of the Criminal Appeal Act 1968), but it would no longer appear to refer to committal proceedings since there are neither jurors nor, at least once the changes to committals elsewhere in the Act are in force, will there be witnesses as such. This latter point may not be too significant since someone whose written statement or deposition is admissible in committal proceedings is a potential witness at the actual trial and therefore comes within the scope of s. 54(1)(b) in any event.

There is nothing in s. 54(1)(b) to prevent the person convicted of the administration of justice offence being the same person who was acquitted of the original offence, although this does not appear to be the primary mischief at which the procedure is aimed. Where the person acquitted of the original offence is convicted of the administration of justice offence, perverting the course of justice for example, he or she can be sentenced for the offence of perverting the course of justice offence (for which the maximum penalty is life imprisonment) without any real need to re-open the original acquittal. There may of course be cases where there is some specific sentencing or related power in relation to the original offence (e.g., in relation to a motoring offence or drug trafficking) which is not available simply on conviction for the administration of justice offence and therefore where the re-opening of the original acquittal may still seem to be desirable or necessary. However, the more obvious case for invoking the tainted acquittal procedure will be where D is acquitted of the original offence, but another person, X, is convicted of the administration of justice offence. Unless D can be proved to have been a party to the administration of justice offence committed by X, D is merely the beneficiary of X's wrongdoing and the only way in which he can be deprived of that benefit is by re-opening his original acquittal. Whether it is right that D should have to undergo double jeopardy (where D is not shown to have caused the flaw at his original trial), is of course another question.

To fully expound the circumstances where s. 54(1)(b) and hence the second precondition will be satisfied it is necessary to take the three types of administration of justice offence in turn.

Perverting the course of justice   For details of the offence, see *Blackstone's Criminal Practice*, B14.26 to B14.33. It has already been pointed out that this offence is considerably wider than, although it certainly includes, offences 'involving interference with or intimidation of a juror or witness' and can be satisfied whether the offence is committed by the person (D) acquitted of the original offence or a third person (X), whether acting independently of or in concert with D.

Intimidating etc. witnesses, jurors and others under s. 51(1) of the Criminal Justice and Public Order Act 1994   For details of the offence, see *Blackstone's Criminal Practice*, B14.34 and Wasik and Taylor, *Blackstone's Guide to the Criminal Justice and Public Order Act 1994*, pp. 131 to 132). Although s. 54(6)(b) of the 1996 Act places the abbreviation 'etc.' after the word 'intimidating' and also refers to 'others' as well as jurors and witnesses (i.e., it copies the full section heading for the whole of s. 51), this is slightly misleading since it is only the offence under s. 51(1) which is relevant and this can only be committed by an act which 'intimidates and is intended to intimidate'. Therefore the reference to 'etc.' should not be thought to refer to interference with witnesses which does not amount to intimidation (even though interference is mentioned in s. 54(1)(b) of the 1996 Act) since interference which is not intimidation is not covered by the offence in s. 51(1) of the 1994 Act (it would of course be covered by perversion of the course of justice under s. 54(6)(a) of the 1996 Act). More significantly perhaps, the reference to 'others' as stated in the title of s. 51(1) is misleading because, although s. 51(1) goes beyond jurors and witnesses and potential witnesses so as to include 'persons assisting in the investigation of' the offence (and also *potential* jurors), as has already been pointed out in discussion of perverting the course of justice, these examples of an administration of justice offence will not satisfy the criterion of 'involving interference with or intimidation of a juror or a witness (or potential witness)'. Note also the absence of any mention of *potential* jurors in s. 54(1)(b), probably because intimidation of *potential* jurors, whilst a problem for the administration of justice, is not normally likely directly to affect the trial itself or produce a tainted acquittal.

Given the limitations just outlined in relation to the inclusion of s. 51(1) of the 1994 Act in s. 54(6)(b) of the 1995 Act, it is tempting to question what useful purpose is achieved by including s. 54(6)(b) in the Act, a sentiment expressed by Wasik and Taylor in relation to the original inclusion of s. 51(1) in the Criminal Justice and Public Order Act 1994. However the point is that, given the existence of the s. 51 offence, many cases of jury or witness nobbling will now be prosecuted under s. 51 rather than under the head of perversion of the course of justice and therefore a conviction under s. 51(1) has to be made an alternative precondition to that of a conviction for the common law offence.

Aiding, abetting, etc., another person to commit an offence under section 1 of the Perjury Act 1911 (perjury in a judicial proceeding)   The failure to mention the commission of perjury by the acquitted person as a principal in this paragraph may seem odd, but it was the result of a deliberate decision by the Government who were anxious not to extend the ambit of the provision beyond cases where there had been intimidation or interference as opposed to an acquittal which was suspect on some other ground. The Government resisted amendments by Lord Ackner to include expressly the commission of perjury by D as a principal (*Hansard*, Lords, 5 February 1996, cols 78–83 and Lords, 19 December 1995, cols 1580–1583). It was in fact at this stage, in response to Lord Ackner's wider amendments, that the more limited inclusion of secondary or inchoate liability for perjury was made. As Baroness Blatch put it:

> No doubt there are many cases in which it might be possible to secure a conviction for perjury because of some deliberate inaccuracy in the evidence given by a defendant or perhaps a witness. Such convictions might be sought more frequently if they could provide a trigger for a retrial. (*Hansard*, Lords, 19 December 1995, col. 1581.)

Whilst the Government was surely right to resist extending the ambit of the exception to the double jeopardy rule any further, the assumption in the House of Lords debates, that s. 56(6)(c) could not include the commission of perjury by D as principal in giving evidence at his trial which led to the initial acquittal, is probably a mistaken one. Perjury by D as principal appears not to be included at first glance both because the subparagraph is limited to aiding, abetting etc. an offence of perjury committed by *another person* and because, under s. 54(1)(b), the administration of justice offence must involve interference with or intimidation of a juror or witness etc. and giving perjured evidence oneself does not satisfy that criterion since one cannot in this sense be said to have interfered with or intimidated oneself.

Despite this appearance, however, it would seem that there may be situations where perjury by D as a principal may come into consideration. The situation to which s. 54(6)(c) will apply will involve at least two and possibly three individuals; i.e., D who has been acquitted of the initial offence, X who has been convicted of aiding and abetting perjury etc. and Y who is the witness aided and abetted etc. to commit the perjury. It is true that there is nothing to stop D and X being the same person and if, as may frequently be the case, D indeed is that same person (i.e., the one who aids and abets the perjury which helps him to be acquitted of the initial offence), he cannot be the person who actually gave the perjured evidence since he has to aid and abet another person, not himself. However, it is also possible that although D and X are *not* the same person, D and Y are, thus D is acquitted of the original offence because X (e.g., a 'gangland boss') has intimidated or pressurised D (perhaps against D's better judgment) to commit perjury in the course of giving evidence as a witness in his own defence at the trial for the initial offence. X may have his own reasons for wishing to ensure that D is acquitted and may even be a co-accused at the original trial.

This may not be the typical situation but it may not necessarily be exceptional either, and it certainly seems to come under s. 51(1)(b) (and indeed it comes under Baroness Blatch's rationale) as involving a person X being convicted of an administration of justice offence involving interference with or intimidation of a witness (in this case D) in any proceedings which led to the initial acquittal of D. D in this situation may therefore not only be prosecuted for the perjury but may also be liable to have his original acquittal re-opened. Indeed this possibility may, in the context of the section's aims, be quite appropriate since it is also possible that D may have a defence of duress to a charge of perjury if the intimidation is severe (*Hudson and Taylor* [1971] 2 QB 202 and cf. *K* (1983) Cr App Rep 82) and yet he may have been acquitted by virtue of his own perjured evidence. The fact that D in this situation may not be guilty of perjury on the grounds of duress is not an absolute bar to the conviction of X for an administration of justice offence consisting of procuring perjury (which conviction is required under s. 54(1)(b)). See *Blackstone's Criminal Practice*, A5.6 and the cases of *Bourne* (1952) 36 Cr App Rep 125 and *Millward* [1994] Crim LR 527, dealing with cases where the procurer is convicted even though the would-be principal has a defence. If the intimidation or interference does not constitute duress this latter problem does not in any event arise.

Having said all that, it will of course be more commonly the case that D is not the person being aided and abetted etc. to commit perjury even where he is not the person doing the aiding and abetting etc. Furthermore, the fact that he has himself committed perjury as principal will normally be of no relevance unless there is another person who has been convicted of aiding and abetting etc. him to do it.

Enough has probably already been said to demonstrate that the meaning of an administration of justice offence and of s. 54(1)(b) has many potential complications with some not very foreseeable (or perhaps intended) results. Where there were two or more co-accused acquitted at the original trial, the permutations become even more complex, particularly if each of them encouraged the other to give perjured evidence.

A further point about s. 54(1)(b) and the administration of justice offence relates to the meaning of 'interference with or intimidation of'. Intimidation is reasonably straightforward and at least corresponds to the offence under s. 51(1) of the Criminal Justice and Public Order Act 1994. Interference however does not equate to the definition of a particular offence and its outer limits are far from clear. It would clearly include bribes and perhaps also economic threats, the latter possibly being included anyway within 'intimidation'. Would it or should it include mere emotional pressure or appeals to loyalty? The Royal Commission referred (Chap. 10, para. 73) to a juror 'bribed or intimidated' and then (in para. 74) used the expression 'interfered with' as a generic term apparently covering both bribery and intimidation. This might suggest that emotional pressure was not intended to be covered if it did not amount to bribery or intimidation. On the other hand, the Royal Commission report may not be too good a guide on this point since the procedure as enacted is much wider than the Commission's proposal in that it covers witnesses as well as jurors and emotional pressure and appeals to loyalty are much more conceivable and relevant in relation to witnesses than in relation to jurors.

It would be more difficult to argue for including within 'interference' influencing the evidence given by a witness, e.g., by tampering with some physical object. For instance, a damaged car is tampered with in order to influence the evidence of an expert witness, or a blood sample is tampered with in order to influence a forensic scientist's evidence. In both cases it might be difficult to describe what had occurred as an interference with the witness as opposed to the evidence of the witness and yet the case for re-opening the acquittal seems as strong as if the witness had been directly interfered with.

A final point to be made about the requirement of a conviction of a person for an administration of justice offence is that quite obviously there must actually be a conviction and therefore the tainted acquittal procedure cannot apply if the person responsible (in the case where it is not D) has died or has fled the jurisdiction before proceedings can be brought against him for the administration of justice offence. This point further underlines the fact that an essential part of the tainted acquittal process is the certification made by the court which convicts of the administration of justice offence. Until that court makes the requisite certification there can be no question of re-opening the original acquittal and it is to that certification which we now turn.

The tainting of the acquittal (1): the certification by the court convicting of the administration of justice offence

The mere fact that s. 54(1)(b) is satisfied and there has been a conviction for an administration of justice offence involving interference or intimidation etc. does not automatically mean that the court should grant a certificate. Under s. 54(2), it is further required that:

it appears to the court before which the person was convicted that—
  (a) there is a real possibility that, but for the interference or intimidation, the acquitted person would not have been acquitted, and
  (b) subsection (5) does not apply, ...

Section 54(2)(a) thus requires that it should appear that there is a real possibility of a causal link between the interference or intimidation and the initial acquittal. It may appear that the acquittals of one or more defendants at a joint trial will satisfy this test but that others may not — in which case only certain acquittals will be eligible for review. (Compare the Royal Commission's (majority) proposal (Chap. 10, para. 74) that all defendants should be liable to be retried; however this has to be seen in the context of their overall proposal which was limited to interference with a juror where it may be more difficult (than with witness interference) to argue that the interference may have influenced some verdicts rather than others.) Since the court doing the certifying will not normally be the court in which the original acquittal was obtained, it may not be easy to judge (at least as far as witness intimidation is concerned) whether there is a 'real possibility' unless the court has a transcript of the original trial showing what other evidence there was both for and against the particular accused. The court convicting of the administration of justice offence may, in the course of that conviction, only have heard a very small part of the evidence (in the case of *juror* intimidation it may not have heard any) which was given at the original trial. Admittedly, in some cases, the issue may be fairly clear cut. As Baroness Blatch put it:

It may be that the witness who was intimidated gave evidence which was of peripheral relevance to the case. In such circumstance, the judge ... may well conclude that there are no grounds for interfering with the original verdict. In other cases it may be clear to the judge that the witness's evidence was so central to the case that the acquittal is unsafe. (*Hansard*, Lords, 27 November 1995, col. 503.)

In the light of the burden of proof on the prosecution in a criminal trial, the notion of an unsafe acquittal as opposed to an unsafe conviction is interesting in itself, but the real problem is that in many cases the effect of the administration of justice offence will not be clear without further reference to the transcript of the original acquittal. In the case of trials on indictment, speculating on a causal link involves delving into the reasoning which may have lain behind the verdict of the jury in a way which is, to say the least, unusual in the current criminal justice system. One can even go so far as to say, given the secrecy which protects the deliberations of the jury, that it is impossible to be sure that the administration of justice offence caused the original acquittal, which is no doubt one reason why the test for certification is only one of 'appearing to be a real possibility' or, in the case of actually quashing the acquittal (see below), appearing to be 'likely'. Whilst these tests of likelihood and real possibility are clearly workable, the question of principle is whether these tests are sufficiently stringent to justify further legal proceedings for an offence for which the accused has already once been acquitted.

At least the phrase 'real possibility' (which also appears in s. 13(1)(a) of the Criminal Appeal Act 1995 dealing with references to the Criminal Cases Review Commission) was retained by the Government in the face of suggested amendments which would have weakened it further by removing the word 'real' (*Hansard*, Lords, 19 December 1995, cols 1583–1585). The adjective 'real' was retained on the basis that it gives more guidance to the certifying court and makes it clear that there must be fairly robust grounds before one can apply for a person's acquittal to be quashed. It should also be remembered that at this stage of the procedure (i.e., at the end of the trial of the administration of justice offence), unless the accused in that trial is the same person who was acquitted of the initial offence, it would appear that the acquitted person will not be represented before the court and will therefore have no opportunity to influence the decision to certify.

Although there has to be a causal link between the interference or intimidation and the *acquittal* of the defendant, there does not have to be shown to have been any connection between the acquitted *defendant* and the intimidation or interference in the sense that he authorised, requested or arranged it. One (unnamed) member of the Royal Commission thought that there should be such a connection but the majority thought not (Chap. 10, para. 74). Neither indeed did the Commission specify any requirement for a causal link between the interference and the acquittal, but then again their proposals were narrower in being limited to intimidation or interference of a juror, but not a witness, at a Crown Court trial. The absence of a requirement of a link between the acquitted defendant and the interference must be a key factor in any debate about the merits of the new procedure. To put an acquitted defendant at risk of a second trial for the same offence where it cannot be shown that he was in any way responsible for or connected with the interference or intimidation which is said to make his acquittal flawed seems to go against the spirit of the double jeopardy rule much more strongly than where the defendant can be shown to have caused the very flaw which is the reason for his retrial. The Royal Commission did indeed comment on this issue as follows:

> The cases we have in mind will normally occur as a result of the efforts of organised, professional criminals for whom it will, in the opinion of the majority, be all too easy to conceal a connection with the defendant or defendants (Chap. 10, para. 74).

Proving a connection may indeed be difficult, but the Act nowhere specifically requires even any prima facie evidence of such a connection. Perhaps the courts would be prepared to regard the absence of any suggestion that the acquitted defendant was in any way connected with or responsible for the intimidation or interference as a factor in deciding the interests of justice question discussed below. Where it can be proved that the acquitted defendant aided and abetted the intimidation or interference, he can of course be convicted of the administration of justice offence anyway and the need to re-open the original acquittal is much less pressing. If he cannot be proved to have committed the administration of justice offence, then re-opening the acquittal is the only way to get at him and the real question is therefore whether it is right to allow the State to pursue again a defendant who cannot be shown to have caused the interference at his own original trial.

Irrespective of the lack of a requirement of a connection between the defendant and the interference etc., the appearance of a real possibility of a causal connection between the interference and the acquittal is not of itself sufficient for a certification. The reference to 'subsection (5)' in s. 54(2)(b) prevents a certification if 'because of lapse of time or for any other reason it would be contrary to the interests of justice to take proceedings against the acquitted person for the offence of which he was acquitted'. Leaving aside for the moment the view that the subsection is tautologous in that it is arguably always contrary to the interests of justice to take proceedings against an acquitted person for an offence of which he was previously acquitted, the exercise of this 'interests of justice' discretion is potentially crucial in limiting any oppressive effects of the derogation from the double jeopardy rule which the tainted acquittals procedure represents. Lapse of time is specifically mentioned as a factor in the discretion and 'any other reason' can be taken into account. This could include, according to Baroness Blatch in the House of Lords, 'that a crucial witness in the original trial had since died or perhaps that the defendant himself was already serving a lengthy sentence for some other offence' (*Hansard*, Lords, 27 November 1995, col. 503).

Such factors, it might be thought, are essentially ones relevant to the feasibility or utility of prosecuting rather than concerned with the interests of justice, although presumably the death of a key witness as a reason for not certifying includes defence as well as prosecution witnesses. Hopefully, the courts will take a broad view of 'any other reason' and take into account factors such as that adumbrated earlier, relating to the extent to which there is evidence that the acquitted defendant was in some way connected with the interference or intimidation or whether, on the other hand, he is one who has been acquitted after undergoing a trial in relation to which he has behaved himself impeccably. This may be particularly important where the defendant was jointly tried with others who are clearly responsible for organising the intimidation for their own ends and of which he knew nothing but which *may* have had an effect on his own acquittal. At the very least, the court may wish to see a higher degree of likelihood, something more than the statutory minimum of 'real possibility', of a causal link between the interference and his acquittal before they conclude that it is not contrary to the interests of justice that he should be tried a second time.

If both parts of s. 54(2) appear to be satisfied (real possibility of causal connection between intimidation and acquittal plus not contrary to the interests of justice), the acquittal is well on the way to being tainted but there is a further application to be made before it can be regarded as sufficiently tainted for proceedings for a retrial to be commenced. To corrupt an anecdote given by Lord Ackner at the report stage

(*Hansard*, Lords, 5 February 1996, col. 82), the acquittal is 'tainted, but 'tain't yet enough'.

The tainting of the acquittal (2): the four conditions for an order quashing the acquittal

An application for an order to quash the original acquittal can be made under s. 54(3) to the High Court if the court which tried the administration of justice offence has certified under s. 54(2) as discussed above. The High Court must make the order if (but only if) four conditions are satisfied, the conditions being set out in s. 55. It may appear that the High Court is given little discretion in the matter once the four conditions are established but in fact it has quite a degree of room for manoeuvre because the conditions are couched in the language of it 'appearing to the High Court' (three conditions) or 'not appearing to the High Court' in the case of the other one.

The first condition, under s. 55(1), is 'that it appears to the High Court likely that, but for the interference or intimidation, the acquitted person would not have been acquitted'. This echoes strongly the first requirement for certification by the trial court in s. 54(2) and the same point can be made about this requiring a causal link and the difficulty the High Court may have unless it looks at a full transcript of the original trial at which the acquittal was obtained. The only difference from s. 54(2)(a) however is that s. 55 requires it to appear 'likely' rather than 'that there is a real possibility' that the acquitted person would not have been acquitted. The intention would appear to be to make the test under s. 55 more strict in that 'likely' could be taken to mean something along the lines of 'more likely than not' or 'on a balance of probabilities' whereas a real possibility may be something rather less than a 50 per cent chance although more than just a bare possibility. It is perhaps unwise to try to paraphrase the two tests, the important point seeming to be that a stricter test is imposed before a quashing order can actually be made as opposed to a certification under s. 54(2), which merely permits the making of an application for a quashing order.

The second condition, under s. 55(2), echoes precisely the test laid down in s. 54(2)(b) and s. 54(5) that further proceedings are not contrary to the interests of justice (whether because of lapse of time or any other reason). Since the trial court will already have found this condition satisfied, the issue is essentially one of whether the High Court agrees with the trial court on this point, but it will have to exercise its discretion independently in the light of any arguments put to it. It should not simply be a case of asking whether the trial court's decision was one that a reasonable tribunal could have come to. Furthermore, it is quite likely that different and fuller arguments may be put to the High Court since the acquitted person himself will have an input (see s. 55(3) below) whereas this may not always be the case at the trial of the administration of justice offence (see above).

The third and fourth conditions, imposed by s. 55(3) and (4), are wholly outside those considered by the trial court. By s. 55(3), 'the third condition is that it appears to the Court that the acquitted person has been given a reasonable opportunity to make *written* representations' (emphasis added). Since the four conditions, if satisfied, automatically lead to the making of an order under s. 55(3), the written representations will of necessity only relate to the other three conditions and will no doubt often concentrate on the issue of likelihood of whether or not D would have been acquitted but for the interference or intimidation (causal link) or, alternatively, on the issue of whether it would be contrary to the interests of justice to take proceedings against the acquitted person (see the discussion above in relation to this factor). Whether D has been given a reasonable opportunity to make written representations must surely be partly dependent on whether he or she has had proper legal advice and/or legal aid. How and to what extent legal aid for these purposes will be made available is not clear, something that can be said about a number of aspects of the procedure for applying to the High Court.

By s. 55(4), 'the fourth condition is that it appears to the court that the conviction for an administration of justice offence will stand'. In relation to this latter condition, s. 55(6) states that 'this condition will have the effect that the Court shall not make an order under section 54(3) if (for instance) it appears to the Court that any time allowed for giving notice of appeal has not expired or that an appeal is pending'. Thus an order will not be made unless the time limit for giving notice of appeal has expired and no appeal has been lodged. However, once this period has expired, the court need not worry about theoretical or hypothetical possibilities such as a possible future reference of the case to the Court of Appeal by the Criminal Cases Review Commission (unless there are positive grounds for believing that such a reference is likely) since, by s. 55(5):

... the Court shall
  (a)   take into account all the information before it, but
  (b)   ignore the possibility of new factors coming to light.

New proceedings against D for the initial offence

If the High Court makes an order quashing the conviction for the original offence, s. 55(4) permits, but does not compel, proceedings to be taken against the acquitted person for the offence of which he was acquitted. Where the case is dealt with by the Crown Prosecution Service, decisions about it will no doubt be governed by the Code for Crown Prosecutors (see *Blackstone's Criminal Practice*, Appendix 5). Since under clause 3.2 of the Code all cases must be subject to continuing review, the decision whether to 'take proceedings against the acquitted person' will be subject to the same tests which apply to the ordinary run of cases initiated by the police and reviewed by a Crown Prosecutor. Thus, the prosecutor must make a judgment of evidential sufficiency and be satisfied that there is a realistic prospect of conviction (clause 4(1)) and must also consider whether it would be in the public interest to proceed (clause 4(2)). Since the High Court must have determined already that it is not contrary to the interests of justice (whether for lapse of time or for any other reason) to proceed, it may be that the Crown Prosecution Service will decide not to proceed only exceptionally. Nevertheless, the Crown Prosecution Service is constitutionally independent and it would be improper for the Crown Prosecution Service to treat the prior court determination as constraining its decision-making. A particular factor which the High Court may have some difficulty in judging is the length of time which might elapse from first acquittal until the commencement of the second trial. Thus, it may be proper not to proceed where it appears that the lapse of time may be significantly greater than anticipated by the High Court.

Although applications for quashing orders will usually be made by the Crown Prosecution Service, there is nothing in the legislation to prevent a private individual applying for such an order or instituting proceedings for the original offence after an order has been successfully obtained. However the Crown Prosecution Service will have its normal powers to take over such a prosecution or to serve a notice of discontinuance, although again the latter move may be highly unlikely given that the High Court has already satisfied itself of the four conditions in s. 55.

It is inherent in the nature of the tainted acquittals procedure that the second prosecution will be some considerable time after the initial acquittal and therefore even longer after the time of the alleged offence. As has been seen, the original acquittal will not be quashed unless it appears to the High Court that it is not against the interests of justice because of, *inter alia*, lapse of time. Nevertheless, in the case of some offences, the lapse of time could present an apparent problem because the offence is one in which proceedings must be commenced within a specified period of time calculated by reference to the commission of the offence. Section 56(1) deals with this issue by providing that the period of time should instead be calculated by reference to the time when the order quashing the original conviction was made. Section 56(2) states that this shall apply no matter how the enactment imposing the time limit is expressed and gives some examples, including the 12-month time limit under the Sexual Offences Act 1956, sch. 2, para. 10 for unlawful sexual intercourse and the six-month time limit for laying an information for summary offences under s. 127 of the Magistrates' Courts Act 1980.

These are only given as examples by s. 56(2), which in general terms is concerned to state that all time limits for prosecution should be calculated in this way from the date of the quashing order. There may however be a potential anomaly in relation to a time limit such as that under s. 19(1) of the Trade Descriptions Act 1968, which provides that prosecutions for indictable offences under the Act must be commenced within three years of the offence or one year from its discovery *whichever is the earlier*. It may be argued that this time limit is unaffected by s. 56 since it is not, solely at least, 'calculated by reference to the commission of the offence' and, more fundamentally, the substitution of the date of the quashing order for the time of the offence makes no difference since a date 12 months from the discovery of the offence will always be earlier, and the 1968 Act imposes whichever is the earliest of the two dates. The argument may not be particularly attractive on its merits but it does seem to have some force given the wording of s. 56(1)(c).

The discussion in the previous paragraph underlines the fact that proceedings against an acquitted person for the offence of which he has already been acquitted constitute a completely fresh set of proceedings, otherwise s. 56 would not be necessary at all since the time limit would have been satisfied by the institution of the proceedings which led to the initial acquittal. Care will need to be taken to avoid or minimise any potential prejudice to the accused in the second set of proceedings arising out of any publicity given to the first trial or to the fact that he has been tried once already or to the fact that a subsequent trial judge and the High Court have thought it, in the first instance, a 'real possibility' and in the second instance, 'likely' that he would not have been acquitted but for interference or intimidation with jurors or witnesses at his first trial. With this in mind, s. 57(2), (3) and (4) amend the Contempt of Court Act 1981 as follows:

(a)   As a result of s. 57(3), the court trying the administration of justice offence can make an order under s. 4(2) of the Contempt of Court Act 1981 ordering the postponement of the publication of any report of the proceedings if it appears to the court that there is a possibility of subsequent proceedings against a person for an offence of which he has already been acquitted (even though the normal test of those proceedings being pending or imminent is not yet satisfied).

(b)   As a result of s. 57(4), a certification under s. 54(2) by the court trying the administration of justice offence shall be treated as commencing the 'active' period of any subsequent proceedings for the original offence for the purposes of the strict liability contempt of court rule. Under this rule (see Contempt of Court Act 1981, ss. 1 and 2 and sch. 1) publication which creates a substantial risk that the course of justice in 'active' proceedings will be seriously impeded or prejudiced may be regarded as contempt of court regardless of intent. Therefore, once a certification under s. 54(2) has been made (which can only come at the end of the trial of the administration of justice offence), any publicity, for example relating to the original tainted acquittal, is potentially liable to be treated as contempt of court as indeed might any publicity relating to the conviction obtained in the administration of justice offence; such publicity would be exempted by s. 4(1) of the Contempt of Court Act 1981 only if it was a contemporaneous report which was not subject to a postponement order under s. 4(2).

No specific mention is made of the application to the High Court for the Order quashing the original conviction. By this stage, as a result of s. 57(4), the (still putative) proceedings against the acquitted person have become 'active' and the strict liability rule might be thought to apply except that s. 4(1) of the Contempt of Court Act 1981 exempts fair and accurate reports of legal proceedings *held in public*. This exemption would of course not apply if an order under s. 4(2) of the 1981 Act postponing any such report applied but such an order does not seem possible since the retrial is not yet pending or imminent and there is no equivalent provision to s. 57(3) of the 1996 Act (which amends s. 4 of the Contempt of Court Act 1981 so as to permit an order in relation to the trial of the administration of justice offence). The implication therefore is that the application to the High Court for an order quashing the original conviction will not be heard *in public* and therefore no exemption under s. 4(1) of the Contempt of Court Act will be available. That the application under s. 54(3) will not be made in public is consistent with the condition in s. 55(3) relating to the acquitted person's opportunity to make *written* representations. Whilst one can see the desirability of this from the point of view of avoiding any publicity which might prejudice the acquitted person at any subsequent trial if the initial acquittal should be quashed, it does seem quite remarkable that a power to quash an acquittal (which is unique as far as acquittal by a jury is concerned and previously confined to errors of law as far as summary trial was concerned) should be exercisable other than in open court. What is more remarkable is that the Act does not spell out in more detail the procedure and safeguards underpinning the application to the High Court which breaks such new ground as a derogation from the fundamental principle against double jeopardy and from the plea in bar of *autrefois acquit*.

Conclusions

Overall, one has to question whether the tortuosity and the complexities of the tainted acquittals procedure, together with the precedent which it constitutes for any further undermining of the double jeopardy rule, are in any way justified by the practical benefits which it may confer in enabling the conviction at some time in the future of a relatively small proportion of the total number of defendants who may have been improperly acquitted. This is not to underestimate the injustice which occurs when an accused person is improperly acquitted but even on its own terms, the new procedure may be thought to be highly selective. As we have seen, it is not every case where an administration of justice offence has been instrumental in securing an acquittal that the new procedure applies; it has to be one involving interference with or intimidation of a juror or witness and it has to be possible to prosecute successfully a living individual for that administration of justice offence. Other (admittedly much less likely) forms of 'nobbling', such as intimidation of counsel or the judge or magistrate, are not included nor normally is straightforward perjury by the accused nor apparently a number of other equally relevant forms of interference with the course of justice, such as destruction, tampering with or concealment of evidence. The idea for the tainted acquittals procedure may have come from a recommendation of the Royal Commission but that recommendation was significantly narrower in that it applied only to bribery or intimidation of jurors and in any event was not given much discussion or indeed justification in the Report which devoted less than one page to it.

It is also regrettable that, in taking up the Royal Commission's proposal, more attention was not paid to the suggestion of the minority member that there should have to be some connection between the acquitted defendant and the act of interference or intimidation (a connection which would perhaps have been easier to assume if the principle were to have been limited to intimidation of jurors) even though some of the justifications in the debates on the Bill tended to assume that this condition was satisfied:

> We believe that it is right therefore to ensure that the guilty are not able to avoid conviction if it later comes to light that they, or others *on their behalf*, have, for example, threatened or intimidated witnesses or jurors in order to secure an acquittal (per Baroness Blatch, *Hansard*, Lords, 27 November 1995, col. 503) (emphasis added).

> ... while I support the provisions dealing with acquittals tainted by the *accused's* interference with the jury or witnesses, it occurs to me that by parity of reasoning, there should be a similar provision for acquittals obtained by the accused's own perjury (per Lord Ackner, *Hansard*, Lords, 27 November 1995, col. 492) (emphasis added).

Certainly any benefits of the new procedure in terms of retrials and convictions of the guilty will not be seen for a considerable time given the fact that it applies only to acquittals in respect of *initial* offences alleged to have been *committed* after the appointed day (s. 54(7)). In the meantime, the tainted acquittal procedure will stand as a symbol of the vulnerability of principles such as those underpinning the double jeopardy rule, which are designed to protect the individual against potential oppression by the State, in an age when a Government Minister can describe acquittals, equally as well as convictions, as 'unsafe' and the acquittal of a guilty person is regarded by some as an injustice equal to that involved in the conviction of the innocent. Such innovations may not appear so dangerous in one set of circumstances but times, Governments and States can change and it is to be hoped that any principles compromised in this new procedure are not breached or undermined any further in the future in ways which may be more patently objectionable.

Chapter Eight
Derogatory Assertions

The provisions in ss. 58 to 61 of the Act impose restrictions on the reporting of certain derogatory assertions made in the course of pleas in mitigation or in analogous situations. They are based on recommendations of the Royal Commission on Criminal Justice (1993, Cm 2263) contained in Chap. 8, para. 46 of the Report which is to be found in a section subtitled 'Victims and other witnesses'. This is a good indicator of the context of the provisions which can be seen as part of the general move towards giving greater recognition to the rights and interests of victims in the criminal justice process as opposed to merely providing safeguards for the accused. In this sense, links can be made with the proposals of the Pigot Committee (Home Office Advisory Group on Video Evidence) on vulnerable witnesses, whose proposals are partially reflected in the provisions of the Criminal Justice Act 1991 on child witnesses, and with s. 31 of the Criminal Justice and Public Order Act 1994 on imputations on the character of a deceased victim. However, it is important not to press such links too far since unlike the latter reforms in the 1991 and 1994 Acts, which do make a substantive change to the rules of evidence and to the manner in which the defence may conduct their case, the provisions on derogatory assertions do not in any way prevent the making of the assertions in the first place but merely affect the question of whether they can be publicly reported. In this sense, they are perhaps more analogous to provisions of the Sexual Offences (Amendment) Acts 1976 and 1992 dealing with anonymity of victims of rape and certain other sexual offences, although they can perhaps be regarded as having a more limited impact. As a limitation on the general principle of open justice they are none the less significant and deserve examination both on that account and also for their potential benefits to victims and others whose reputations may be unjustifiably damaged by statements made ostensibly in mitigation of sentence.

The basic case for the provisions on derogatory assertions can be found in para. 47 of the Royal Commission Report:

... particularly if a plea of guilty has been entered, the victim may have slurs cast upon him or her during the defence speech in mitigation of the likely sentence. Such remarks are privileged and may be reported by the press with impunity and with no opportunity for the victim to obtain redress. This is a difficult problem since we have no desire to restrict the freedom of the press and the defendant's counsel is under a duty to carry out his or her client's instructions. Nevertheless, we believe that it should be possible to prevent wholly unfair attacks on the victim during speeches in mitigation. In appropriate cases the prosecution should intervene and the CPS have told us that it is their policy to do so where the defence depart from the facts in a material aspect. Such a course, however, cannot be embarked upon lightly since there may have to be a separate hearing, following an adjournment, if the defence persist in their version of the facts. We believe that, if prosecuting counsel intervened more often, defendants would become less prone to launching unsupported attacks on the characters of victims and other witnesses (or even on occasion people who have not appeared at the trial at all), since such attacks would be likely to be counter-productive when it came to sentence. We recommend, however, that a power be vested in the judge to prohibit in the last resort the reporting of unsupported allegations made during a speech in mitigation. We envisage this as a discretionary power to be used in the extreme case of a defendant apparently using the opportunity of a speech in mitigation to do as much damage as possible to the reputation of the victim or a third party without any risk of retaliation.

The power of last resort referred to in the above recommendation is now provided for in s. 58 of the 1996 Act, and discussion of this and the other provisions on derogatory assertions can best be dealt with in terms of:

(a)   the power to make an order (s. 58);
(b)   the effect of an order once made (s. 59);
(c)   offences committed by persons contravening an order (s. 60);
(d)   commencement and supplementary provisions (s. 61).

The power to make an order under s. 58

By virtue of s. 58(1), s. 58 applies to the normal case where 'a person has been convicted of an offence and a speech in mitigation is made by him or on his behalf' before either a court determining sentence or a magistrates' court determining whether he should be committed for sentence. In addition to such pleas in mitigation *before* sentence, s. 58(2) provides that s. 58 can also apply where sentence has already been passed and 'a submission relating to the sentence is made by him or on his behalf' on the hearing of an appeal against the sentence, a review of the sentence or an application for leave to appeal against the sentence.

In any of the above situations (speeches in mitigation prior to sentence or defence submissions as to sentence to appellate courts after sentence), the court may make an order by virtue of s. 58(4):

where there are substantial grounds for believing—

(a)   that an assertion forming part of the speech or submission is derogatory to a person's character (for instance, because it suggests that this conduct is or has been criminal, immoral or improper), and
(b)   that the assertion is false or that the facts asserted are irrelevant to the sentence . . .

It will be noticed that, under s. 58(4), there are two cumulative conditions the second of which has two alternative ways of being satisfied. The two conditions are (a) that the assertion is derogatory, *and* (b) that the assertion is *either* false *or* irrelevant. The two conditions do not have to be proved to exist either beyond a reasonable doubt or on a balance of probabilities but there must be 'substantial grounds for believing' that the two conditions are satisfied.

As to the first requirement that the assertion is derogatory, it is noticeable that the civil law standard of 'defamatory' is not utilised, no doubt in an attempt to prevent the technicalities of the law of libel entering into the picture. It is clear, however, that there will be a substantial overlap between what is defamatory of a person's reputation for the purposes of the law of libel and what is 'derogatory to a person's character' for the purposes of s. 58. Section 58(4)(a) helpfully gives some examples of reasons why an assertion may be regarded as derogatory ('because it suggests that ... conduct is or has been criminal, immoral or improper'). Most cases where the court is considering prohibiting the reporting of an assertion will tend to come under one of these examples and it will thus be clear that the allegation is derogatory, this being precisely why the court is considering preventing its publication. There will no doubt be less clear cases however. Take an assertion that a person is insane or suffering from some specific mental illness. This would probably be defamatory (if untrue) but is it derogatory to his character? If character means nothing more nor less than reputation (cf. *Rowton* (1865) Le & Ca 520) then the answer is probably yes, but then the distinction between defamatory and derogatory becomes almost completely illusory. But character may refer more directly to notions of virtue as contrasted with wrongdoing (as might be suggested by the examples of 'criminal, immoral or improper') — in which case it would not be derogatory to suggest a person is insane since this involves no judgment of censure or blame. It would also follow that whether or not it would today be regarded as defamatory to say of a person that she had been raped (cf. *Youssoupoff* v *MGM Pictures Ltd* (1934) 50 TLR 581), it would not be derogatory of her character. On the other hand this is a type of assertion which, if false or irrelevant, it may be desirable to prevent being reported and that consideration may encourage the courts to adopt a wider view of the meaning of 'derogatory to a person's character'.

Similar arguments may arise in relation to assertions which may appear derogatory to certain sections of society but not others. For example, to say of a member of the League against Cruel Sports that she took part in a foxhunt, may be highly damaging to her reputation (with other members of the League), but is it derogatory to her character? Or if a member of a political party which campaigns against private education or health care is asserted to make use of the private sector, would this be regarded as derogatory to his character? On a literal view, possibly not; but, if the assertion is false or irrelevant, there may be an argument that the defence should not be able to use the forum of the criminal courts to give the assertion publicity, which consideration again may encourage the courts to take a wider view of the meaning of derogatory. In any case it may be argued that even if the assertion is not in itself derogatory, the *implication* of inconsistency, doing one thing whilst belonging to an organisation which campaigns for the opposite, is derogatory to a person's character.

That an assertion is derogatory is not enough, there must also be substantial grounds for believing it is either false or irrelevant to the sentence. The court itself is in as good a position as anyone to judge whether the assertion is relevant to sentence.

A common reason for putting forward an apparently derogatory assertion may be to attempt to show that the accused was responding to an attack by the victim or by (or on) a third party. Even if the court considers the assertion may be relevant in this sense, if there are substantial grounds for believing it to be untrue, then the court can still make an order. The court may find this question of truth more difficult than the question of relevance, but it may be assisted in this regard by the holding of a *Newton* hearing (see *Blackstone's Criminal Practice*, D16.2–D16.14 and D16.28–D16.30) whereby the defence and prosecution can adduce evidence as to the facts to be accepted for the purposes of sentencing the accused (after a plea of guilty or indeed a verdict of guilty). Paragraph 11.8 of Annexe H of the Code of Conduct of the Bar is particularly relevant here. It provides:

> In relation to sentence, prosecuting counsel:
> ...
> (e)   should draw the attention of the defence to any assertion of material fact made in mitigation which the prosecution believes to be untrue: if the defence persists in that assertion, prosecution counsel should invite the court to consider requiring the issue to be determined by the calling of evidence in accordance with the decision of the Court of Appeal in *Newton* (1982) 77 Cr App Rep 13.

In addition to the requirements relating to the assertion set out in s. 58(4), the assertion must not be one previously made at the trial or during any other proceedings relating to the offence (s. 58(5)). This is an important limitation on the protection given against derogatory assertions but without it the provisions would go much further than the Royal Commission's recommendations and would interfere too much with the principle of open justice. In any case, assertions made (by the accused) in evidence at the trial are subject to much more powerful control in terms of the possible loss of the accused's own shield against cross-examination on his own character and can themselves be tested and challenged in cross-examination. It is the fact that assertions in speeches in mitigation can sometimes go unchallenged which is partly behind the provisions in ss. 58 to 61. In connection both with assertions during the trial and with pleas in mitigation, the terms of para. 610(e) to (h) of the Code of Conduct of the Bar should be borne in mind which state, *inter alia*, that a barrister:

> ... must not make statements or ask questions which are merely scandalous or intended or calculated only to vilify, insult or annoy either a witness or some other person ...
> ... must if possible avoid the naming in open court of third parties whose character would thereby be impugned ...

Interim orders and full orders

Assuming that the substantial grounds for believing there to be a derogatory assertion under s. 58(4) are established (and provided that it does not appear to the court that the assertion was previously made at the trial), an order may be made under s. 58(8). Such an order can conveniently be referred to as a full order. It is not a permanent order since, as will be noted, it will last only for a maximum of 12 months. It is here referred to as a full order to contrast it with what might conveniently be called an interim order under s. 58(7). An interim order is one which is made prior to the 'determination with regard to sentencing', an expression which is defined in s. 58(9) but which essentially means the decision which the plea or submission is designed to influence (i.e., the sentencing decision or the decision whether to commit for sentence or the decision of the appellate court as to sentence or as to leave to appeal).

The power to make the interim order is necessary to allow the court to prevent the reporting of a potentially derogatory assertion as soon as it is made and before an evaluation has been made as to whether it is believed to be either irrelevant to the defence or false. The interim order cannot last beyond (it may be revoked earlier) the time of the sentencing determination. At that point, if the restriction on reporting the assertion is to be continued, a full order under s. 58(8) must be made. Since a restriction under s. 58(7) is very much a temporary restriction, the test which must be satisfied is not 'substantial grounds for believing' but 'a real possibility' that a full order under s. 58(8) may in due course be made; this means that there must be a real possibility that there will be substantial grounds for believing as required under s. 58(4) and that the court will exercise its discretion to make an order.

Whilst the power under s. 58(7) to make the interim order is obviously useful, there is no indication in the Act as to the mechanism for triggering consideration of whether to make an order under s. 58(7) or (8). Will it be up to the court to notice that an allegation has been made which may be derogatory and untrue or irrelevant or will the prosecution be expected to point this out? The prosecution may be better placed to intervene where the assertion relates to a victim or a prosecution witness whom they may be expected to know a good deal about, but if the allegation relates to some other person (as is perfectly possible under s. 58(4)(a)), it may be more difficult for the prosecution to judge whether the allegation is false or even derogatory. However, given that the power to make an order is designed to be one of last resort, it would seem that courts should not indulge in making interim orders every time something potentially derogatory is said by way of mitigation. Certainly, the fact that no interim order has been made in advance of sentencing determination does not prevent a full order being made subsequently (see s. 58(9)(d)) if that later proves to be appropriate (assuming the damage has not already been done by widespread publication).

Perhaps the most curious aspect of the whole section at first sight is that even for a full order under s. 58(8), which has to be made as soon as is reasonably practicable after the sentencing determination, the order can last only for 12 months (less if revoked before then). On the face of it, this would seem to imply that the derogatory assertion can be published with impunity provided the publisher is prepared to wait for 12 months. This is not the case however. What has to be remembered is that the reason why the subject of a derogatory assertion needs protection is that contemporaneous reports of judicial proceedings are privileged in relation to defamation (under s. 3 of the Law of Libel Amendment Act 1888). That privilege will no longer apply 12 months after the making of an order under s. 58 since the report will not be published contemporaneously. The protection of an order under s. 58 is therefore no longer necessary and the law of defamation can be invoked if necessary by the subject of the derogatory assertion if it is reported. Indeed it would be inappropriate for the assertion to be permanently stifled merely because the criminal court believed on substantial grounds that the assertion was derogatory and false. It would be even less appropriate if the order was based on the view that the assertion was derogatory and irrelevant to the defence plea or submission but not false. That is a good ground for refusing to allow a contemporaneous report to be issued which thereby automatically attracts privilege in relation to defamation as a report of judicial proceedings, but it is no ground for permanently banning the statement being reported if it is not shown subsequently to be libellous.

The effect under s. 59 of orders made under s. 58

Whilst an order under s. 58(7) or (8) is in force, s. 59(1) provides that the derogatory assertion:

> must not—
> (a)   be published in Great Britain in a written publication available to the public; or
> (b)   be included in a relevant programme for reception in Great Britain.

It will be noticed that this restriction does not extend to Northern Ireland; ss. 58 to 60 do apply to derogatory assertions made in Northern Ireland proceedings (see s. 79(3) and sch. 4, paras 23 and 24), but the ban on publication is correspondingly restricted to publication in Northern Ireland (see sch. 4, para. 24). In other respects s. 59(1) is quite wide, applying both to reporting via radio and television and also by a 'written publication', which is widely defined in s. 59(2) to include 'a film, a soundtrack and any other record in permanent form'. It does not however include 'an indictment or other document prepared for use in particular legal proceedings', an exclusion presumably designed to cater for the exceptional case where the derogatory assertion, whilst perhaps being irrelevant to the defence, appears likely to be true and leads to criminal proceedings being taken against the subject of the assertion.

Section 59(3) clarifies the circumstances in which an assertion will be regarded as published or included in a programme. The publication etc. must both *name* the person about whom the assertion is made (*or*, without naming him, contain enough to make it likely that members of the public will *identify* him) and *reproduce* the actual wording of the matter asserted *or* contain its *substance*. Thus the clearest breach of an order will reproduce the assertion verbatim, including the actual name of the subject of the assertion, but equally a report which does neither of these things may contravene an order if it makes it likely that the subject will be identified and also contains the substance of the allegation. The substance of the allegation will include at least those aspects of the allegation that make it derogatory, but it will not normally be essential that the precise words used in the allegation are utilised.

The offence of contravening an order

The consequences of reporting an assertion which contravenes s. 59 are set out in s. 60 which essentially provides that it is a summary offence punishable by a fine not exceeding level 5 (currently £5,000). The person liable for the offence varies according to the manner in which the assertion is reported. In the case of publication, it is the publisher, although in the case of publication in a newspaper or periodical, 'any proprietor' and 'any editor' of the newspaper or periodical may additionally be liable (s. 60(1)(a)). In the case of an assertion included in a relevant programme, 'any body corporate engaged in providing the service in which the programme is included and any person having functions in relation to the programme corresponding to those of an editor of a newspaper' may be guilty of the offence. This would therefore include the television or radio company and also the producer, director or news editor of the particular programme, depending on which of those three persons had responsibility for the content of the programme. In the case of offences committed by a body corporate (such as a television company), s. 60(4) provides also for the liability of individual officers where the offence has been committed with their consent or connivance or is attributable to their neglect.

Although the offence created by s. 60 does not seem to require any particular *mens rea*, by virtue of s. 60(3), it is a defence for a person charged to prove that he was not aware and neither suspected nor had reason to suspect that an order under s. 58 was in force or that the publication or programme in question included the assertion in question.

Commencement and supplementary

The power to make orders under s. 58 will apply only to speeches in mitigation etc. in relation to offences *committed* after the day appointed under s. 61(1), which is intended to be early in 1997. It is intended that rules of court will be made and laid before Parliament before implementation which will perhaps cover, *inter alia*, questions such as how and by whom the potentially derogatory effect of an assertion should or can be raised.

The provisions of ss. 58 and 59 do not affect any other restrictions or prohibitions on reporting imposed by virtue of any other enactment (s. 61(3)), such as restrictions under s. 4(2) of the Contempt of Court Act 1981 for the avoidance of a substantial risk of prejudice to the administration of justice. Neither, as a result of s. 61(4), do they affect the privilege of newspaper reports of court proceedings under s. 3 of the Law of Libel Amendment Act 1888. Thus, if a newspaper contravenes an order under s. 58 and is found guilty of an offence under s. 60, there will normally still be no liability for libel as the privilege under s. 3 of the 1888 Act will remain available.

Although the prosecution of a newspaper for libel requires the leave of a judge in chambers (s. 8 of the Law of Libel Amendment Act 1888) and an offence under s. 60 *may* involve the publication of a libel, s. 61(5) makes it clear that no such leave is required for a prosecution for an offence under s. 60.

It will be interesting to see how often it is necessary or possible to use the powers contained in s. 58 which, it has been repeatedly said both in the Royal Commission Report and in Parliament, have been provided for use as a last resort. It may be that, as the Royal Commission hoped, a greater readiness by the prosecution to test defence versions of the facts through *Newton* hearings coupled with the very existence of the new provisions will discourage defendants from putting forward unjustified derogatory assertions in the first place, in which case the new powers will be little used. This is perhaps the best that one can hope for although one might also hope that, on the relatively rare occasions where it should prove necessary to use the new powers, they can be used effectively and expeditiously. The rules of court to be introduced before implementation may well have a significant impact on whether or not this proves to be the case.

Chapter Nine
Evidence and Miscellaneous Provisions

This chapter deals with a small number of reforms to the law of evidence and a number of other miscellaneous provisions of the Act which it has not been appropriate to deal with in other chapters of this Guide. These miscellaneous matters relate to witness orders, indemnification of justices and justices' clerks and the meaning of the preliminary stage of criminal proceedings for the purposes of custody time-limits. First, however, the three unrelated evidential reforms will be considered.

Television links and video recordings

Because of the stress and trauma which can be caused to child witnesses by their having to give evidence in open court in trials of sexual or violent offences, s. 32 of the Criminal Justice Act 1988 introduced a procedure whereby such evidence could be given by way of live television link. This was supplemented by the Criminal Justice Act 1991, which inserted a new s. 32A into the 1988 Act to permit a child's evidence-in-chief in such cases to be given by means of a video recording (see Wasik and Taylor, *Blackstone's Guide to the Criminal Justice Act 1991*, Chap. 6). The child witness still has to be available at the trial for cross-examination but such cross-examination can at least be done via the live television link rather than in the physical presence of the accused (who is also precluded by s. 34A of the Criminal Justice Act 1988 from conducting the cross-examination in person). In each case, before evidence is given by live television link or by means of a video recording, the leave of the court is required (see in relation to evidence in a video recording *Practice Direction (Crime: Child's Video Evidence)* (1992) 1 WLR 839).

The amendments introduced in s. 62 of the 1996 Act relate to the leave of the court referred to above. Sections 32 and 32A of the Criminal Justice Act 1988 are amended so as to make it more difficult, once leave has been given, to reverse that decision. The decision can be changed only if there has been a 'material change of circumstances since the leave was given' (see the new s. 32(3E) and s. 32A(6C)). The reason for the amendments was given by Baroness Blatch at report stage (*Hansard*, Lords, 5 February 1996, col. 87):

> If decisions can be taken at an early stage in proceedings, and if those decisions can be made to stick, there will be enormous benefits for the children concerned. They can be reasonably confident that they will be able to give their evidence by

live television link or by video recording. They will be able to prepare themselves on that basis which is likely to make their evidence all the more valuable. It will be very much less likely that they will be faced at short notice, and with insufficient preparation, with the trauma of having to give evidence in court . . . this new clause will help to reduce uncertainty. It seeks to ensure that, once a decision has been made that a child should give evidence by live television link or video recording, it cannot lightly be reversed. But we have retained some flexibility to take account of changes in circumstances. Either party to the proceedings will be able to make an application for the child to give evidence in person if there has been a material change in circumstances. The child might, for example, have a last minute change of heart about using the live television link. Judges will retain discretion to vary an earlier ruling if it appears to be in the interests of justice to do so.

Whatever the benefits of the change as explained by Baroness Blatch, the next 12 columns of *Hansard* were taken up with the discussion and ultimate rejection of a number of other amendments tabled by the late Baroness Faithfull and others which were designed to improve further the position for child witnesses, including in particular a clause designed to enable not only evidence-in-chief but also cross-examination of the child to take place on video in advance of the trial. Similar amendments were unsuccessfully pressed during the passage of both the Criminal Justice Act 1991 and the Criminal Justice and Public Order Act 1994 even though a similar procedure is available in Scotland by virtue of s. 33 of the Prisoners and Criminal Proceedings (Scotland) Act 1993.

A minor anomaly in the wording of the amendment to s. 32A arises because the evidence to be given by video recording need not be the whole of the child witnesses' evidence-in-chief. The child may still give evidence-in-chief at the trial but not on any matter which 'has been *adequately* dealt with in his recorded testimony' (s. 32A(5)(b): emphasis added). The word 'adequately' was specifically added by s. 51 of the Criminal Justice and Public Order Act 1994 (see Wasik and Taylor *Blackstone's Guide to the Criminal Justice and Public Order Act 1994*, para. 3.19) to enable the child to supplement the video recording by oral evidence at the trial where a matter was not fully or adequately dealt with in the video recording. This amendment appears to have been overlooked in the new s. 32A(6D) which refers merely to matter 'dealt with in the recording'. The result seems to be that unless there has been a change of circumstances, the effect of s. 32A(6A) and (6D) is to prevent evidence being given other than by means of the video recording 'if it relates to matter . . . dealt with in the recording' whether or not it is 'adequately' dealt with in that recording. Unless some explanation can be found for the absence of the word 'adequately' in s. 32A(6D)(b), it would seem unfortunately that the effect of s. 51 of the 1994 Act might have been largely nullified.

The amendments contained in s. 62 come into force where leave has been given on or after the appointed day, which is expected to be early 1997.

Provision of blood and urine specimens: road traffic and transport offences

Section 7(3) of the Road Traffic Act 1988 allows, in the course of investigations into drink-driving offences, the police to require a specimen of blood or urine to be provided at a police station in certain circumstances, including where (s. 7(3)(b)):

at the time the requirement is made, a device or a reliable device of the type [approved by the Secretary of State for analysis of specimens of breath] is not available at the police station or it is then for any other reason not practicable to use such a device there ...

Section 31(4) of the Transport and Works Act 1992 is to similar effect in relation to railway employees suspected of being over the alcohol limits.

These provisions authorise the requirement of a blood or urine sample in cases where it is decided *not* to require an evidential *breath* test at the police station because there is no machine available or no reliable machine or because the presence of an interfering agent (such as drugs) is suspected and no reliable result will be produced. They do not, however, authorise a blood or urine sample to be required where a breath test *is* taken using an apparently perfectly reliable machine but the results obtained cannot be relied on for some reason (such as the difference between the reading for two breath samples being greater than 15 per cent).

Section 63(1) of the 1996 Act therefore inserts a new s. 7(3)(bb) into the Road Traffic Act 1988 to authorise the requirement of a blood or urine sample at the police station in this type of situation, i.e., where:

a device of the type mentioned in subsection (1)(a) above has been used at the police station but the constable who required the specimens of breath has reasonable cause to believe that the device has not produced a reliable indication of the proportion of alcohol in the breath of the person concerned ...

Similarly, s. 63(2) inserts a new s. 31(4)(bb) into the Transport and Works Act 1992, to the same effect. The change is prompted mainly by the imminent availability of new evidential breath-testing equipment. Baroness Blatch explained the section as follows in the House of Lords (*Hansard*, Lords, 26 June 1996, col. 970).

The new clause ensures that the police can make full use of new evidential breath-testing equipment, which will shortly be available, by continuing to exercise their discretion to require blood or urine samples from suspected drink drivers in certain situations ... The existing breath-test equipment at police stations was introduced in 1983 and we need to plan ahead for its replacement. Technology has moved on since 1983, as have the international standards on breath-testing. The new equipment therefore incorporates some new software which enables it to identify and flag up automatically certain situations which are currently catered for by operational arrangements. Put simply, these cover situations where it is suspected an interfering substance may be present, or the alleged offender produces mouth alcohol or the difference between the reading for two breath samples is greater than 15 per cent. In such situations the machine will advise the operator and the constable should then be able to require a blood or urine sample as an alternative.

The existing provisions in section 7 of the Road Traffic Act 1988 do not currently allow specimens to be required in a situation where a properly working machine indicates such readings. The new clause therefore extends the police's existing discretion to allow specimens to be taken in such situations.

Whilst this explanation makes sense in terms of the new technology to be introduced, which will itself provide reasonable grounds for the constable to believe that the reading is not a reliable indication of the proportion of alcohol in the breath of the person concerned, s. 7(3)(bb) does not seem to be limited to these situations. For example, if a machine indicates a reading which is not in excess of the permitted limit but the constable, on the basis of the apparently drunken condition of the suspect, believes it must be under-recording, could that constitute 'reasonable cause to believe that the device has not produced a reliable indication of the proportion of alcohol in the breath of the person concerned'? In the light of the explanation given by Baroness Blatch, it would seem to be more proper to take the view that the results of an apparently reliable machine should be accepted unless the machine itself, as it is capable of doing, indicates that the reading given cannot be regarded as reliable. Otherwise, one would be getting very close to a situation where the police could disregard the result and insist on a blood or urine sample at the police station merely because the result given by the machine is not the one that they strongly anticipated. They can of course in any event under s. 7(3) insist on a blood or urine sample being taken at a hospital.

Checks against fingerprints or samples etc.

A new s. 63A(1) was inserted into PACE by s. 56 of the Criminal Justice and Public Order Act 1994 to enable a 'speculative search' to be made where fingerprints or samples have been taken from a person arrested on suspicion of being involved in a recordable offence. Such speculative searches check for a match between the fingerprints or samples or information derived from the samples (e.g., DNA profiles) on the one hand and fingerprints or samples or information etc. already held by the police in respect of other offences. In other words they enable the police to check whether the person arrested on one occasion is also implicated in other offences.

Section 64 of the 1996 Act now replaces s. 63A(1) with a somewhat broader s. 63A(1) and a new s. 63A(1A). Section 63A(1) is broadened in that it now authorises a speculative search not only where fingerprints or samples etc. have been taken from a person who has been *arrested* in connection with a recordable offence, but also from a person who has been charged with such an offence or has been informed that he will be reported for such an offence. Furthermore, the new s. 63A(1A) specifically authorises the cross-checking to be done with fingerprints, samples and information etc. held by or on behalf of police forces in the different jurisdictions of England and Wales, Scotland, Northern Ireland, Jersey, Guernsey, and the Isle of Man. (As far as Jersey, Guernsey and the Isle of Man are concerned, this is apparently effectively confined to fingerprints since police there do not currently have the power to take samples.)

The new subsections come into force immediately and apply (see s. 64(2)) where a person is arrested, charged or informed that he will be reported after Royal Assent (4 July 1996).

Abolition of witness orders

Section 1 of the Criminal Procedure (Attendance of Witnesses) Act 1965, which required a magistrates' court conducting committal proceedings to make witness orders (to attend and give evidence at the Crown Court) in respect of each witness examined by the court, is repealed by s. 65. This function was regarded as no longer appropriate given the changes to committal proceedings effected via sch. 1 to the Act (see Chapter 5) and the fact that witnesses will no longer give oral evidence at committals and thus will not be 'examined' by the court. Furthermore, although s. 102(10) of the Magistates' Courts Act 1980 treated a person whose written statement had been tendered in evidence at committal proceedings as a witness who has been examined by the court, s. 102 is also repealed by para. 9 of sch. 1 to the 1996 Act. When s. 65 comes into force and repeals s. 1 of the 1965 Act (expected to be Spring 1997), the notification of witnesses to attend court is apparently to be effected by means of a new administrative procedure. It is not at the moment clear how this procedure will operate and how in particular it will distinguish between and make judgments about those witnesses whose evidence is likely to be admitted in written form and those who will be required to give oral evidence at the Crown Court. (See the discussion of s. 68 and sch. 2 in Chapter Five.)

Summons to (reluctant) witness to attend Crown Court

Sections 66 and 67 make a number of substantial changes to ss. 2 to 4 of the Criminal Procedure (Attendance of Witnesses) Act 1965, which deal with summonses to witnesses to attend the Crown Court to give evidence or produce any document or thing. Section 2 of the 1965 Act was, prior to the amendments, much shorter and was used primarily to secure the attendance of witnesses whose evidence was not given or tendered at the committal proceedings and in respect of whom therefore a witness order had not been made under the now-repealed s. 1. The attendance of such witnesses will now presumably be secured by means of the new administrative procedure to be introduced, but s. 66 inserts a new much lengthier s. 2 to deal with witnesses who will not *voluntarily* attend to give evidence which is likely to be material evidence or produce any document or thing which is likely to be material evidence. The procedure is analogous to that provided for witnesses at summary trial by s. 97 of the Magistrates' Courts Act 1980 (as amended by s. 51 of the 1996 Act: see Chapter 6) in that, under the new s. 2(4), an application for a summons must be made as soon as is reasonably practicable after the committal (or, under s. 2(5), where the notice of transfer procedure has been used, as soon as possible after the transfer).

Provision is also made (by means of a new s. 2A of the 1965 Act) for advance production and inspection of a document or thing. Following such inspection, the person applying for the summons may apply for the summons to be of no further effect if he concludes that the summons is no longer required (s. 2B). A person summonsed may also apply under s. 2C for the summons to be of no effect either:

(a)   because the court is satisfied that he was not served with notice of the application to issue the summons and was neither present nor represented at the hearing of the application; or

(b)   because the court is satisfied that he cannot give any evidence, or produce any document or thing, likely to be material evidence.

Applications for summonses to be issued, and for them to be of no effect, are to be made to the Crown Court which can also, under s. 2D, issue a witness summons of its own motion. Prior to the amendments by the 1996 Act, the High Court was an alternative source of a witness summons but this is no longer the case. In addition, under s. 4 of the 1965 Act, it was only a judge of the High Court who could issue a warrant for the arrest of a witness who was unlikely to comply with the summons. This too is changed by s. 67 of the 1996 Act, which amends s. 4 of the 1965 Act so as to refer to a judge of the Crown Court rather than the High Court.

The changes introduced by ss. 66 and 67 are expected to come into force in Spring 1997.

Indemnification of justices and justices' clerks

Justices and justices' clerks can be personally liable for costs orders made against them after successful appeals against their decisions, whether the decision was made in the exercise of their criminal or civil jurisdiction. They are however entitled to be provided with an indemnity out of local funds (of the Magistrates' Court Committee) under s. 53 of the Justices of the Peace Act 1979, provided that they have acted 'reasonably and in good faith'. In introducing, at report stage in the Lords (*Hansard*, Lords, 5 February 1996, col. 64) the amendment which ultimately led to what is now s. 70 of the 1996 Act, Lord Ackner pointed out that:

What is reasonable may be a matter of dispute, more easily determined with the benefit of hindsight ... I am informed that at least one instance has been traced, some years ago, of a magistrate being left to bear the costs personally. I am told that there have been other such instances. Magistrates have expressed fears concerning bankruptcy and at least one has resigned because of her concern.

Lord Ackner's amendment sought to alleviate this problem, at least as far as criminal proceedings are concerned, by providing an entitlement to an indemnity in the absence of proof that the justice or justice's clerk acted in bad faith. In other words, the requirement of reasonableness would disappear and there would be no burden of proving good faith, it would be up to whoever was seeking to resist the indemnity to prove bad faith. The Government resisted this amendment on the grounds that it would prefer to await the outcome of consultations as to how best to tackle the problem generally, dealing not just with criminal proceedings and also looking at questions of immunity as well as of indemnity. Lord Ackner's amendment could only cover criminal proceedings, otherwise it would go outside the scope of the Bill. Nevertheless, to provide an interim solution, Lord Ackner successfully pressed his amendment to a Division and the Government then relented and substituted its preferred form of drafting at third reading (*Hansard*, Lords, 19 February 1996, cols 895 and 905).

Section 70 amends s. 53 of the Justices of the Peace Act 1979 by inserting a new subsection (1A) which has the effect that, in criminal proceedings, a justice of the peace or justices' clerk *shall* rather than *may* be indemnified out of local funds 'unless it is proved ... that he acted in bad faith'. The position as far as civil proceedings is concerned for the moment remains unchanged, i.e., '... the Magistrates' Court Committee has a general power to provide indemnity and is obliged to provide indemnity if the justice or justices' clerk acted reasonably and in good faith. In criminal cases, indemnity will have to be given unless bad faith is proved' (per Baroness Blatch, *Hansard*, Lords, 19 February 1996, col. 896).

The section applies to things done or omitted to be done (i.e., decisions of magistrates giving rise to liability for costs) on or after the appointed day, which is expected to be in Autumn 1996. Meanwhile, the Government has undertaken to press ahead with its review of the wider issues of indemnity and immunity for magistrates across both their criminal and civil jurisdiction in order to provide a more long-term and consistent solution to the issues.

Meaning of preliminary stage of criminal proceedings

Section 22 of the Prosecution of Offences Act 1985 empowers the Secretary of State to make provision by regulations as to the maximum period 'with respect to any specified preliminary stage of proceedings'.

Regulations may prescribe 'overall time-limits' during which the prosecution must complete the particular stage (failure to comply would result in the accused being treated for all purposes as having been acquitted but no such overall time-limits have yet been set). Alternatively regulations may set custody time-limits which limit the maximum period for which an accused may be kept in custody whilst awaiting the completion of a preliminary stage. If a custody time-limit has expired and is not extended before completion of the relevant preliminary stage, the accused must be granted bail but the proceedings are otherwise unaffected. Regulations prescribing custody time-limits have been made (Prosecution of Offences (Custody Time-Limits) Regulations 1987 (SI 1987 No. 299)) in respect of indictable offences and these prescribe, essentially, a maximum of 70 days from first appearance to committal proceedings (or to the start of prosecution evidence if the case is tried summarily) and 112 days from committal to arraignment if the accused is committed for trial to the Crown Court.

The custody time-limits can have no effect once the accused has been arraigned because the power to make regulations is limited by s. 22(1) of the 1985 Act 'with respect to any specified preliminary stage of the proceedings' and preliminary stage, it is stated in s. 22(11), '*does not include any stage of the proceedings after the accused has been arraigned in the Crown Court* or, in the case of a summary trial, *the magistrates' court has begun to hear evidence for the prosecution at the trial'* (emphasis added).

This definition made sense in 1985 when arraignment was normally contemporaneous with the start of the trial but with the growth of the use of plea and directions hearings (PDHs) at which arraignment takes place several weeks before the start of the trial, the accused could spend a considerable time in custody after arraignment in excess of the prescribed maximum periods but before the start of the trial proper (cf. *Croydon Crown Court, ex parte Lewis* (1994) 158 JP 886). In order to restore the full benefit of the custody time-limit to the accused in such cases, s. 71 of the 1996 Act substitutes the following definition into s. 22(10) of the 1985 Act in place of the original definition of 'preliminary stage' quoted above:

'preliminary stage' in relation to any proceedings, does not include any stage after the start of the trial (within the meaning given by subsections (11A) and (11B) below).

A new s. 22(11A) then defines the start of a trial on indictment by reference to the swearing of the jury or a plea of guilty rather than by reference to arraignment. However, it should be noted that this is expressly made subject to s. 8 of the Criminal Justice Act 1987 and s. 30 of the 1996 Act (preparatory hearings for serious or complex frauds or for long or complex cases, which hearings are treated as the start of the trial even though the jury is not sworn at that stage — see Chapter Three).

The result is that custody time-limits will now be relevant beyond the holding of plea and directions hearings or *pre-trial* hearings under Part IV of the 1996 Act (see Chapter 4) which, by definition (s. 39(1)), take place *before* the start of the trial. Custody time-limits will still not be relevant, however, once a *preparatory* hearing has commenced either in a complex or potentially long case under Part III of the 1996 Act or in a case of complex or serious fraud under the Criminal Justice Act 1987; since such a preparatory hearing is regarded as part of the trial itself.

Section 22(11B) of the 1985 Act, inserted by s. 71(3) of the 1996 Act, defines the start of a *summary* trial in similar terms to the old definition ('when the court begins to hear evidence for the prosecution at the trial'), but also now provides the alternatives of when it begins to consider whether to exercise its power under s. 37(3) of the Mental Health Act 1983 to make a hospital order without convicting the accused or when the court accepts a guilty plea if it does so before getting to either of the above stages. Section 71 also makes some consequential amendments to the Prosecution of Offences (Custody Time-Limits) Regulations 1987.

The changes effected by s. 71 apply to time-limits which begin on or after the appointed day or which have begun but not expired before that day except where arraignment has already taken place before that day. The appointed day is expected to be in Autumn 1996.

Chapter Ten
Serious Fraud

Introduction

Schedule 3, which is given effect by s. 72, makes various amendments to Part I of the Criminal Justice Act 1987, dealing with serious fraud. These amendments are consequent on the changes to criminal procedure made by the 1996 Act. In particular, the system of preparatory hearings is made consistent with the new system of preparatory hearings for long or complex cases, introduced by Part III of the 1996 Act. Schedule 3 will come into effect in relation to cases which are committed or transferred to the Crown Court, or in which a voluntary bill of indictment is preferred, after a day to be appointed by order of the Secretary of State (sch. 3, para. 8), which is likely to be in early 1997.

The Government has chosen to retain the transfer for trial procedure for serious fraud notwithstanding the abandonment of a similar procedure for offences in general (Part V). This is surprising in view of the fact that many of the practitioners' criticisms which influenced the Government to drop the procedure stemmed from experience with serious fraud. Doubts about the effectiveness of transfers had also been expressed in an academic study conducted for the Royal Commission (M. Levi *The investigation, prosecution and trial of serious fraud*, 1993, Royal Commission on Criminal Justice Research Study No. 14). Perhaps the single factor which justifies retention of the procedure for serious frauds is that their legal complexity requires the skills of a judge to determine whether there is sufficient evidence to justify trial (under s. 6 of the Criminal Justice Act 1987). The retention of the transfer procedure provides a significant procedural advantage for the accused. On an application to the Crown Court to dismiss charges of serious fraud, the defence may tender documentary evidence and, with leave of the court, oral evidence (s. 6(3) of the Criminal Justice Act 1987). In contrast, an accused who submits that there is no case to answer under the new streamlined committal procedure can make representations but can tender no evidence (see Chapter Five at p. 78).

Pre-trial disclosure

Part I of the Act creates a new system of pre-trial disclosure applicable to all indictable offences, including those involving serious fraud. Under s. 7(3) to (5) of the Criminal Justice Act 1987, where a judge proposes to hold a preparatory hearing in a serious fraud case, he also has a discretion to order both parties to make pre-trial disclosure. These provisions are now rendered superfluous and are omitted from the 1987 Act by virtue of para. 2 of sch. 3.

A significant difference between the specific scheme of pre-trial disclosure which is abolished and the general scheme which replaces it is that deviation from a disclosed defence may be subject to adverse comment and inferences in court under the new scheme (s. 11(1)), whereas this was not the case under the old. The Government probably assume that attaching sanctions to both stages of defence disclosure will improve the process of narrowing and clarification of the issues pre-trial. This aspiration may not be realised since defence lawyers will sensibly wish to avoid committing the accused to a firm line of defence at the earlier stage, for fear that disparities between the first and second stages of disclosure may be seized upon by the prosecution as evidence of fabrication.

Power to make orders in advance of preparatory hearings

The new scheme of preparatory hearings for long or complex cases in Part III largely follows the existing scheme for serious fraud under the 1987 Act, but contains one significant development — a power of the judge to make orders in advance of the preparatory hearing (s. 32). The new power should speed up the proceedings by enabling the judge to order the parties to commence reciprocal disclosure of case statements prior to the first hearing. This benefit is extended to preparatory hearings for serious fraud by virtue of para. 4 of sch. 3. Disclosure required under these provisions will be more extensive than that required by the ordinary disclosure scheme in Part I, and will take place after disclosure under the ordinary scheme has been completed.

Paragraph 4 inserts a new s. 9A into the Criminal Justice Act 1987. This provides that, where a judge orders a preparatory hearing under that Act, he may make any order under s. 9(4) or (5) prior to the hearing.

Under s. 9(4) of the 1987 Act, the prosecution may be ordered:

(a)   to supply the court and the accused with a case statement including the principal facts, witnesses, exhibits, and propositions of law to be relied upon and any consequences in terms of the counts on the indictment which flow from the matters in the case statement (i.e., that the accused is guilty of a particular offence);

(b)   to prepare and supply its evidence in a form likely to aid comprehension by the jury;

(c)   to notify the court and the defendant of any documents which in the view of the prosecution ought to be admitted as true;

(d)   to make amendments to any case statement supplied by the prosecution that appear to be appropriate in the light of the objections made by the defendant.

Where a case statement has been supplied by the prosecution as ordered under s. 9(4), the judge may then make the following orders to the accused under s. 9(5):

(a)   to provide to the court and the prosecution with a written statement of the general nature of the defence and which indicates the principal matters on which he takes issue with the prosecution;

(b)   to notify the court and the prosecution of any objections to the case statement;
(c)   to notify the court and the prosecution of any points of law or authorities on which he intends to rely;
(d)   to notify the court and the prosecution of the extent to which he agrees with the prosecution about which documents or other matters should be admitted and to give reasons for any disagreement.

If it appears to the judge that the reasons given for disagreeing with the prosecution are inadequate, then the accused must be informed of this and may be ordered to give further reasons (s. 9(8)).

By virtue of the new s. 9A(2)(b), s. 9(6) to (10), subject to two minor amendments, applies to orders made prior to preparatory hearing. Under s. 9(6), Crown Court Rules may be made to provide that defence disclosure under s. 9(5) need not disclose the identity of defence witnesses except for expert witnesses and alibi witnesses. In this respect, it should be noted also that in s. 9(6) the reference to s. 11 of the Criminal Justice Act 1967 (alibi) is substituted by a reference to s. 5(7) of the 1996 Act (s. 74 of the 1996 Act).

Under s. 9(7), a judge ordering the defence to make disclosure under s. 9(5) must warn the defendant of the possibilities of adverse comment by the judge at trial and adverse inferences drawn by the jury under s. 10 of the 1987 Act, if the defendant fails to comply with the disclosure order. Orders under s. 9 may specify time limits within which disclosure must be made, and these time limits may be made subject to maxima and minima under Crown Court Rules (s. 9(9)). Any order made prior to the preparatory hearing will continue in effect during the trial unless an application is made to vary or discharge it and the judge is satisfied that it is in the interests of justice to do so (s. 9(10)).

Failure to disclose and departures from cases disclosed

Section 10 of the Criminal Justice Act 1987 provides for the consequences of departure from the case disclosed or for failure to disclose when ordered to do so. Paragraph 5 of sch. 3 substitutes a new s. 10 of the 1987 Act which is similar in form to s. 34 of the 1996 Act (which deals with preparatory hearings for long or complex cases).

Section 10 of the 1987 Act provides that where a judge has ordered disclosure under s. 9 any party may depart from the case disclosed. However, where a party fails to comply with a disclosure order or departs from the case disclosed, the judge may comment on the failure or departure, and may give leave to any other party to comment, and the jury may draw inferences as appropriate.

There is no stated restriction on the type of comment which may be made, except that it must be such as appears appropriate to the maker of the comment, whether the judge, prosecutor or other party. The latitude given is remarkable in that it could permit either the prosecutor or co-accused to go beyond the bounds of comment permitted at common law and, for instance, suggest that failure to disclose indicates guilt. Whatever the latitude permitted by the statute, the Court of Appeal might feel constrained to quash any conviction following a comment of this sort. In view of that, judges should consider carefully whether it would be best to avoid risks attached to comment by co-accused, and reserve the power to make comment to themselves and the prosecution.

There are two specific differences between the old and the new versions of s. 10.

(a)   Whereas the old s. 10 was concerned only with disclosure at preparatory hearing, the new s. 10 applies to any disclosure ordered under s. 9, i.e., including disclosure prior to the preparatory hearing under s. 9A of the 1987 Act (as inserted by sch. 3), which is discussed above.

(b)   Under the old s. 10, in deciding whether to give leave for comment, the judge was required to have regard to the extent of departure from the disclosed case and also to whether there was any justification for it. This is repeated in the new s. 10, but the judge must also have regard to the extent of failure to comply with an order to disclose, and any justification for that.

This amendment may add little since for the accused to depart at trial from the defence as originally disclosed amounts to the same as failing to disclose fully the eventual defence. However, it is important to emphasise that inferences should not necessarily be drawn where there is a failure of defence disclosure. In very complex fraud cases, lines of defence may emerge late in the development of the case, not least because of the difficulties which defence lawyers may have in getting to grips with a mass of documentation. Although this might be considered an explanation rather than a justification for late disclosure, it should nevertheless be a factor for the judge in deciding whether to make comment and whether to invite the jury to draw adverse inferences.

A particular issue which is not addressed by the new s. 10 is what approach the court should take to significant differences between initial pre-trial disclosure under s. 5 of the 1996 Act and later disclosure which is ordered by the judge under s. 9 or 9A of the 1987 Act. Where the defence ultimately relied upon at trial departs from what was disclosed at both stages, the judge is entitled to invite the jury to draw inferences from both departures. Should this be done, the attention of the jury would necessarily be drawn to the differences between the two stages of disclosure. Whether it would be sensible for a judge to exploit the opportunities for adverse comment and inference fully in these circumstances is debatable. Excessive emphasis by the judge on variations between defences raised at three different stages of the process and possible inferences therefrom might lead the jury away from a proper consideration of the weight of the positive evidence. It is submitted that a better course, which would avoid the risk of confusing or misleading the jury, would be for the judge to ignore the initial defence disclosure and focus only on any departures from the more considered and better informed disclosure made under the 1987 Act.

Reporting restrictions

Section 11 of the Criminal Justice Act 1987 established restrictions on the reporting of preparatory hearings, applications for dismissal and related applications and appeals, and also created offences for breach of those restrictions. Paragraph 6 of sch. 3 now substitutes a new s. 11, which deals with reporting restrictions, and a new s. 11A, which deals with related offences. The new provisions are similar in form to those applying to preparatory hearings for long or complex cases (ss. 37 and 38 of the 1996 Act), but with necessary modifications for the special procedures operating for serious fraud.

The only substantial difference between the old and the new provisions is that, whereas formerly the power to lift reporting restrictions did not apply to final appeals to the House of Lords, the House is now given a power to lift restrictions on reporting appeals to it and applications to appeal to it (s. 11(6)). Notwithstanding similarity in substance, the new provisions differ from the old in form and arrangement. For convenience the new sections are explained below.

The new s. 11 creates reporting restrictions in relation to applications to dismiss charges under s. 6(1) of the 1987 Act, preparatory hearings, applications for leave to appeal and also appeals in relation to such hearings (s. 11(2)). The restrictions cover written reports which are published in Great Britain and reports which are included in programmes broadcast for reception in Great Britain (s. 11(1)). The restrictions cease and reports may be published after the conclusion of the trial of the accused, or where there is more than one accused, at the conclusion of the trial of the last one to be tried (s. 11(11)).

Certain formal details are exempted from the restrictions. These fall into two categories: those details which may also be published in relation to committal proceedings (s. 11(12)) and a further list of relevant business information (s. 11(14)). The basic list of publishable details includes:

(a)   the identity of the court and the name of the judge;

(b)   the names, ages, home addresses (either at the time of the events leading to the charge or the time of the publication or programme: s. 11(10)) and occupations of the accused and witnesses;

(c)   relevant business information (categories listed below);

(d)   the offence or offences, or a summary of them, with which the accused is or are charged;

(e)   the names of counsel and solicitors in the proceedings;

(f)   in the event of adjournment, the date and place to which proceedings are adjourned;

(g)   any arrangements as to bail;

(h)   whether legal aid was granted to any of the accused.

The relevant business information which may also be published includes the name and addresses of any business carried on by the accused on his own account, or as a partner, or by which he was employed at a relevant time, and the name and address of any company of which he was a director or for which he worked at any relevant time (s. 11(14)).

Lifting restrictions

Restrictions on reporting may be lifted by the judge in respect of applications to the Crown Court to dismiss the charges, preparatory hearings and applications to the judge for leave to appeal against an order made at preparatory hearing (s. 11(3) and (4)). The Court of Appeal and House of Lords are given similar powers to lift reporting restrictions relating to applications for leave to appeal and appeals heard by those courts (s. 11(5) and (6)). In each case the relevant court may lift restrictions completely or to a specified extent.

The Act does not provide a procedure for applying to have reporting restrictions lifted, nor does it specify the criteria to be applied in determining the issue. It thus appears that the court may act of its own motion and for whatever reason it chooses. It may be expected however that generally the issue will be considered only where there has been a request by a party that the court should consider the matter. Where the court is considering the issue, the accused must all be given an opportunity to make representations, and if any one of them objects, the restrictions should be lifted if (and only if) the court is satisfied that it is in the interests of justice to do so (s. 11(7) and (8)).

Since reporting restrictions afford a protection for the integrity of criminal trials generally and for the accused personally, the presumption should be that restrictions should remain unless a very strong case relating to the interests of justice is made out (cf. *Leeds Justices, ex parte Sykes* [1983] 1 WLR 132). The case for maintaining the restrictions will be particularly strong where one or more accused objects to their being lifted. Should restrictions be lifted without one or more of the accused making representations, the lifting order will be a nullity (*Wirral District Magistrates' Court, ex parte Meikle* (1990) 154 JP 1035), unless adequate opportunity for making representations was given.

Breach of reporting restrictions

Section 11A makes it an offence to publish or broadcast a report of an application to dismiss charges, a preparatory hearing or appeal or an application for leave to appeal relating thereto. The prohibition extends to publications in, and programmes for reception in, Great Britain. In relation to a report in a newspaper or periodical, the offence is committed by any proprietor, editor or publisher (s. 11A(1)(a)). In relation to a written report which is published in some other form, the offence is committed by the person who publishes it (s. 11A(1)(b)). In the case of a report included in a broadcast programme, the offence is committed by any body corporate providing the service in which the report is included and any person performing the functions corresponding to those of editor of a newspaper (s. 11A(1)(c)).

The offence is punishable on summary conviction by a fine not exceeding level 5 on the standard scale (currently £5,000) (s. 11A(2)). Proceedings for the offence may be instituted only with the consent of the Attorney-General (s. 11(3)).

Criminal Procedure and Investigations Act 1996

CHAPTER 25
ARRANGEMENT OF SECTIONS

PART I
DISCLOSURE

Introduction

Criminal Procedure and Investigations Act 1996

1996 CHAPTER 25

An Act to make provision about criminal procedure and criminal investigations.

[4th July 1996]

BE IT ENACTED by the Queen's most Excellent Majesty, by and with the advice and consent of the Lords Spiritual and Temporal, and Commons, in this present Parliament assembled, and by the authority of the same, as follows:—

PART I
DISCLOSURE

Introduction

1. Application of this Part

(1) This Part applies where—

(a) a person is charged with a summary offence in respect of which a court proceeds to summary trial and in respect of which he pleads not guilty,

(b) a person who has attained the age of 18 is charged with an offence which is triable either way, in respect of which a court proceeds to summary trial and in respect of which he pleads not guilty, or

(c) a person under the age of 18 is charged with an indictable offence in respect of which a court proceeds to summary trial and in respect of which he pleads not guilty.

(2) This Part also applies where—

(a) a person is charged with an indictable offence and he is committed for trial for the offence concerned,

(b) a person is charged with an indictable offence and proceedings for the trial of the person on the charge concerned are transferred to the Crown Court by virtue of a notice of transfer given under section 4 of the Criminal Justice Act 1987 (serious or complex fraud),

(c) a person is charged with an indictable offence and proceedings for the trial of the person on the charge concerned are transferred to the Crown Court by virtue of a notice of transfer served on a magistrates' court under section 53 of the Criminal Justice Act 1991 (certain cases involving children),

(d) a count charging a person with a summary offence is included in an indictment under the authority of section 40 of the Criminal Justice Act 1988 (common assault etc.), or

(e) a bill of indictment charging a person with an indictable offence is preferred under the authority of section 2(2)(b) of the Administration of Justice (Miscellaneous Provisions) Act 1933 (bill preferred by direction of Court of Appeal, or by direction or with consent of a judge).

(3) This Part applies in relation to alleged offences into which no criminal investigation has begun before the appointed day.

(4) For the purposes of this section a criminal investigation is an investigation which police officers or other persons have a duty to conduct with a view to it being ascertained—

(a) whether a person should be charged with an offence, or

(b) whether a person charged with an offence is guilty of it.

(5) The reference in subsection (3) to the appointed day is to such day as is appointed for the purposes of this Part by the Secretary of State by order.

2. General interpretation

(1) References to the accused are to the person mentioned in section 1(1) or (2).

(2) Where there is more than one accused in any proceedings this Part applies separately in relation to each of the accused.

(3) References to the prosecutor are to any person acting as prosecutor, whether an individual or a body.

(4) References to material are to material of all kinds, and in particular include references to—

(a) information, and

(b) objects of all descriptions.

(5) References to recording information are to putting it in a durable or retrievable form (such as writing or tape).

(6) This section applies for the purposes of this Part.

The main provisions

3. Primary disclosure by prosecutor

(1) The prosecutor must—

(a) disclose to the accused any prosecution material which has not previously been disclosed to the accused and which in the prosecutor's opinion might undermine the case for the prosecution against the accused, or

(b) give to the accused a written statement that there is no material of a description mentioned in paragraph (a).

(2) For the purposes of this section prosecution material is material—

(a) which is in the prosecutor's possession, and came into his possession in connection with the case for the prosecution against the accused, or

(b) which, in pursuance of a code operative under Part II, he has inspected in connection with the case for the prosecution against the accused.

(3) Where material consists of information which has been recorded in any form the prosecutor discloses it for the purposes of this section—

(a) by securing that a copy is made of it and that the copy is given to the accused, or

(b) if in the prosecutor's opinion that is not practicable or not desirable, by allowing the accused to inspect it at a reasonable time and a reasonable place or by taking steps to secure that he is allowed to do so;

and a copy may be in such form as the prosecutor thinks fit and need not be in the same form as that in which the information has already been recorded.

(4)   Where material consists of information which has not been recorded the prosecutor discloses it for the purposes of this section by securing that it is recorded in such form as he thinks fit and—

(a)   by securing that a copy is made of it and that the copy is given to the accused, or

(b)   if in the prosecutor's opinion that is not practicable or not desirable, by allowing the accused to inspect it at a reasonable time and a reasonable place or by taking steps to secure that he is allowed to do so.

(5)   Where material does not consist of information the prosecutor discloses it for the purposes of this section by allowing the accused to inspect it at a reasonable time and a reasonable place or by taking steps to secure that he is allowed to do so.

(6)   Material must not be disclosed under this section to the extent that the court, on an application by the prosecutor, concludes it is not in the public interest to disclose it and orders accordingly.

(7)   Material must not be disclosed under this section to the extent that—

(a)   it has been intercepted in obedience to a warrant issued under section 2 of the Interception of Communications Act 1985, or

(b)   it indicates that such a warrant has been issued or that material has been intercepted in obedience to such a warrant.

(8)   The prosecutor must act under this section during the period which, by virtue of section 12, is the relevant period for this section.

4.   Primary disclosure: further provisions

(1)   This section applies where—

(a)   the prosecutor acts under section 3, and

(b)   before so doing he was given a document in pursuance of provision included, by virtue of section 24(3), in a code operative under Part II.

(2)   In such a case the prosecutor must give the document to the accused at the same time as the prosecutor acts under section 3.

5.   Compulsory disclosure by accused

(1)   Subject to subsections (2) to (4), this section applies where—

(a)   this Part applies by virtue of section 1(2), and

(b)   the prosecutor complies with section 3 or purports to comply with it.

(2)   Where this Part applies by virtue of section 1(2)(b), this section does not apply unless—

(a)   a copy of the notice of transfer, and

(b)   copies of the documents containing the evidence,

have been given to the accused under regulations made under section 5(9) of the Criminal Justice Act 1987.

(3)   Where this Part applies by virtue of section 1(2)(c), this section does not apply unless—

(a)   a copy of the notice of transfer, and

(b)   copies of the documents containing the evidence,

have been given to the accused under regulations made under paragraph 4 of Schedule 6 to the Criminal Justice Act 1991.

(4)   Where this Part applies by virtue of section 1(2)(e), this section does not apply unless the prosecutor has served on the accused a copy of the indictment and

a copy of the set of documents containing the evidence which is the basis of the charge.

(5)   Where this section applies, the accused must give a defence statement to the court and the prosecutor.

(6)   For the purposes of this section a defence statement is a written statement—

(a)   setting out in general terms the nature of the accused's defence,

(b)   indicating the matters on which he takes issue with the prosecution, and

(c)   setting out, in the case of each such matter, the reason why he takes issue with the prosecution.

(7)   If the defence statement discloses an alibi the accused must give particulars of the alibi in the statement, including—

(a)   the name and address of any witness the accused believes is able to give evidence in support of the alibi, if the name and address are known to the accused when the statement is given;

(b)   any information in the accused's possession which might be of material assistance in finding any such witness, if his name or address is not known to the accused when the statement is given.

(8)   For the purposes of this section evidence in support of an alibi is evidence tending to show that by reason of the presence of the accused at a particular place or in a particular area at a particular time he was not, or was unlikely to have been, at the place where the offence is alleged to have been committed at the time of its alleged commission.

(9)   The accused must give a defence statement under this section during the period which, by virtue of section 12, is the relevant period for this section.

6.   Voluntary disclosure by accused

(1)   This section applies where—

(a)   this Part applies by virtue of section 1(1), and

(b)   the prosecutor complies with section 3 or purports to comply with it.

(2)   The accused—

(a)   may give a defence statement to the prosecutor, and

(b)   if he does so, must also give such a statement to the court.

(3)   Subsections (6) to (8) of section 5 apply for the purposes of this section as they apply for the purposes of that.

(4)   If the accused gives a defence statement under this section he must give it during the period which, by virtue of section 12, is the relevant period for this section.

7.   Secondary disclosure by prosecutor

(1)   This section applies where the accused gives a defence statement under section 5 or 6.

(2)   The prosecutor must—

(a)   disclose to the accused any prosecution material which has not previously been disclosed to the accused and which might be reasonably expected to assist the accused's defence as disclosed by the defence statement given under section 5 or 6, or

(b)   give to the accused a written statement that there is no material of a description mentioned in paragraph (a).

(3)   For the purposes of this section prosecution material is material—

(a)   which is in the prosecutor's possession and came into his possession in connection with the case for the prosecution against the accused, or

(b) which, in pursuance of a code operative under Part II, he has inspected in connection with the case for the prosecution against the accused.

(4) Subsections (3) to (5) of section 3 (method by which prosecutor discloses) apply for the purposes of this section as they apply for the purposes of that.

(5) Material must not be disclosed under this section to the extent that the court, on an application by the prosecutor, concludes it is not in the public interest to disclose it and orders accordingly.

(6) Material must not be disclosed under this section to the extent that—

(a) it has been intercepted in obedience to a warrant issued under section 2 of the Interception of Communications Act 1985, or

(b) it indicates that such a warrant has been issued or that material has been intercepted in obedience to such a warrant.

(7) The prosecutor must act under this section during the period which, by virtue of section 12, is the relevant period for this section.

8. Application by accused for disclosure

(1) This section applies where the accused gives a defence statement under section 5 or 6 and the prosecutor complies with section 7 or purports to comply with it or fails to comply with it.

(2) If the accused has at any time reasonable cause to believe that—

(a) there is prosecution material which might be reasonably expected to assist the accused's defence as disclosed by the defence statement given under section 5 or 6, and

(b) the material has not been disclosed to the accused,

the accused may apply to the court for an order requiring the prosecutor to disclose such material to the accused.

(3) For the purposes of this section prosecution material is material—

(a) which is in the prosecutor's possession and came into his possession in connection with the case for the prosecution against the accused,

(b) which, in pursuance of a code operative under Part II, he has inspected in connection with the case for the prosecution against the accused, or

(c) which falls within subsection (4).

(4) Material falls within this subsection if in pursuance of a code operative under Part II the prosecutor must, if he asks for the material, be given a copy of it or be allowed to inspect it in connection with the case for the prosecution against the accused.

(5) Material must not be disclosed under this section to the extent that the court, on an application by the prosecutor, concludes it is not in the public interest to disclose it and orders accordingly.

(6) Material must not be disclosed under this section to the extent that—

(a) it has been intercepted in obedience to a warrant issued under section 2 of the Interception of Communications Act 1985, or

(b) it indicates that such a warrant has been issued or that material has been intercepted in obedience to such a warrant.

9. Continuing duty of prosecutor to disclose

(1) Subsection (2) applies at all times—

(a) after the prosecutor complies with section 3 or purports to comply with it, and

(b)   before the accused is acquitted or convicted or the prosecutor decides not to proceed with the case concerned.

(2)   The prosecutor must keep under review the question whether at any given time there is prosecution material which—

(a)   in his opinion might undermine the case for the prosecution against the accused, and

(b)   has not been disclosed to the accused;

and if there is such material at any time the prosecutor must disclose it to the accused as soon as is reasonably practicable.

(3)   In applying subsection (2) by reference to any given time the state of affairs at that time (including the case for the prosecution as it stands at that time) must be taken into account.

(4)   Subsection (5) applies at all times—

(a)   after the prosecutor complies with section 7 or purports to comply with it, and

(b)   before the accused is acquitted or convicted or the prosecutor decides not to proceed with the case concerned.

(5)   The prosecutor must keep under review the question whether at any given time there is prosecution material which—

(a)   might be reasonably expected to assist the accused's defence as disclosed by the defence statement given under section 5 or 6, and

(b)   has not been disclosed to the accused;

and if there is such material at any time the prosecutor must disclose it to the accused as soon as is reasonably practicable.

(6)   For the purposes of this section prosecution material is material—

(a)   which is in the prosecutor's possession and came into his possession in connection with the case for the prosecution against the accused, or

(b)   which, in pursuance of a code operative under Part II, he has inspected in connection with the case for the prosecution against the accused.

(7)   Subsections (3) to (5) of section 3 (method by which prosecutor discloses) apply for the purposes of this section as they apply for the purposes of that.

(8)   Material must not be disclosed under this section to the extent that the court, on an application by the prosecutor, concludes it is not in the public interest to disclose it and orders accordingly.

(9)   Material must not be disclosed under this section to the extent that—

(a)   it has been intercepted in obedience to a warrant issued under section 2 of the Interception of Communications Act 1985, or

(b)   it indicates that such a warrant has been issued or that material has been intercepted in obedience to such a warrant.

10.   Prosecutor's failure to observe time limits

(1)   This section applies if the prosecutor—

(a)   purports to act under section 3 after the end of the period which, by virtue of section 12, is the relevant period for section 3, or

(b)   purports to act under section 7 after the end of the period which, by virtue of section 12, is the relevant period for section 7.

(2)   Subject to subsection (3), the failure to act during the period concerned does not on its own constitute grounds for staying the proceedings for abuse of process.

(3)   Subsection (2) does not prevent the failure constituting such grounds if it involves such delay by the prosecutor that the accused is denied a fair trial.

11.   Faults in disclosure by accused
(1)   This section applies where section 5 applies and the accused—
  (a)   fails to give a defence statement under that section,
  (b)   gives a defence statement under that section but does so after the end of the period which, by virtue of section 12, is the relevant period for section 5,
  (c)   sets out inconsistent defences in a defence statement given under section 5,
  (d)   at his trial puts forward a defence which is different from any defence set out in a defence statement given under section 5,
  (e)   at his trial adduces evidence in support of an alibi without having given particulars of the alibi in a defence statement given under section 5, or
  (f)   at his trial calls a witness to give evidence in support of an alibi without having complied with subsection (7)(a) or (b) of section 5 as regards the witness in giving a defence statement under that section.
(2)   This section also applies where section 6 applies, the accused gives a defence statement under that section, and the accused—
  (a)   gives the statement after the end of the period which, by virtue of section 12, is the relevant period for section 6,
  (b)   sets out inconsistent defences in the statement,
  (c)   at his trial puts forward a defence which is different from any defence set out in the statement,
  (d)   at his trial adduces evidence in support of an alibi without having given particulars of the alibi in the statement, or
  (e)   at his trial calls a witness to give evidence in support of an alibi without having complied with subsection (7)(a) or (b) of section 5 (as applied by section 6) as regards the witness in giving the statement.
(3)   Where this section applies—
  (a)   the court or, with the leave of the court, any other party may make such comment as appears appropriate;
  (b)   the court or jury may draw such inferences as appear proper in deciding whether the accused is guilty of the offence concerned.
(4)   Where the accused puts forward a defence which is different from any defence set out in a defence statement given under section 5 or 6, in doing anything under subsection (3) or in deciding whether to do anything under it the court shall have regard—
  (a)   to the extent of the difference in the defences, and
  (b)   to whether there is any justification for it.
(5)   A person shall not be convicted of an offence solely on an inference drawn under subsection (3).
(6)   Any reference in this section to evidence in support of an alibi shall be construed in accordance with section 5.

Time limits

12.   Time limits
(1)   This section has effect for the purpose of determining the relevant period for sections 3, 5, 6 and 7.

(2) Subject to subsection (3), the relevant period is a period beginning and ending with such days as the Secretary of State prescribes by regulations for the purposes of the section concerned.

(3) The regulations may do one or more of the following—

(a) provide that the relevant period for any section shall if the court so orders be extended (or further extended) by so many days as the court specifies;

(b) provide that the court may only make such an order if an application is made by a prescribed person and if any other prescribed conditions are fulfilled;

(c) provide that an application may only be made if prescribed conditions are fulfilled;

(d) provide that the number of days by which a period may be extended shall be entirely at the court's discretion;

(e) provide that the number of days by which a period may be extended shall not exceed a prescribed number;

(f) provide that there shall be no limit on the number of applications that may be made to extend a period;

(g) provide that no more than a prescribed number of applications may be made to extend a period;

and references to the relevant period for a section shall be construed accordingly.

(4) Conditions mentioned in subsection (3) may be framed by reference to such factors as the Secretary of State thinks fit.

(5) Without prejudice to the generality of subsection (4), so far as the relevant period for section 3 or 7 is concerned—

(a) conditions may be framed by reference to the nature or volume of the material concerned;

(b) the nature of material may be defined by reference to the prosecutor's belief that the question of non-disclosure on grounds of public interest may arise.

(6) In subsection (3) 'prescribed' means prescribed by regulations under this section.

13. Time limits: transitional

(1) As regards a case in relation to which no regulations under section 12 have come into force for the purposes of section 3, section 3(8) shall have effect as if it read—

'(8) The prosecutor must act under this section as soon as is reasonably practicable after—

(a) the accused pleads not guilty (where this Part applies by virtue of section 1(1)),

(b) the accused is committed for trial (where this Part applies by virtue of section 1(2)(a)),

(c) the proceedings are transferred (where this Part applies by virtue of section 1(2)(b) or (c)),

(d) the count is included in the indictment (where this Part applies by virtue of section 1(2)(d)), or

(e) the bill of indictment is preferred (where this Part applies by virtue of section 1(2)(e)).'

(2) As regards a case in relation to which no regulations under section 12 have come into force for the purposes of section 7, section 7(7) shall have effect as if it read—

'(7)   The prosecutor must act under this section as soon as is reasonably practicable after the accused gives a defence statement under section 5 or 6.'

Public interest

14.   Public interest: review for summary trials
(1)   This section applies where this Part applies by virtue of section 1(1).
(2)   At any time—
    (a)   after a court makes an order under section 3(6), 7(5), 8(5) or 9(8), and
    (b)   before the accused is acquitted or convicted or the prosecutor decides not to proceed with the case concerned,
the accused may apply to the court for a review of the question whether it is still not in the public interest to disclose material affected by its order.
(3)   In such a case the court must review that question, and if it concludes that it is in the public interest to disclose material to any extent—
    (a)   it shall so order, and
    (b)   it shall take such steps as are reasonable to inform the prosecutor of its order.
(4)   Where the prosecutor is informed of an order made under subsection (3) he must act accordingly having regard to the provisions of this Part (unless he decides not to proceed with the case concerned).

15.   Public interest: review in other cases
(1)   This section applies where this Part applies by virtue of section 1(2).
(2)   This section applies at all times—
    (a)   after a court makes an order under section 3(6), 7(5), 8(5) or 9(8), and
    (b)   before the accused is acquitted or convicted or the prosecutor decides not to proceed with the case concerned.
(3)   The court must keep under review the question whether at any given time it is still not in the public interest to disclose material affected by its order.
(4)   The court must keep the question mentioned in subsection (3) under review without the need for an application; but the accused may apply to the court for a review of that question.
(5)   If the court at any time concludes that it is in the public interest to disclose material to any extent—
    (a)   it shall so order, and
    (b)   it shall take such steps as are reasonable to inform the prosecutor of its order.
(6)   Where the prosecutor is informed of an order made under subsection (5) he must act accordingly having regard to the provisions of this Part (unless he decides not to proceed with the case concerned).

16.   Applications: opportunity to be heard
Where—
    (a)   an application is made under section 3(6), 7(5), 8(5), 9(8), 14(2) or 15(4),
    (b)   a person claiming to have an interest in the material applies to be heard by the court, and
    (c)   he shows that he was involved (whether alone or with others and whether directly or indirectly) in the prosecutor's attention being brought to the material,

the court must not make an order under section 3(6), 7(5), 8(5), 9(8), 14(3) or 15(5) (as the case may be) unless the person applying under paragraph (b) has been given an opportunity to be heard.

Confidentiality

17. Confidentiality of disclosed information

(1) If the accused is given or allowed to inspect a document or other object under—

    (a)   section 3, 4, 7, 9, 14 or 15, or

    (b)   an order under section 8,

then, subject to subsections (2) to (4), he must not use or disclose it or any information recorded in it.

(2) The accused may use or disclose the object or information—

    (a)   in connection with the proceedings for whose purposes he was given the object or allowed to inspect it,

    (b)   with a view to the taking of further criminal proceedings (for instance, by way of appeal) with regard to the matter giving rise to the proceedings mentioned in paragraph (a), or

    (c)   in connection with the proceedings first mentioned in paragraph (b).

(3) The accused may use or disclose—

    (a)   the object to the extent that it has been displayed to the public in open court, or

    (b)   the information to the extent that it has been communicated to the public in open court;

but the preceding provisions of this subsection do not apply if the object is displayed or the information is communicated in proceedings to deal with a contempt of court under section 18.

(4) If—

    (a)   the accused applies to the court for an order granting permission to use or disclose the object or information, and

    (b)   the court makes such an order,

the accused may use or disclose the object or information for the purpose and to the extent specified by the court.

(5) An application under subsection (4) may be made and dealt with at any time, and in particular after the accused has been acquitted or convicted or the prosecutor has decided not to proceed with the case concerned; but this is subject to rules made by virtue of section 19(2).

(6) Where—

    (a)   an application is made under subsection (4), and

    (b)   the prosecutor or a person claiming to have an interest in the object or information applies to be heard by the court,

the court must not make an order granting permission unless the person applying under paragraph (b) has been given an opportunity to be heard.

(7) References in this section to the court are to—

    (a)   a magistrates' court, where this Part applies by virtue of section 1(1);

    (b)   the Crown Court, where this Part applies by virtue of section 1(2).

(8) Nothing in this section affects any other restriction or prohibition on the use or disclosure of an object or information, whether the restriction or prohibition arises under an enactment (whenever passed) or otherwise.

18. Confidentiality: contravention

(1)   It is a contempt of court for a person knowingly to use or disclose an object or information recorded in it if the use or disclosure is in contravention of section 17.

(2)   The following courts have jurisdiction to deal with a person who is guilty of a contempt under this section—

  (a)   a magistrates' court, where this Part applies by virtue of section 1(1);

  (b)   the Crown Court, where this Part applies by virtue of section 1(2).

(3)   A person who is guilty of a contempt under this section may be dealt with as follows—

  (a)   a magistrates' court may commit him to custody for a specified period not exceeding six months or impose on him a fine not exceeding £5,000 or both;

  (b)   the Crown Court may commit him to custody for a specified period not exceeding two years or impose a fine on him or both.

(4)   If—

  (a)   a person is guilty of a contempt under this section, and

  (b)   the object concerned is in his possession,

the court finding him guilty may order that the object shall be forfeited and dealt with in such manner as the court may order.

(5)   The power of the court under subsection (4) includes power to order the object to be destroyed or to be given to the prosecutor or to be placed in his custody for such period as the court may specify.

(6)   If—

  (a)   the court proposes to make an order under subsection (4), and

  (b)   the person found guilty, or any other person claiming to have an interest in the object, applies to be heard by the court,

the court must not make the order unless the applicant has been given an opportunity to be heard.

(7)   If—

  (a)   a person is guilty of a contempt under this section, and

  (b)   a copy of the object concerned is in his possession,

the court finding him guilty may order that the copy shall be forfeited and dealt with in such manner as the court may order.

(8)   Subsections (5) and (6) apply for the purposes of subsection (7) as they apply for the purposes of subsection (4), but as if references to the object were references to the copy.

(9)   An object or information shall be inadmissible as evidence in civil proceedings if to adduce it would in the opinion of the court be likely to constitute a contempt under this section; and 'the court' here means the court before which the civil proceedings are being taken.

(10)   The powers of a magistrates' court under this section may be exercised either of the court's own motion or by order on complaint.

Other provisions

19. Rules of court

(1)   Without prejudice to the generality of subsection (1) of—

  (a)   section 144 of the Magistrates' Courts Act 1980 (magistrates' court rules), and

  (b)   section 84 of the Supreme Court Act 1981 (rules of court), the power to make rules under each of those sections includes power to make provision mentioned in subsection (2).

(2) The provision is provision as to the practice and procedure to be followed in relation to—

(a) proceedings to deal with a contempt of court under section 18;

(b) an application under section 3(6), 7(5), 8(2) or (5), 9(8), 14(2), 15(4), 16(b), 17(4) or (6)(b) or 18(6);

(c) an application under regulations made under section 12;

(d) an order under section 3(6), 7(5), 8(2) or (5), 9(8), 14(3), 17(4) or 18(4) or (7);

(e) an order under section 15(5) (whether or not an application is made under section 15(4));

(f) an order under regulations made under section 12.

(3) Rules made under section 144 of the Magistrates' Courts Act 1980 by virtue of subsection (2)(a) above may contain or include provision equivalent to Schedule 3 to the Contempt of Court Act 1981 (proceedings for disobeying magistrates' court order) with any modifications which the Lord Chancellor considers appropriate on the advice of or after consultation with the rule committee for magistrates' courts.

(4) Rules made by virtue of subsection (2)(b) in relation to an application under section 17(4) may include provision—

(a) that an application to a magistrates' court must be made to a particular magistrates' court;

(b) that an application to the Crown Court must be made to the Crown Court sitting at a particular place;

(c) requiring persons to be notified of an application:

(5) Rules made by virtue of this section may make different provision for different cases or classes of case.

20. Other statutory rules as to disclosure

(1) A duty under any of the disclosure provisions shall not affect or be affected by any duty arising under any other enactment with regard to material to be provided to or by the accused or a person representing him; but this is subject to subsection (2).

(2) In making an order under section 9 of the Criminal Justice Act 1987 or section 31 of this Act (preparatory hearings) the judge may take account of anything which—

(a) has been done,

(b) has been required to be done, or

(c) will be required to be done,

in pursuance of any of the disclosure provisions.

(3) Without prejudice to the generality of section 144(1) of the Magistrates' Courts Act 1980 (magistrates' court rules) the power to make rules under that section includes power to make, with regard to any proceedings before a magistrates' court which relate to an alleged offence, provision for—

(a) requiring any party to the proceedings to disclose to the other party or parties any expert evidence which he proposes to adduce in the proceedings;

(b) prohibiting a party who fails to comply in respect of any evidence with any requirement imposed by virtue of paragraph (a) from adducing that evidence without the leave of the court.

(4) Rules made by virtue of subsection (3)—

    (a) may specify the kinds of expert evidence to which they apply;
    (b) may exempt facts or matters of any description specified in the rules.
  (5) For the purposes of this section—
    (a) the disclosure provisions are sections 3 to 9;
    (b) 'enactment' includes an enactment comprised in subordinate legislation
(which here has the same meaning as in the Interpretation Act 1978).

21. Common law rules as to disclosure

  (1) Where this Part applies as regards things falling to be done after the relevant
time in relation to an alleged offence, the rules of common law which—
    (a) were effective immediately before the appointed day, and
    (b) relate to the disclosure of material by the prosecutor,
do not apply as regards things falling to be done after that time in relation to the
alleged offence.
  (2) Subsection (1) does not affect the rules of common law as to whether
disclosure is in the public interest.
  (3) References in subsection (1) to the relevant time are to the time when—
    (a) the accused pleads not guilty (where this Part applies by virtue of section 1(1)),
    (b) the accused is committed for trial (where this Part applies by virtue of
section 1(2)(a)),
    (c) the proceedings are transferred (where this Part applies by virtue of section
1(2)(b) or (c)),
    (d) the count is included in the indictment (where this Part applies by virtue
of section 1(2)(d)), or
    (e) the bill of indictment is preferred (where this Part applies by virtue of
section 1(2)(e)).
  (4) The reference in subsection (1) to the appointed day is to the day appointed
under section 1(5).

PART II
CRIMINAL INVESTIGATIONS

22. Introduction

  (1) For the purposes of this Part a criminal investigation is an investigation
conducted by police officers with a view to it being ascertained—
    (a) whether a person should be charged with an offence, or
    (b) whether a person charged with an offence is guilty of it.
  (2) In this Part references to material are to material of all kinds, and in particular
include references to—
    (a) information, and
    (b) objects of all descriptions.
  (3) In this Part references to recording information are to putting it in a durable
or retrievable form (such as writing or tape).

23. Code of practice

  (1) The Secretary of State shall prepare a code of practice containing provisions
designed to secure—
    (a) that where a criminal investigation is conducted all reasonable steps are
taken for the purposes of the investigation and, in particular, all reasonable lines of
inquiry are pursued;

(b)   that information which is obtained in the course of a criminal investigation and may be relevant to the investigation is recorded;

(c)   that any record of such information is retained;

(d)   that any other material which is obtained in the course of a criminal investigation and may be relevant to the investigation is retained;

(e)   that information falling within paragraph (b) and material falling within paragraph (d) is revealed to a person who is involved in the prosecution of criminal proceedings arising out of or relating to the investigation and who is identified in accordance with prescribed provisions;

(f)   that where such a person inspects information or other material in pursuance of a requirement that it be revealed to him, and he requests that it be disclosed to the accused, the accused is allowed to inspect it or is given a copy of it;

(g)   that where such a person is given a document indicating the nature of information or other material in pursuance of a requirement that it be revealed to him, and he requests that it be disclosed to the accused, the accused is allowed to inspect it or is given a copy of it;

(h)   that the person who is to allow the accused to inspect information or other material or to give him a copy of it shall decide which of those (inspecting or giving a copy) is appropriate;

(i)   that where the accused is allowed to inspect material as mentioned in paragraph (f) or (g) and he requests a copy, he is given one unless the person allowing the inspection is of opinion that it is not practicable or not desirable to give him one;

(j)   that a person mentioned in paragraph (e) is given a written statement that prescribed activities which the code requires have been carried out.

(2)   The code may include provision—

(a)   that a police officer identified in accordance with prescribed provisions must carry out a prescribed activity which the code requires;

(b)   that a police officer so identified must take steps to secure the carrying out by a person (whether or not a police officer) of a prescribed activity which the code requires;

(c)   that a duty must be discharged by different people in succession in prescribed circumstances (as where a person dies or retires).

(3)   The code may include provision about the form in which information is to be recorded.

(4)   The code may include provision about the manner in which and the period for which—

(a)   a record of information is to be retained, and

(b)   any other material is to be retained;

and if a person is charged with an offence the period may extend beyond a conviction or an acquittal.

(5)   The code may include provision about the time when, the form in which, the way in which, and the extent to which, information or any other material is to be revealed to the person mentioned in subsection (1)(e).

(6)   The code must be so framed that it does not apply to material intercepted in obedience to a warrant issued under section 2 of the Interception of Communications Act 1985.

(7)   The code may—

(a)   make different provision in relation to different cases or descriptions of case;

(b)   contain exceptions as regards prescribed cases or descriptions of case.

(8)   In this section 'prescribed' means prescribed by the code.

24. Examples of disclosure provisions

(1)   This section gives examples of the kinds of provision that may be included in the code by virtue of section 23(5).

(2)   The code may provide that if the person required to reveal material has possession of material which he believes is sensitive he must give a document which—

(a)   indicates the nature of that material, and

(b)   states that he so believes.

(3)   The code may provide that if the person required to reveal material has possession of material which is of a description prescribed under this subsection and which he does not believe is sensitive he must give a document which—

(a)   indicates the nature of that material, and

(b)   states that he does not so believe.

(4)   The code may provide that if—

(a)   a document is given in pursuance of provision contained in the code by virtue of subsection (2), and

(b)   a person identified in accordance with prescribed provisions asks for any of the material,

the person giving the document must give a copy of the material asked for to the person asking for it or (depending on the circumstances) must allow him to inspect it.

(5)   The code may provide that if—

(a)   a document is given in pursuance of provision contained in the code by virtue of subsection (3),

(b)   all or any of the material is of a description prescribed under this subsection, and

(c)   a person is identified in accordance with prescribed provisions as entitled to material of that description,

the person giving the document must give a copy of the material of that description to the person so identified or (depending on the circumstances) must allow him to inspect it.

(6)   The code may provide that if—

(a)   a document is given in pursuance of provision contained in the code by virtue of subsection (3),

(b)   all or any of the material is not of a description prescribed under subsection (5), and

(c)   a person identified in accordance with prescribed provisions asks for any of the material not of that description,

the person giving the document must give a copy of the material asked for to the person asking for it or (depending on the circumstances) must allow him to inspect it.

(7)   The code may provide that if the person required to reveal material has possession of material which he believes is sensitive and of such a nature that provision contained in the code by virtue of subsection (2) should not apply with regard to it—

(a)   that provision shall not apply with regard to the material,

(b)   he must notify a person identified in accordance with prescribed provisions of the existence of the material, and

(c)   he must allow the person so notified to inspect the material.

(8)   For the purposes of this section material is sensitive to the extent that its disclosure under Part I would be contrary to the public interest.

(9)   In this section 'prescribed' means prescribed by the code.

25.   Operation and revision of code

(1)   When the Secretary of State has prepared a code under section 23—

(a)   he shall publish it in the form of a draft,

(b)   he shall consider any representations made to him about the draft, and

(c)   he may modify the draft accordingly.

(2)   When the Secretary of State has acted under subsection (1) he shall lay the code before each House of Parliament, and when he has done so he may bring it into operation on such day as he may appoint by order.

(3)   A code brought into operation under this section shall apply in relation to suspected or alleged offences into which no criminal investigation has begun before the day so appointed.

(4)   The Secretary of State may from time to time revise a code previously brought into operation under this section; and the preceding provisions of this section shall apply to a revised code as they apply to the code as first prepared.

26.   Effect of code

(1)   A person other than a police officer who is charged with the duty of conducting an investigation with a view to it being ascertained—

(a)   whether a person should be charged with an offence, or

(b)   whether a person charged with an offence is guilty of it,

shall in discharging that duty have regard to any relevant provision of a code which would apply if the investigation were conducted by police officers.

(2)   A failure—

(a)   by a police officer to comply with any provision of a code for the time being in operation by virtue of an order under section 25, or

(b)   by a person to comply with subsection (1),

shall not in itself render him liable to any criminal or civil proceedings.

(3)   In all criminal and civil proceedings a code in operation at any time by virtue of an order under section 25 shall be admissible in evidence.

(4)   If it appears to a court or tribunal conducting criminal or civil proceedings that—

(a)   any provision of a code in operation at any time by virtue of an order under section 25, or

(b)   any failure mentioned in subsection (2)(a) or (b),

is relevant to any question arising in the proceedings, the provision or failure shall be taken into account in deciding the question.

27.   Common law rules as to criminal investigations

(1)   Where a code prepared under section 23 and brought into operation under section 25 applies in relation to a suspected or alleged offence, the rules of common law which—

(a)   were effective immediately before the appointed day, and

(b)   relate to the matter mentioned in subsection (2),

shall not apply in relation to the suspected or alleged offence.

(2)   The matter is the revealing of material—

(a)   by a police officer or other person charged with the duty of conducting an investigation with a view to it being ascertained whether a person should be charged with an offence or whether a person charged with an offence is guilty of it;

(b)   to a person involved in the prosecution of criminal proceedings.

(3)   In subsection (1) 'the appointed day' means the day appointed under section 25 with regard to the code as first prepared.

PART III
PREPARATORY HEARINGS

Introduction

28.   Introduction

(1)   This Part applies in relation to an offence if—

(a)   on or after the appointed day the accused is committed for trial for the offence concerned,

(b)   proceedings for the trial on the charge concerned are transferred to the Crown Court on or after the appointed day, or

(c)   a bill of indictment relating to the offence is preferred on or after the appointed day under the authority of section 2(2)(b) of the Administration of Justice (Miscellaneous Provisions) Act 1933 (bill preferred by direction of Court of Appeal, or by direction or with consent of a judge).

(2)   References in subsection (1) to the appointed day are to such day as is appointed for the purposes of this section by the Secretary of State by order.

(3)   If an order under this section so provides, this Part applies only in relation to the Crown Court sitting at a place or places specified in the order.

(4)   References in this Part to the prosecutor are to any person acting as prosecutor, whether an individual or a body.

Preparatory hearings

29.   Power to order preparatory hearing

(1)   Where it appears to a judge of the Crown Court that an indictment reveals a case of such complexity, or a case whose trial is likely to be of such length, that substantial benefits are likely to accrue from a hearing—

(a)   before the jury are sworn, and

(b)   for any of the purposes mentioned in subsection (2),

he may order that such a hearing (in this Part referred to as a preparatory hearing) shall be held.

(2)   The purposes are those of—

(a)   identifying issues which are likely to be material to the verdict of the jury;

(b)   assisting their comprehension of any such issues;

(c)   expediting the proceedings before the jury;

(d)   assisting the judge's management of the trial.

(3)   No order may be made under subsection (1) where it appears to a judge of the Crown Court that the evidence on an indictment reveals a case of fraud of such seriousness or complexity as is mentioned in section 7(1) of the Criminal Justice Act 1987 (preparatory hearings in cases of serious or complex fraud).

(4)   A judge may make an order under subsection (1)—
   (a)   on the application of the prosecutor,
   (b)   on the application of the accused or, if there is more than one, any of them,
or
   (c)   of the judge's own motion.

30.   Start of trial and arraignment

If a judge orders a preparatory hearing—
   (a)   the trial shall start with that hearing, and
   (b)   arraignment shall take place at the start of that hearing, unless it has taken place before then.

31.   The preparatory hearing

(1)   At the preparatory hearing the judge may exercise any of the powers specified in this section.

(2)   The judge may adjourn a preparatory hearing from time to time.

(3)   He may make a ruling as to—
   (a)   any question as to the admissibility of evidence;
   (b)   any other question of law relating to the case.

(4)   He may order the prosecutor—
   (a)   to give the court and the accused or, if there is more than one, each of them a written statement (a case statement) of the matters falling within subsection (5);
   (b)   to prepare the prosecution evidence and any explanatory material in such a form as appears to the judge to be likely to aid comprehension by the jury and to give it in that form to the court and to the accused or, if there is more than one, to each of them;
   (c)   to give the court and the accused or, if there is more than one, each of them written notice of documents the truth of the contents of which ought in the prosecutor's view to be admitted and of any other matters which in his view ought to be agreed;
   (d)   to make any amendments of any case statement given in pursuance of an order under paragraph (a) that appear to the judge to be appropriate, having regard to objections made by the accused or, if there is more than one, by any of them.

(5)   The matters referred to in subsection (4)(a) are—
   (a)   the principal facts of the case for the prosecution;
   (b)   the witnesses who will speak to those facts;
   (c)   any exhibits relevant to those facts;
   (d)   any proposition of law on which the prosecutor proposes to rely;
   (e)   the consequences in relation to any of the counts in the indictment that appear to the prosecutor to flow from the matters falling within paragraphs (a) to (d).

(6)   Where a judge has ordered the prosecutor to give a case statement and the prosecutor has complied with the order, the judge may order the accused or, if there is more than one, each of them—
   (a)   to give the court and the prosecutor a written statement setting out in general terms the nature of his defence and indicating the principal matters on which he takes issue with the prosecution;
   (b)   to give the court and the prosecutor written notice of any objections that he has to the case statement;

(c)   to give the court and the prosecutor written notice of any point of law (including any point as to the admissibility of evidence) which he wishes to take, and any authority on which he intends to rely for that purpose.

(7)   Where a judge has ordered the prosecutor to give notice under subsection (4)(c) and the prosecutor has complied with the order, the judge may order the accused or, if there is more than one, each of them to give the court and the prosecutor a written notice stating—

(a)   the extent to which he agrees with the prosecutor as to documents and other matters to which the notice under subsection (4)(c) relates, and

(b)   the reason for any disagreement.

(8)   A judge making an order under subsection (6) or (7) shall warn the accused or, if there is more than one, each of them of the possible consequence under section 34 of not complying with it.

(9)   If it appears to a judge that reasons given in pursuance of subsection (7) are inadequate, he shall so inform the person giving them and may require him to give further or better reasons.

(10)   An order under this section may specify the time within which any specified requirement contained in it is to be complied with.

(11)   An order or ruling made under this section shall have effect throughout the trial, unless it appears to the judge on application made to him that the interests of justice require him to vary or discharge it.

32.   Orders before preparatory hearing

(1)   This section applies where—

(a)   a judge orders a preparatory hearing, and

(b)   he decides that any order which could be made under section 31(4) to (7) at the hearing should be made before the hearing.

(2)   In such a case—

(a)   he may make any such order before the hearing (or at the hearing), and

(b)   section 31(4) to (11) shall apply accordingly.

33.   Crown Court Rules

(1)   Crown Court Rules may provide that except to the extent that disclosure is required—

(a)   by rules under section 81 of the Police and Criminal Evidence Act 1984 (expert evidence), or

(b)   by section 5(7) of this Act,

anything required to be given by an accused in pursuance of a requirement imposed under section 31 need not disclose who will give evidence.

(2)   Crown Court Rules may make provision as to the minimum or maximum time that may be specified under section 31(10).

34.   Later stages of trial

(1)   Any party may depart from the case he disclosed in pursuance of a requirement imposed under section 31.

(2) Where—

(a)   a party departs from the case he disclosed in pursuance of a requirement imposed under section 31, or

(b)   a party fails to comply with such a requirement,

the judge or, with the leave of the judge, any other party may make such comment as appears to the judge or the other party (as the case may be) to be appropriate and the jury may draw such inference as appears proper.

(3) In deciding whether to give leave the judge shall have regard—
(a) to the extent of the departure or failure, and
(b) to whether there is any justification for it.

(4) Except as provided by this section no part—
(a) of a statement given under section 31(6)(a), or
(b) of any other information relating to the case for the accused or, if there is more than one, the case for any of them, which was given in pursuance of a requirement imposed under section 31,
may be disclosed at a stage in the trial after the jury have been sworn without the consent of the accused concerned.

Appeals

35. Appeals to Court of Appeal
(1) An appeal shall lie to the Court of Appeal from any ruling of a judge under section 31(3), but only with the leave of the judge or of the Court of Appeal.

(2) The judge may continue a preparatory hearing notwithstanding that leave to appeal has been granted under subsection (1), but no jury shall be sworn until after the appeal has been determined or abandoned.

(3) On the termination of the hearing of an appeal, the Court of Appeal may confirm, reverse or vary the decision appealed against.

(4) Subject to rules of court made under section 53(1) of the Supreme Court Act 1981 (power by rules to distribute business of Court of Appeal between its civil and criminal divisions)—
(a) the jurisdiction of the Court of Appeal under subsection (1) above shall be exercised by the criminal division of the court;
(b) references in this Part to the Court of Appeal shall be construed as references to that division.

36. Appeals to House of Lords
(1) In the Criminal Appeal Act 1968, in—
(a) section 33(1) (right of appeal to House of Lords), and
(b) section 36 (bail),
after '1987' there shall be inserted 'or section 35 of the Criminal Procedure and Investigations Act 1996'.

(2) The judge may continue a preparatory hearing notwithstanding that leave to appeal has been granted under Part II of the Criminal Appeal Act 1968, but no jury shall be sworn until after the appeal has been determined or abandoned.

Reporting restrictions

37. Restrictions on reporting
(1) Except as provided by this section—
(a) no written report of proceedings falling within subsection (2) shall be published in Great Britain;
(b) no report of proceedings falling within subsection (2) shall be included in a relevant programme for reception in Great Britain.

(2)   The following proceedings fall within this subsection—
  (a)   a preparatory hearing;
  (b)   an application for leave to appeal in relation to such a hearing;
  (c)   an appeal in relation to such a hearing.
(3)   The judge dealing with a preparatory hearing may order that subsection (1) shall not apply, or shall not apply to a specified extent, to a report of—
  (a)   the preparatory hearing, or
  (b)   an application to the judge for leave to appeal to the Court of Appeal under section 35(1) in relation to the preparatory hearing.
(4)   The Court of Appeal may order that subsection (1) shall not apply, or shall not apply to a specified extent, to a report of—
  (a)   an appeal to the Court of Appeal under section 35(1) in relation to a preparatory hearing,
  (b)   an application to that Court for leave to appeal to it under section 35(1) in relation to a preparatory hearing, or
  (c)   an application to that Court for leave to appeal to the House of Lords under Part II of the Criminal Appeal Act 1968 in relation to a preparatory hearing.
(5)   The House of Lords may order that subsection (1) shall not apply, or shall not apply to a specified extent, to a report of—
  (a)   an appeal to that House under Part II of the Criminal Appeal Act 1968 in relation to a preparatory hearing, or
  (b)   an application to that House for leave to appeal to it under Part II of the Criminal Appeal Act 1968 in relation to a preparatory hearing.
(6)   Where there is only one accused and he objects to the making of an order under subsection (3), (4) or (5) the judge or the Court of Appeal or the House of Lords shall make the order if (and only if) satisfied after hearing the representations of the accused that it is in the interests of justice to do so; and if the order is made it shall not apply to the extent that a report deals with any such objection or representations.
(7)   Where there are two or more accused and one or more of them objects to the making of an order under subsection (3), (4) or (5) the judge or the Court of Appeal or the House of Lords shall make the order if (and only if) satisfied after hearing the representations of each of the accused that it is in the interests of justice to do so; and if the order is made it shall not apply to the extent that a report deals with any such objection or representations.
(8)   Subsection (1) does not apply to—
  (a)   the publication of a report of a preparatory hearing,
  (b)   the publication of a report of an appeal in relation to a preparatory hearing or of an application for leave to appeal in relation to such a hearing,
  (c)   the inclusion in a relevant programme of a report of a preparatory hearing, or
  (d)   the inclusion in a relevant programme of a report of an appeal in relation to a preparatory hearing or of an application for leave to appeal in relation to such a hearing,
at the conclusion of the trial of the accused or of the last of the accused to be tried.
(9)   Subsection (1) does not apply to a report which contains only one or more of the following matters—
  (a)   the identity of the court and the name of the judge;
  (b)   the names, ages, home addresses and occupations of the accused and witnesses;

(c)　the offence or offences, or a summary of them, with which the accused is or are charged;

(d)　the names of counsel and solicitors in the proceedings;

(e)　where the proceedings are adjourned, the date and place to which they are adjourned;

(f)　any arrangements as to bail;

(g)　whether legal aid was granted to the accused or any of the accused.

(10)　The addresses that may be published or included in a relevant programme under subsection (9) are addresses—

(a)　at any relevant time, and

(b)　at the time of their publication or inclusion in a relevant programme; and 'relevant time' here means a time when events giving rise to the charges to which the proceedings relate occurred.

(11)　Nothing in this section affects any prohibition or restriction imposed by virtue of any other enactment on a publication or on matter included in a programme.

(12)　In this section—

(a)　'publish', in relation to a report, means publish the report, either by itself or as part of a newspaper or periodical, for distribution to the public;

(b)　expressions cognate with 'publish' shall be construed accordingly;

(c)　'relevant programme' means a programme included in a programme service, within the meaning of the Broadcasting Act 1990.

38.　Offences in connection with reporting

(1)　If a report is published or included in a relevant programme in contravention of section 37 each of the following persons is guilty of an offence—

(a)　in the case of a publication of a written report as part of a newspaper or periodical, any proprietor, editor or publisher of the newspaper or periodical;

(b)　in the case of a publication of a written report otherwise than as part of a newspaper or periodical, the person who publishes it;

(c)　in the case of the inclusion of a report in a relevant programme, any body corporate which is engaged in providing the service in which the programme is included and any person having functions in relation to the programme corresponding to those of an editor of a newspaper.

(2)　A person guilty of an offence under this section is liable on summary conviction to a fine of an amount not exceeding level 5 on the standard scale.

(3)　Proceedings for an offence under this section shall not be instituted in England and Wales otherwise than by or with the consent of the Attorney General.

(4)　Subsection (12) of section 37 applies for the purposes of this section as it applies for the purposes of that.

PART IV
RULINGS

39.　Meaning of pre-trial hearing

(1)　For the purposes of this Part a hearing is a pre-trial hearing if it relates to a trial on indictment and it takes place—

(a)　after the accused has been committed for trial for the offence concerned or after the proceedings for the trial have been transferred to the Crown Court, and

(b)　before the start of the trial.

(2) For the purposes of this Part a hearing is also a pre-trial hearing if—
  (a) it relates to a trial on indictment to be held in pursuance of a bill of indictment preferred under the authority of section 2(2)(b) of the Administration of Justice (Miscellaneous Provisions) Act 1933 (bill preferred by direction of Court of Appeal, or by direction or with consent of a judge), and
  (b) it takes place after the bill of indictment has been preferred and before the start of the trial.

(3) For the purposes of this section the start of a trial on indictment occurs when a jury is sworn to consider the issue of guilt or fitness to plead or, if the court accepts a plea of guilty before a jury is sworn, when that plea is accepted; but this is subject to section 8 of the Criminal Justice Act 1987 and section 30 of this Act (preparatory hearings).

40. Power to make rulings

(1) A judge may make at a pre-trial hearing a ruling as to—
  (a) any question as to the admissibility of evidence;
  (b) any other question of law relating to the case concerned.

(2) A ruling may be made under this section—
  (a) on an application by a party to the case, or
  (b) of the judge's own motion.

(3) Subject to subsection (4), a ruling made under this section has binding effect from the time it is made until the case against the accused or, if there is more than one, against each of them is disposed of; and the case against an accused is disposed of if—
  (a) he is acquitted or convicted, or
  (b) the prosecutor decides not to proceed with the case against him.

(4) A judge may discharge or vary (or further vary) a ruling made under this section if it appears to him that it is in the interests of justice to do so; and a judge may act under this subsection—
  (a) on an application by a party to the case, or
  (b) of the judge's own motion.

(5) No application may be made under subsection (4)(a) unless there has been a material change of circumstances since the ruling was made or, if a previous application has been made, since the application (or last application) was made.

(6) The judge referred to in subsection (4) need not be the judge who made the ruling or, if it has been varied, the judge (or any of the judges) who varied it.

(7) For the purposes of this section the prosecutor is any person acting as prosecutor, whether an individual or a body.

41. Restrictions on reporting

(1) Except as provided by this section—
  (a) no written report of matters falling within subsection (2) shall be published in Great Britain;
  (b) no report of matters falling within subsection (2) shall be included in a relevant programme for reception in Great Britain.

(2) The following matters fall within this subsection—
  (a) a ruling made under section 40;
  (b) proceedings on an application for a ruling to be made under section 40;
  (c) an order that a ruling made under section 40 be discharged or varied or further varied;

(d)   proceedings on an application for a ruling made under section 40 to be discharged or varied or further varied.

(3)   The judge dealing with any matter falling within subsection (2) may order that subsection (1) shall not apply, or shall not apply to a specified extent, to a report of the matter.

(4)   Where there is only one accused and he objects to the making of an order under subsection (3) the judge shall make the order if (and only if) satisfied after hearing the representations of the accused that it is in the interests of justice to do so; and if the order is made it shall not apply to the extent that a report deals with any such objection or representations.

(5)   Where there are two or more accused and one or more of them objects to the making of an order under subsection (3) the judge shall make the order if (and only if) satisfied after hearing the representations of each of the accused that it is in the interests of justice to do so; and if the order is made it shall not apply to the extent that a report deals with any such objection or representations.

(6)   Subsection (1) does not apply to—
(a)   the publication of a report of matters, or
(b)   the inclusion in a relevant programme of a report of matters,
at the conclusion of the trial of the accused or of the last of the accused to be tried.

(7)   Nothing in this section affects any prohibition or restriction imposed by virtue of any other enactment on a publication or on matter included in a programme.

(8)   In this section—
(a)   'publish', in relation to a report, means publish the report, either by itself or as part of a newspaper or periodical, for distribution to the public;
(b)   expressions cognate with 'publish' shall be construed accordingly;
(c)   'relevant programme' means a programme included in a programme service, within the meaning of the Broadcasting Act 1990.

42.   Offences in connection with reporting

(1)   If a report is published or included in a relevant programme in contravention of section 41 each of the following persons is guilty of an offence—
(a)   in the case of a publication of a written report as part of a newspaper or periodical, any proprietor, editor or publisher of the newspaper or periodical;
(b)   in the case of a publication of a written report otherwise than as part of a newspaper or periodical, the person who publishes it;
(c)   in the case of the inclusion of a report in a relevant programme, any body corporate which is engaged in providing the service in which the programme is included and any person having functions in relation to the programme corresponding to those of an editor of a newspaper.

(2)   A person guilty of an offence under this section is liable on summary conviction to a fine of an amount not exceeding level 5 on the standard scale.

(3)   Proceedings for an offence under this section shall not be instituted in England and Wales otherwise than by or with the consent of the Attorney General.

(4)   Subsection (8) of section 41 applies for the purposes of this section as it applies for the purposes of that.

43.   Application of this Part

(1)   This Part applies in relation to pre-trial hearings beginning on or after the appointed day.

(2)   The reference in subsection (1) to the appointed day is to such day as is appointed for the purposes of this section by the Secretary of State by order.

PART V
COMMITTAL, TRANSFER, ETC.

44.   Reinstatement of certain provisions

(1)   The Criminal Justice and Public Order Act 1994 shall be amended as follows.

(2)   Section 44 and Schedule 4 (which provide for transfer for trial instead of committal proceedings) shall be omitted.

(3)   In each of sections 34, 36 and 37 for paragraph (a) of subsection (2) (magistrates' court proceeding with a view to transfer) there shall be substituted—

'(a)   a magistrates' court inquiring into the offence as examining justices;'.

(4)   Sections 34(7), 36(8) and 37(7) (transitional) shall be omitted.

(5)   In Schedule 11 (repeals) the entries relating to the following (which concern committal, transfer and other matters) shall be omitted—

(a)   sections 13(3) and 49(2) of the Criminal Justice Act 1925;

(b)   section 1 of the Criminal Procedure (Attendance of Witnesses) Act 1965;

(c)   section 7 of the Criminal Justice Act 1967 and in section 36(1) of that Act the definition of 'committal proceedings';

(d)   in paragraph 1 of Schedule 2 to the Criminal Appeal Act 1968 the words from 'section 13(3)' to 'but';

(e)   in section 46(1) of the Criminal Justice Act 1972 the words 'Section 102 of the Magistrates' Courts Act 1980 and', 'which respectively allow', 'committal proceedings and in other', 'and section 106 of the said Act of 1980', 'which punish the making of', '102 or' and ', as the case may be', and section 46(2) of that Act;

(f)   in section 32(1)(b) of the Powers of Criminal Courts Act 1973 the words 'tried or';

(g)   in Schedule 1 to the Interpretation Act 1978, paragraph (a) of the definition of 'Committed for trial';

(h)   in section 97(1) of the Magistrates' Courts Act 1980 the words from 'at an inquiry' to 'be) or', sections 102, 103,105,106 and 145(1)(e) of that Act, in section 150(1) of that Act the definition of 'committal proceedings', and paragraph 2 of Schedule 5 to that Act;

(i)   in section 2(2)(g) of the Criminal Attempts Act 1981 the words 'or committed for trial';

(j)   in section 1(2) of the Criminal Justice Act 1982 the words 'trial or';

(k)   paragraphs 10 and 11 of Schedule 2 to the Criminal Justice Act 1987;

(l)   in section 20(4)(a) of the Legal Aid Act 1988 the words 'trial or', and section 20(4)(bb) and (5) of that Act;

(m)   in section 1(4) of the War Crimes Act 1991 the words 'England, Wales or', and Part I of the Schedule to that Act.

(6)   The 1994 Act shall be treated as having been enacted with the amendments made by subsections (2) and (5).

(7)   Subsections (3) and (4) apply where a magistrates' court begins to inquire into an offence as examining justices after the day on which this Act is passed.

45.   Notices of tranfer

(1)   Section 5 of the Criminal Justice Act 1987 (notices of transfer in cases of serious or complex fraud) shall be amended as mentioned in subsections (2) and (3).

(2)   In subsection (9)(a) (regulations) for the words 'a statement of the evidence' there shall be substituted 'copies of the documents containing the evidence (including oral evidence)'.

(3)   The following subsection shall be inserted after subsection (9)—

'(9A)   Regulations under subsection (9)(a) above may provide that there shall be no requirement for copies of documents to accompany the copy of the notice of transfer if they are referred to, in documents sent with the notice of transfer, as having already been supplied.'

(4)   In Schedule 6 to the Criminal Justice Act 1991 (notices of transfer in certain cases involving children) paragraph 4 (regulations) shall be amended as mentioned in subsections (5) and (6).

(5)   In sub-paragraph (1)(a) for the words 'a statement of the evidence' there shall be substituted 'copies of the documents containing the evidence (including oral evidence)'.

(6)   The following sub-paragraph shall be inserted after subparagraph (1)—

'(1A)   Regulations under sub-paragraph (1)(a) above may provide that there shall be no requirement for copies of documents to accompany the copy of the notice of transfer if they are referred to, in documents sent with the notice of transfer, as having already been supplied.'

(7)   In paragraph 6 of Schedule 6 to the 1991 Act (reporting restrictions) in sub-paragraph (8) for the words 'sub-paragraphs (5) and (6)' there shall be substituted 'sub-paragraphs (5) and (7)'.

(8)   This section applies where a notice of transfer is given under section 4 of the 1987 Act or served under section 53 of the 1991 Act (as the case may be) on or after the appointed day.

(9)   The reference in subsection (8) to the appointed day is to such day as is appointed for the purposes of this section by the Secretary of State by order.

46.   War crimes: abolition of transfer procedure

(1)   In the War Crimes Act 1991—

(a)   in section 1(4) (which introduces the Schedule providing a procedure for use instead of committal proceedings for certain war crimes) the words 'England, Wales or' shall be omitted, and

(b)   Part I of the Schedule (procedure for use in England and Wales instead of committal proceedings) shall be omitted.

(2)   In section 20(4) of the Legal Aid Act 1988 (power of magistrates' court to grant legal aid for Crown Court proceedings)—

(a)   the word 'or' shall be inserted at the end of paragraph (b), and

(b)   paragraph (bb) (which relates to a notice of transfer under Part I of the Schedule to the War Crimes Act 1991) shall be omitted.

47.   Committal proceedings

Schedule 1 to this Act (which contains provisions about committal proceedings and related matters) shall have effect.

PART VI
MAGISTRATES' COURTS

48.   Non-appearance of accused: issue of warrant

(1)   Section 13 of the Magistrates' Courts Act 1980 (non-appearance of accused: issue of warrant) shall be amended as follows.

(2) In subsection (2) (no warrant where summons has been issued unless certain conditions fulfilled) for the words from 'unless' to the end of the subsection there shall be substituted 'unless the condition in subsection (2A) below or that in subsection (2B) below is fulfilled'.

(3) The following subsections shall be inserted after subsection (2)—

'(2A) The condition in this subsection is that it is proved to the satisfaction of the court, on oath or in such other manner as may be prescribed, that the summons was served on the accused within what appears to the court to be a reasonable time before the trial or adjourned trial.

(2B) The condition in this subsection is that—

(a) the adjournment now being made is a second or subsequent adjournment of the trial,

(b) the accused was present on the last (or only) occasion when the trial was adjourned, and

(c) on that occasion the court determined the time for the hearing at which the adjournment is now being made.'

(4) This section applies where the court proposes to issue a warrant under section 13 on or after the appointed day.

(5) The reference in subsection (4) to the appointed day is to such day as is appointed for the purposes of this section by the Secretary of State by order.

49. Either way offences: accused's intention as to plea

(1) The Magistrates' Courts Act 1980 shall be amended as follows.

(2) The following sections shall be inserted after section 17 (offences triable on indictment or summarily)—

'**17A. Initial procedure: accused to indicate intention as to plea**

(1) This section shall have effect where a person who has attained the age of 18 years appears or is brought before a magistrates' court on an information charging him with an offence triable either way.

(2) Everything that the court is required to do under the following provisions of this section must be done with the accused present in court.

(3) The court shall cause the charge to be written down, if this has not already been done, and to be read to the accused.

(4) The court shall then explain to the accused in ordinary language that he may indicate whether (if the offence were to proceed to trial) he would plead guilty or not guilty, and that if he indicates that he would plead guilty—

(a) the court must proceed as mentioned in subsection (6) below; and

(b) he may be committed for sentence to the Crown Court under section 38 below if the court is of such opinion as is mentioned in subsection (2) of that section.

(5) The court shall then ask the accused whether (if the offence were to proceed to trial) he would plead guilty or not guilty.

(6) If the accused indicates that he would plead guilty the court shall proceed as if—

(a) the proceedings constituted from the beginning the summary trial of the information; and

(b) section 9(1) above was complied with and he pleaded guilty under it.

(7) If the accused indicates that he would plead not guilty section 18(1) below shall apply.

(8)   If the accused in fact fails to indicate how he would plead, for the purposes of this section and section 18(1) below he shall be taken to indicate that he would plead not guilty.

(9)   Subject to subsection (6) above, the following shall not for any purpose be taken to constitute the taking of a plea—

(a)   asking the accused under this section whether (if the offence were to proceed to trial) he would plead guilty or not guilty;

(b)   an indication by the accused under this section of how he would plead.

17B.   Intention as to plea: absence of accused

(1)   This section shall have effect where—

(a)   a person who has attained the age of 18 years appears or is brought before a magistrates' court on an information charging him with an offence triable either way,

(b)   the accused is represented by a legal representative,

(c)   the court considers that by reason of the accused's disorderly conduct before the court it is not practicable for proceedings under section 17A above to be conducted in his presence, and

(d)   the court considers that it should proceed in the absence of the accused.

(2)   In such a case—

(a)   the court shall cause the charge to be written down, if this has not already been done, and to be read to the representative;

(b)   the court shall ask the representative whether (if the offence were to proceed to trial) the accused would plead guilty or not guilty;

(c)   if the representative indicates that the accused would plead guilty the court shall proceed as if the proceedings constituted from the beginning the summary trial of the information, and as if section 9(1) above was complied with and the accused pleaded guilty under it;

(d)   if the representative indicates that the accused would plead not guilty section 18(1) below shall apply.

(3)   If the representative in fact fails to indicate how the accused would plead, for the purposes of this section and section 18(1) below he shall be taken to indicate that the accused would plead not guilty.

(4)   Subject to subsection (2)(c) above, the following shall not for any purpose be taken to constitute the taking of a plea—

(a)   asking the representative under this section whether (if the offence were to proceed to trial) the accused would plead guilty or not guilty;

(b)   an indication by the representative under this section of how the accused would plead.

17C.   Intention as to plea: adjournment

A magistrates' court proceeding under section 17A or 17B above may adjourn the proceedings at any time, and on doing so on any occasion when the accused is present may remand the accused, and shall remand him if—

(a)   on the occasion on which he first appeared, or was brought, before the court to answer to the information he was in custody or, having been released on bail, surrendered to the custody of the court; or

(b)   he has been remanded at any time in the course of proceedings on the information;

and where the court remands the accused, the time fixed for the resumption of proceedings shall be that at which he is required to appear or be brought before the court in pursuance of the remand or would be required to be brought before the court but for section 128(3A) below.'

(3)   In section 18(1) (initial procedure) after 'either way' there shall be inserted 'and—

    (a)   he indicates under section 17A above that (if the offence were to proceed to trial) he would plead not guilty, or

    (b)   his representative indicates under section 17B above that (if the offence were to proceed to trial) he would plead not guilty'.

(4)   In section 19 (court to consider which mode of trial appears more suitable) paragraph (a) of subsection (2) (charge to be read to accused) shall be omitted.

(5)   In—

    (a)   subsections (1A), (3A), (3C) and (3E) of section 128 (remand), and

    (b)   subsection (1) of section 130 (transfer of remand hearings), after '10(1)' there shall be inserted ', 17C'.

(6)   This section applies where a person appears or is brought before a magistrates' court on or after the appointed day, unless he has appeared or been brought before such a court in respect of the same offence on a previous occasion falling before that day.

(7)   The reference in subsection (6) to the appointed day is to such day as is appointed for the purposes of this section by the Secretary of State by order.

50.   Enforcement of payment of fines

(1)   In section 87 of the Magistrates' Courts Act 1980 (enforcement of fines) in subsection (3) (no proceedings unless court authorises it after inquiry into means) for the words from 'authorised' to the end of the subsection there shall be substituted 'there has been an inquiry under section 82 above into that person's means and he appeared to the court to have sufficient means to pay the sum forthwith.'

(2)   This section applies where the clerk of a magistrates' court proposes to take proceedings by virtue of section 87(1) on or after the appointed day.

(3)   The reference in subsection (2) to the appointed day is to such day as is appointed for the purposes of this section by the Secretary of State by order.

51.   Summons to witness and warrant for his arrest

(1)   In section 97 of the Magistrates' Courts Act 1980 (summons to witness and warrant for his arrest) the following subsections shall be inserted after subsection (2A)—

    '(2B)   A justice may refuse to issue a summons under subsection (1) above in relation to the summary trial of an information if he is not satisfied that an application for the summons was made by a party to the case as soon as reasonably practicable after the accused pleaded not guilty.

    (2C)   In relation to the summary trial of an information, subsection (2) above shall have effect as if the reference to the matters mentioned in subsection (1) above included a reference to the matter mentioned in subsection (2B) above.'

(2)   This section applies in relation to any proceedings for the purpose of which no summons has been issued under section 97(1), and no warrant has been issued under section 97(2), before the appointed day.

(3)   The reference in subsection (2) to the appointed day is to such day as is appointed for the purposes of this section by the Secretary of State by order.

52. Remand

(1)   In section 128 of the Magistrates' Courts Act 1980 (remand in custody or on bail) paragraph (c) of subsection (1A) and paragraph (c) of subsection (3A) (which restrict certain provisions about remand to persons who have attained the age of 17) shall be omitted.

(2)   In section 128A(1) of that Act (power to make order allowing remand in custody for more than 8 clear days if accused has attained the age of 17) the words 'who has attained the age of 17' shall be omitted.

(3)   Subsection (1) applies where the offence with which the person concerned is charged is alleged to be committed on or after the appointed day.

(4)   The reference in subsection (3) to the appointed day is to such day as is appointed for the purposes of this section by the Secretary of State by order.

53. Attachment of earnings

(1)   In section 3 of the Attachment of Earnings Act 1971 (court's power to make order) the following subsections shall be inserted after subsection (3A)—

'(3B)   Where—

(a)   a magistrates' court imposes a fine on a person in respect of an offence, and

(b)   that person consents to an order being made under this subsection,

the court may at the time it imposes the fine, and without the need for an application, make an attachment of earnings order to secure the payment of the fine.

(3C)   Where—

(a)   a magistrates' court makes in the case of a person convicted of an offence an order under section 35 of the Powers of Criminal Courts Act 1973 (a compensation order) requiring him to pay compensation or to make other payments, and

(b)   that person consents to an order being made under this subsection,

the court may at the time it makes the compensation order, and without the need for an application, make an attachment of earnings order to secure the payment of the compensation or other payments.'

(2)   This section applies in relation to—

(a)   fines imposed in respect of offences committed on or after the appointed day;

(b)   compensation orders made on convictions for offences committed on or after that day.

(3)   The reference in subsection (2) to the appointed day is to such day as is appointed for the purposes of this section by the Secretary of State by order.

PART VII
MISCELLANEOUS AND GENERAL

Tainted acquittals

54. Acquittals tainted by intimidation etc.

(1)   This section applies where—

(a)   a person has been acquitted of an offence, and

    (b) a person has been convicted of an administration of justice offence
involving interference with or intimidation of a juror or a witness (or potential
witness) in any proceedings which led to the acquittal.

    (2) Where it appears to the court before which the person was convicted that—
    (a) there is a real possibility that, but for the interference or intimidation, the
acquitted person would not have been acquitted, and
    (b) subsection (5) does not apply,
the court shall certify that it so appears.

    (3) Where a court certifies under subsection (2) an application may be made to
the High Court for an order quashing the acquittal, and the Court shall make the order
if (but shall not do so unless) the four conditions in section 55 are satisfied.

    (4) Where an order is made under subsection (3) proceedings may be taken
against the acquitted person for the offence of which he was acquitted.

    (5) This subsection applies if, because of lapse of time or for any other reason,
it would be contrary to the interests of justice to take proceedings against the acquitted
person for the offence of which he was acquitted.

    (6) For the purposes of this section the following offences are administration of
justice offences—
    (a) the offence of perverting the course of justice;
    (b) the offence under section 51(1) of the Criminal Justice and Public Order
Act 1994 (intimidation etc. of witnesses, jurors and others);
    (c) an offence of aiding, abetting, counselling, procuring, suborning or inciting
another person to commit an offence under section 1 of the Perjury Act 1911.

    (7) This section applies in relation to acquittals in respect of offences alleged to
be committed on or after the appointed day.

    (8) The reference in subsection (7) to the appointed day is to such day as is
appointed for the purposes of this section by the Secretary of State by order.

55. Conditions for making order
    (1) The first condition is that it appears to the High Court likely that, but for the
interference or intimidation, the acquitted person would not have been acquitted.

    (2) The second condition is that it does not appear to the Court that, because of
lapse of time or for any other reason, it would be contrary to the interests of justice
to take proceedings against the acquitted person for the offence of which he was
acquitted.

    (3) The third condition is that it appears to the Court that the acquitted person
has been given a reasonable opportunity to make written representations to the Court.

    (4) The fourth condition is that it appears to the Court that the conviction for the
administration of justice offence will stand.

    (5) In applying subsection (4) the Court shall—
    (a) take into account all the information before it, but
    (b) ignore the possibility of new factors coming to light.

    (6) Accordingly, the fourth condition has the effect that the Court shall not make
an order under section 54(3) if (for instance) it appears to the Court that any time
allowed for giving notice of appeal has not expired or that an appeal is pending.

56. Time limits for proceedings
    (1) Where—

(a)   an order is made under section 54(3) quashing an acquittal,

(b)   by virtue of section 54(4) it is proposed to take proceedings against the acquitted person for the offence of which he was acquitted, and

(c)   apart from this subsection, the effect of an enactment would be that the proceedings must be commenced before a specified period calculated by reference to the commission of the offence,

in relation to the proceedings the enactment shall have effect as if the period were instead one calculated by reference to the time the order is made under section 54(3).

(2)   Subsection (1)(c) applies however the enactment is expressed so that (for instance) it applies in the case of—

(a)   paragraph 10 of Schedule 2 to the Sexual Offences Act 1956 (prosecution for certain offences may not be commenced more than 12 months after offence);

(b)   section 127(1) of the Magistrates' Courts Act 1980 (magistrates' court not to try information unless it is laid within 6 months from time when offence committed);

(c)   an enactment that imposes a time limit only in certain circumstances (as where proceedings are not instituted by or with the consent of the Director of Public Prosecutions).

57.   Tainted acquittals: supplementary

(1)   Section 45 of the Offences Against the Person Act 1861 (which releases a person from criminal proceedings in certain circumstances) shall have effect subject to section 54(4) of this Act.

(2)   The Contempt of Court Act 1981 shall be amended as mentioned in subsections (3) and (4).

(3)   In section 4 (contemporary reports of proceedings) after subsection (2) there shall be inserted—

'(2A)   Where in proceedings for any offence which is an administration of justice offence for the purposes of section 54 of the Criminal Procedure and Investigations Act 1996 (acquittal tainted by an administration of justice offence) it appears to the court that there is a possibility that (by virtue of that section) proceedings may be taken against a person for an offence of which he has been acquitted, subsection (2) of this section shall apply as if those proceedings were pending or imminent.'

(4)   In Schedule 1 (time when proceedings are active for purposes of section 2) in paragraph 3 (period for which criminal proceedings are active) after '4' there shall be inserted 'or 4A', and after paragraph 4 there shall be inserted—

'4A.   Where as a result of an order under section 54 of the Criminal Procedure and Investigations Act 1996 (acquittal tainted by an administration of justice offence) proceedings are brought against a person for an offence of which he has previously been acquitted, the initial step of the proceedings is a certification under subsection (2) of that section; and paragraph 4 has effect subject to this.'

Derogatory assertions

58.   Orders in respect of certain assertions

(1)   This section applies where a person has been convicted of an offence and a speech in mitigation is made by him or on his behalf before—

(a)   a court determining what sentence should be passed on him in respect of the offence, or

(b)   a magistrates' court determining whether he should be committed to the Crown Court for sentence.

(2)   This section also applies where a sentence has been passed on a person in respect of an offence and a submission relating to the sentence is made by him or on his behalf before—

(a)   a court hearing an appeal against or reviewing the sentence, or

(b)   a court determining whether to grant leave to appeal against the sentence.

(3)   Where it appears to the court that there is a real possibility that an order under subsection (8) will be made in relation to the assertion, the court may make an order under subsection (7) in relation to the assertion.

(4)   Where there are substantial grounds for believing—

(a)   that an assertion forming part of the speech or submission is derogatory to a person's character (for instance, because it suggests that his conduct is or has been criminal, immoral or improper), and

(b)   that the assertion is false or that the facts asserted are irrelevant to the sentence, the court may make an order under subsection (8) in relation to the assertion.

(5)   An order under subsection (7) or (8) must not be made in relation to an assertion if it appears to the court that the assertion was previously made—

(a)   at the trial at which the person was convicted of the offence, or

(b)   during any other proceedings relating to the offence.

(6)   Section 59 has effect where a court makes an order under subsection (7) or (8).

(7)   An order under this subsection—

(a)   may be made at any time before the court has made a determination with regard to sentencing;

(b)   may be revoked at any time by the court;

(c)   subject to paragraph (b), shall cease to have effect when the court makes a determination with regard to sentencing.

(8)   An order under this subsection—

(a)   may be made after the court has made a determination with regard to sentencing, but only if it is made as soon as is reasonably practicable after the making of the determination;

(b)   may be revoked at any time by the court;

(c)   subject to paragraph (b), shall cease to have effect at the end of the period of 12 months beginning with the day on which it is made;

(d)   may be made whether or not an order has been made under subsection (7) with regard to the case concerned.

(9)   For the purposes of subsections (7) and (8) the court makes a determination with regard to sentencing—

(a)   when it determines what sentence should be passed (where this section applies by virtue of subsection (1)(a));

(b)   when it determines whether the person should be committed to the Crown Court for sentence (where this section applies by virtue of subsection (1)(b));

(c)   when it determines what the sentence should be (where this section applies by virtue of subsection (2)(a));

(d)   when it determines whether to grant leave to appeal (where this section applies by virtue of subsection (2)(b)).

59.　Restriction on reporting of assertions

(1)　Where a court makes an order under section 58(7) or (8) in relation to any assertion, at any time when the order has effect the assertion must not—

　　(a)　be published in Great Britain in a written publication available to the public, or

　　(b)　be included in a relevant programme for reception in Great Britain.

(2)　In this section—

'relevant programme' means a programme included in a programme service, within the meaning of the Broadcasting Act 1990;

'written publication' includes a film, a soundtrack and any other record in permanent form but does not include an indictment or other document prepared for use in particular legal proceedings.

(3)　For the purposes of this section an assertion is published or included in a programme if the material published or included—

　　(a)　names the person about whom the assertion is made or, without naming him, contains enough to make it likely that members of the public will identify him as the person about whom it is made, and

　　(b)　reproduces the actual wording of the matter asserted or contains its substance.

60.　Reporting of assertions: offences

(1)　If an assertion is published or included in a relevant programme in contravention of section 59, each of the following persons is guilty of an offence—

　　(a)　in the case of publication in a newspaper or periodical, any proprietor, any editor and any publisher of the newspaper or periodical;

　　(b)　in the case of publication in any other form, the person publishing the assertion;

　　(c)　in the case of an assertion included in a relevant programme, any body corporate engaged in providing the service in which the programme is included and any person having functions in relation to the programme corresponding to those of an editor of a newspaper.

(2)　A person guilty of an offence under this section is liable on summary conviction to a fine of an amount not exceeding level 5 on the standard scale.

(3)　Where a person is charged with an offence under this section it is a defence to prove that at the time of the alleged offence—

　　(a)　he was not aware, and neither suspected nor had reason to suspect, that an order under section 58(7) or (8) had effect at that time, or

　　(b)　he was not aware, and neither suspected nor had reason to suspect, that the publication or programme in question was of, or (as the case may be) included, the assertion in question.

(4)　Where an offence under this section committed by a body corporate is proved to have been committed with the consent or connivance of, or to be attributable to any neglect on the part of—

　　(a)　a director, manager, secretary or other similar officer of the body corporate, or

　　(b)　a person purporting to act in any such capacity,

he as well as the body corporate is guilty of the offence and liable to be proceeded against and punished accordingly.

(5)   In relation to a body corporate whose affairs are managed by its members 'director' in subsection (4) means a member of the body corporate.

(6)   Subsections (2) and (3) of section 59 apply for the purposes of this section as they apply for the purposes of that.

61.   Reporting of assertions: commencement and supplementary

(1)   Section 58 applies where the offence mentioned in subsection (1) or (2) of that section is committed on or after the appointed day.

(2)   The reference in subsection (1) to the appointed day is to such day as is appointed for the purposes of this section by the Secretary of State by order.

(3)   Nothing in section 58 or 59 affects any prohibition or restriction imposed by virtue of any other enactment on a publication or on matter included in a programme.

(4)   Nothing in section 58 or 59 affects section 3 of the Law of Libel Amendment Act 1888 (privilege of newspaper reports of court proceedings).

(5)   Section 8 of the Law of Libel Amendment Act 1888 (order of judge required for prosecution for libel published in a newspaper) does not apply to a prosecution for an offence under section 60.

(6)   In section 159 of the Criminal Justice Act 1988 (appeal to Court of Appeal against orders restricting reports etc.) in subsection (1) the following paragraph shall be inserted after paragraph (a)—

'(aa)   an order made by the Crown Court under section 58(7) or (8) of the Criminal Procedure and Investigations Act 1996 in a case where the Court has convicted a person on a trial on indictment;'.

Evidence: special provisions

62.   Television links and video recordings

(1)   In section 32 of the Criminal Justice Act 1988 (evidence through television links) the following subsections shall be inserted after subsection (3B)—

'(3C)   Where—

(a)   the court gives leave for a person to give evidence through a live television link, and

(b)   the leave is given by virtue of subsection (1)(b) above,

then, subject to subsection (3D) below, the person concerned may not give evidence otherwise than through a live television link.

(3D)   In a case falling within subsection (3C) above the court may give permission for the person to give evidence otherwise than through a live television link if it appears to the court to be in the interests of justice to give such permission.

(3E)   Permission may be given under subsection (3D) above—

(a)   on an application by a party to the case, or

(b)   of the court's own motion;

but no application may be made under paragraph (a) above unless there has been a material change of circumstances since the leave was given by virtue of subsection (1)(b) above.'

(2)   In section 32A of the Criminal Justice Act 1988 (video recordings of testimony from child witnesses) the following subsections shall be inserted after subsection (6)—

'(6A)   Where the court gives leave under subsection (2) above the child witness shall not give relevant evidence (within the meaning given by subsection (6D) below) otherwise than by means of the video recording; but this is subject to subsection (6B) below.

(6B) In a case falling within subsection (6A) above the court may give permission for the child witness to give relevant evidence (within the meaning given by subsection (6D) below) otherwise than by means of the video recording if it appears to the court to be in the interests of justice to give such permission.

(6C) Permission may be given under subsection (6B) above—
(a) on an application by a party to the case, or
(b) of the court's own motion;
but no application may be made under paragraph (a) above unless there has been a material change of circumstances since the leave was given under subsection (2) above.

(6D) For the purposes of subsections (6A) and (6B) above evidence is relevant evidence if—
(a) it is evidence in chief on behalf of the party who tendered the video recording, and
(b) it relates to matter which, in the opinion of the court, is dealt with in the recording and which the court has not directed to be excluded under subsection (3) above.'

(3) This section applies where the leave concerned is given on or after the appointed day.

(4) The reference in subsection (3) to the appointed day is to such day as is appointed for the purposes of this section by the Secretary of State by order.

63. Road traffic and transport: provision of specimens

(1) In section 7(3) of the Road Traffic Act 1988 (provision of blood or urine in course of investigating whether certain road traffic offences have been committed) after paragraph (b) there shall be inserted—
'(bb) a device of the type mentioned in subsection (1)(a) above has been used at the police station but the constable who required the specimens of breath has reasonable cause to believe that the device has not produced a reliable indication of the proportion of alcohol in the breath of the person concerned, or'.

(2) In section 31(4) of the Transport and Works Act 1992 (provision of blood or urine in course of investigating whether certain offences have been committed by persons working on transport systems) the word 'or' at the end of paragraph (b) shall be omitted and after that paragraph there shall be inserted—
'(bb) a device of the type mentioned in subsection (1)(a) above has been used at the police station but the constable who required the specimens of breath has reasonable cause to believe that the device has not produced a reliable indication of the proportion of alcohol in the breath of the person concerned, or'.

(3) This section applies where it is proposed to make a requirement mentioned in section 7(3) of the 1988 Act or section 31(3) of the 1992 Act after the appointed day.

(4) The reference in subsection (3) to the appointed day is to such day as is appointed for the purposes of this section by the Secretary of State by order.

64. Checks against fingerprints etc.

(1) In section 63A of the Police and Criminal Evidence Act 1984 the following subsections shall be substituted for subsection (1) (checks against fingerprints etc.

where a person has been arrested on suspicion of being involved in a recordable offence)—
'(1) Where a person has been arrested on suspicion of being involved in a recordable offence or has been charged with such an offence or has been informed that he will be reported for such an offence, fingerprints or samples or the information derived from samples taken under any power conferred by this Part of this Act from the person may be checked against—
    (a)   other fingerprints or samples to which the person seeking to check has access and which are held by or on behalf of a police force (or police forces) falling within subsection (1A) below or are held in connection with or as a result of an investigation of an offence;
    (b)   information derived from other samples if the information is contained in records to which the person seeking to check has access and which are held as mentioned in paragraph (a) above.
    (1A)   Each of the following police forces falls within this subsection—
    (a)   a police force within the meaning given by section 62 of the Police Act 1964 (which relates to England and Wales);
    (b)   a police force within the meaning given by section 50 of the Police (Scotland) Act 1967;
    (c)   the Royal Ulster Constabulary and the Royal Ulster Constabulary Reserve;
    (d)   the States of Jersey Police Force;
    (e)   the salaried police force of the Island of Guernsey;
    (f)   the Isle of Man Constabulary.'
    (2)   This section applies where a person—
    (a)   is arrested on suspicion of being involved in a recordable offence,
    (b)   is charged with a recordable offence, or
    (c)   is informed that he will be reported for a recordable offence,
after the day on which this Act is passed.

Witness orders and summonses

65.   Abolition of witness orders
    (1)   Section 1 of the Criminal Procedure (Attendance of Witnesses) Act 1965 (examining justices to order witness to attend and give evidence before Crown Court) shall be omitted.
    (2)   In that Act the following words shall be omitted—
    (a)   in section 3(1) the words 'witness order or';
    (b)   in section 4(1) the words 'witness order or' and (where they next occur) 'order or';
    (c)   in the proviso to section 4(1) the words from 'in the case' (where they first occur) to 'witness summons';
    (d)   in section 4(2) the words 'a witness order or' and (where they next occur) 'order or'.
    (3)   In section 145 of the Magistrates' Courts Act 1980 (rules) subsection (1)(e) (which relates to witness orders) shall be omitted.
    (4)   This section shall have effect in accordance with provision made by the Secretary of State by order.

66. Summons to witness to attend Crown Court

(1)   The Criminal Procedure (Attendance of Witnesses) Act 1965 shall be amended as follows.

(2)   The following shall be substituted for section 2 (summons to witness to attend Crown Court)—

'Issue of witness summons on application

2.   Issue of witness summons on application to Crown Court

(1)   This section applies where the Crown Court is satisfied that—

(a)   a person is likely to be able to give evidence likely to be material evidence, or produce any document or thing likely to be material evidence, for the purpose of any criminal proceedings before the Crown Court, and

(b)   the person will not voluntarily attend as a witness or will not voluntarily produce the document or thing.

(2)   In such a case the Crown Court shall, subject to the following provisions of this section, issue a summons (a witness summons) directed to the person concerned and requiring him to—

(a)   attend before the Crown Court at the time and place stated in the summons, and

(b)   give the evidence or produce the document or thing.

(3)   A witness summons may only be issued under this section on an application; and the Crown Court may refuse to issue the summons if any requirement relating to the application is not fulfilled.

(4)   Where a person has been committed for trial for any offence to which the proceedings concerned relate, an application must be made as soon as is reasonably practicable after the committal.

(5)   Where the proceedings concerned have been transferred to the Crown Court, an application must be made as soon as is reasonably practicable after the transfer.

(6)   Where the proceedings concerned relate to an offence in relation to which a bill of indictment has been preferred under the authority of section 2(2)(b) of the Administration of Justice (Miscellaneous Provisions) Act 1933 (bill preferred by direction of Court of Appeal, or by direction or with consent of judge) an application must be made as soon as is reasonably practicable after the bill was preferred.

(7)   An application must be made in accordance with Crown Court rules; and different provision may be made for different cases or descriptions of case.

(8)   Crown Court rules—

(a)   may, in such cases as the rules may specify, require an application to be made by a party to the case;

(b)   may, in such cases as the rules may specify, require the service of notice of an application on the person to whom the witness summons is proposed to be directed;

(c)   may, in such cases as the rules may specify, require an application to be supported by an affidavit containing such matters as the rules may stipulate;

(d)   may, in such cases as the rules may specify, make provision for enabling the person to whom the witness summons is proposed to be directed to be present or represented at the hearing of the application for the witness summons.

(9)　Provision contained in Crown Court rules by virtue of subsection (8)(c) above may in particular require an affidavit to—

(a)　set out any charge on which the proceedings concerned are based;

(b)　specify any stipulated evidence, document or thing in such a way as to enable the directed person to identify it;

(c)　specify grounds for believing that the directed person is likely to be able to give any stipulated evidence or produce any stipulated document or thing;

(d)　specify grounds for believing that any stipulated evidence is likely to be material evidence;

(e)　specify grounds for believing that any stipulated document or thing is likely to be material evidence.

(10)　In subsection (9) above—

(a)　references to any stipulated evidence, document or thing are to any evidence, document or thing whose giving or production is proposed to be required by the witness summons;

(b)　references to the directed person are to the person to whom the witness summons is proposed to be directed.

2A.　Power to require advance production
A witness summons which is issued under section 2 above and which requires a person to produce a document or thing as mentioned in section 2(2) above may also require him to produce the document or thing—

(a)　at a place stated in the summons, and

(b)　at a time which is so stated and precedes that stated under section 2(2) above,

for inspection by the person applying for the summons.

2B.　Summons no longer needed
(1)　If—

(a)　a document or thing is produced in pursuance of a requirement imposed by a witness summons under section 2A above,

(b)　the person applying for the summons concludes that a requirement imposed by the summons under section 2(2) above is no longer needed, and

(c)　he accordingly applies to the Crown Court for a direction that the summons shall be of no further effect,

the court may direct accordingly.

(2)　An application under this section must be made in accordance with Crown Court rules; and different provision may be made for different cases or descriptions of case.

(3)　Crown Court rules may, in such cases as the rules may specify, require the effect of a direction under this section to be notified to the person to whom the summons is directed.

2C.　Application to make summons ineffective
(1)　If a witness summons issued under section 2 above is directed to a person who—

(a)　applies to the Crown Court,

(b)　satisfies the court that he was not served with notice of the application to issue the summons and that he was neither present nor represented at the hearing of the application, and

(c)   satisfies the court that he cannot give any evidence likely to be material evidence or, as the case may be, produce any document or thing likely to be material evidence,

the court may direct that the summons shall be of no effect.

(2)   For the purposes of subsection (1) above it is immaterial—

(a)   whether or not Crown Court rules require the person to be served with notice of the application to issue the summons;

(b)   whether or not Crown Court rules enable the person to be present or represented at the hearing of the application.

(3)   In subsection (l)(b) above 'served' means—

(a)   served in accordance with Crown Court rules, in a case where such rules require the person to be served with notice of the application to issue the summons;

(b)   served in such way as appears reasonable to the court to which the application is made under this section, in any other case.

(4)   The Crown Court may refuse to make a direction under this section if any requirement relating to the application under this section is not fulfilled.

(5)   An application under this section must be made in accordance with Crown Court rules; and different provision may be made for different cases or descriptions of case.

(6)   Crown Court rules may, in such cases as the rules may specify, require the service of notice of an application under this section on the person on whose application the witness summons was issued.

(7)   Crown Court rules may, in such cases as the rules may specify, require that where—

(a)   a person applying under this section can produce a particular document or thing, but

(b)   he seeks to satisfy the court that the document or thing is not likely to be material evidence,

he must arrange for the document or thing to be available at the hearing of the application.

(8)   Where a direction is made under this section that a witness summons shall be of no effect, the person on whose application the summons was issued may be ordered to pay the whole or any part of the costs of the application under this section.

(9)   Any costs payable under an order made under subsection (8) above shall be taxed by the proper officer of the court, and payment of those costs shall be enforceable in the same manner as an order for payment of costs made by the High Court in a civil case or as a sum adjudged summarily to be paid as a civil debt.

Issue of witness summons of court's own motion

2D.   Issue of witness summons of Crown Court's own motion

For the purpose of any criminal proceedings before it, the Crown Court may of its own motion issue a summons (a witness summons) directed to a person and requiring him to—

(a)   attend before the court at the time and place stated in the summons, and

(b)   give evidence, or produce any document or thing specified in the summons.

2E.   Application to make summons ineffective

(1)   If a witness summons issued under section 2D above is directed to a person who—

(a)   applies to the Crown Court, and

(b)   satisfies the court that he cannot give any evidence likely to be material evidence or, as the case may be, produce any document or thing likely to be material evidence,

the court may direct that the summons shall be of no effect.

(2)   The Crown Court may refuse to make a direction under this section if any requirement relating to the application under this section is not fulfilled.

(3)   An application under this section must be made in accordance with Crown Court rules; and different provision may be made for different cases or descriptions of case.

(4)   Crown Court rules may, in such cases as the rules may specify, require that where—

(a)   a person applying under this section can produce a particular document or thing, but

(b)   he seeks to satisfy the court that the document or thing is not likely to be material evidence,

he must arrange for the document or thing to be available at the hearing of the application.

Other provisions'.

(3)   In section 3 (punishment for disobedience to witness summons) after subsection (1) there shall be inserted—

'(1A)   Any person who without just excuse disobeys a requirement made by any court under section 2A above shall be guilty of contempt of that court and may be punished summarily by that court as if his contempt had been committed in the face of the court.'

(4)   In section 3, in subsection (2) for the words 'such disobedience' there shall be substituted 'any disobedience mentioned in subsection (1) or (1A) above'.

(5)   In section 4 (further process to secure attendance of witness) in the proviso to subsection (1) after the word 'give' there shall be inserted 'evidence likely to be'.

(6)   Schedule 1 (application for direction that witness summons shall be of no effect) shall be omitted.

(7)   This section applies in relation to any proceedings for the purpose of which no witness summons has been issued under section 2 of the 1965 Act before the appointed day.

(8)   The reference in subsection (7) to the appointed day is to such day as is appointed for the purposes of this section by the Secretary of State by order.

67.   Witness summons: securing attendance of witness

(1)   In section 4(1) of the Criminal Procedure (Attendance of Witnesses) Act 1965 (judge of High Court may issue warrant to arrest witness in respect of whom witness summons is in force) for the words 'High Court' there shall be substituted 'Crown Court'.

(2)   This section shall have effect in accordance with provision made by the Secretary of State by order.

Other miscellaneous provisions

68. Use of written statements and depositions at trial
Schedule 2 to this Act (which relates to the use at the trial of written statements and depositions admitted in evidence in committal proceedings) shall have effect.

69. Proof by written statement
(1)   In section 9 of the Criminal Justice Act 1967 (proof by written statement) in subsection (3)(a) (statement by person under 21 must give his age) for 'twenty-one' there shall be substituted 'eighteen'.

(2)   This section applies in relation to statements tendered in evidence on or after the appointed day.

(3)   The reference in subsection (2) to the appointed day is to such day as is appointed for the purposes of this section by the Secretary of State by order.

70. Indemnification of justices and justices' clerks
(1)   In section 53 of the Justices of the Peace Act 1979 (indemnification of justices and justices' clerks) the following subsection shall be inserted after subsection (1)—
'(1A)   So far as the duty mentioned in subsection (1) above relates to criminal matters, that subsection shall have effect as if—
(a)   for the word 'may' there were substituted 'shall', and
(b)   for the words following paragraph (c) there were substituted 'unless it is proved, in respect of the matters giving rise to the proceedings or claim, that he acted in bad faith'.

(2)   This section applies in relation to things done or omitted on or after the appointed day.

(3)   The reference in subsection (2) to the appointed day is to such day as is appointed for the purposes of this section by the Secretary of State by order.

71. Meaning of preliminary stage of criminal proceedings
(1)   Section 22 of the Prosecution of Offences Act 1985 (power of Secretary of State to set time limits in relation to preliminary stages of criminal proceedings) shall be amended as mentioned in subsections (2) and (3).

(2)   In subsection (11) the following shall be substituted for the definition of 'preliminary stage'—
'''preliminary stage'', in relation to any proceedings, does not include any stage after the start of the trial (within the meaning given by subsections (11A) and (11B) below);'.

(3)   The following subsections shall be inserted after subsection (11)—
'(11A)   For the purposes of this section, the start of a trial on indictment shall be taken to occur when a jury is sworn to consider the issue of guilt or fitness to plead or, if the court accepts a plea of guilty before a jury is sworn, when that plea is accepted; but this is subject to section 8 of the Criminal Justice Act 1987 and section 30 of the Criminal Procedure and Investigations Act 1996 (preparatory hearings).

(11B)   For the purposes of this section, the start of a summary trial shall be taken to occur—
(a)   when the court begins to hear evidence for the prosecution at the trial or to consider whether to exercise its power under section 37(3) of the Mental Health Act 1983 (power to make hospital order without convicting the accused), or

(b)   if the court accepts a plea of guilty without proceeding as mentioned above, when that plea is accepted.'

(4)   The Prosecution of Offences (Custody Time Limits) Regulations 1987 shall be amended as follows, but without prejudice to the power to make further regulations amending or revoking the provisions amended—

(a)   in regulation 2 (interpretation) for paragraph (3) there shall be substituted—

'(3)   In these Regulations any reference to the start of the trial shall be construed in accordance with section 22(11A) and (11B) of the 1985 Act.';

(b)   in regulation 4 (custody time limits in magistrates' courts) in paragraphs (2) and (3) for 'commencement' there shall be substituted 'start';

(c)   in regulation 5 (custody time limits in Crown Court) for 'his arraignment' in paragraphs (3)(a) and (b) and (6)(a) and (b), and for 'the accused's arraignment' in paragraph (5), there shall be substituted 'the start of the trial';

(d)   regulation 5(7) (when arraignment occurs) shall be omitted.

(5)   This section applies in relation to—

(a)   any time limit which begins to run on or after the appointed day, and

(b)   any time limit which has begun to run and has not expired before that day,

except that it does not apply in relation to proceedings for an offence for which the accused has been duly arraigned in the Crown Court before that day.

(6)   The reference in subsection (5) to the appointed day is to such day as is appointed for the purposes of this section by the Secretary of State by order.

72.   Fraud

Schedule 3 (which amends provisions relating to serious or complex fraud) shall have effect.

73.   Amendments to the Criminal Procedure (Scotland) Act 1995

(1)   The Criminal Procedure (Scotland) Act 1995 shall be amended as follows.

(2)   In section 27 (breach of bail conditions: offences) the following subsection shall be inserted after subsection (4)—

'(4A)   The fact that the subsequent offence was committed while the accused was on bail shall, unless challenged—

(a)   in the case of proceedings on indictment, by giving notice of a preliminary objection under paragraph (b) of section 72(1) of this Act or under that paragraph as applied by section 71(2) of this Act; or

(b)   in summary proceedings, by preliminary objection before his plea is recorded,

be held as admitted.'.

(3)   In subsection (1) of section 65 (prevention of delay in trials), for the words from 'shall be discharged forthwith' to the end of the subsection there shall be substituted—

'(a)   shall be discharged forthwith from any indictment as respects the offence; and

(b)   shall not at any time be proceeded against on indictment as respects the offence'.

(4)   In Schedule 9 (certificates as to proof of certain routine matters), in the entry relating to the Social Security Administration Act 1992, for 'Section 114(4)' in column 1 there shall be substituted 'Section 112(1)'.

74. Alibi

(1)   Section 11 of the Criminal Justice Act 1967 (notice of alibi) shall cease to have effect, but subject to the following provisions of this section.

(2)   Subsection (1) does not affect the application of section 11 of the Criminal Justice Act 1967 to proceedings before courts martial by virtue of section 12 of that Act.

(3)   The reference in section 12 of the Criminal Justice Act 1967 to section 11 as it applies to proceedings on indictment shall be construed as a reference to it as it would apply to proceedings on indictment apart from subsection (1) of this section.

(4)   In section 9(6) of the Criminal Justice Act 1987 (disclosure in cases involving fraud) in paragraph (a) for the words 'section 11 of the Criminal Justice Act 1967' there shall be substituted 'section 5(7) of the Criminal Procedure and Investigations Act 1996'.

(5)   This section applies in relation to alleged offences into which no criminal investigation, within the meaning given by section 1(4), has begun before the day appointed under section 1(5).

General

75. Time when alleged offence committed

(1)   Subsection (2) applies for the purposes of sections 52(3) and 54(7).

(2)   Where an offence is alleged to be committed over a period of more than one day, or at some time during a period of more than one day, it must be taken to be alleged to be committed on the last of the days in the period.

(3)   Subsection (2) applies for the purposes of section 61(1) as if 'alleged to be' (in each place) were omitted.

76. Power of magistrates' courts

In section 148(2) of the Magistrates' Courts Act 1980 (power of court to act where another may act) the reference to that Act includes a reference to this Act.

77. Orders and regulations

(1)   This section concerns the powers of the Secretary of State to make orders or regulations under this Act.

(2)   Any power to make an order or regulations may be exercised differently in relation to different areas or in relation to other different cases or descriptions of case.

(3)   Any order or regulations may include such supplementary, incidental, consequential or transitional provisions as appear to the Secretary of State to be necessary or expedient.

(4)   Any power to make an order or regulations shall be exercisable by statutory instrument.

(5)   No order under section 25 shall have effect unless approved by a resolution of each House of Parliament.

(6)   A statutory instrument containing—
    (a)   an order under section 78, or
    (b)   regulations,
shall be subject to annulment in pursuance of a resolution of either House of Parliament.

78. Application to armed forces

(1) Subject to subsection (2) and to section 74(2) and (3), nothing in this Act applies to—

(a) proceedings before a court martial constituted under the Army Act 1955, the Air Force Act 1955 or the Naval Discipline Act 1957;

(b) proceedings before a Standing Civilian Court;

(c) any investigation conducted with a view to it being ascertained whether a person should be charged with an offence under any of those Acts or whether a person charged with such an offence is guilty of it.

(2) The Secretary of State may by order—

(a) make as regards any proceedings falling within subsection (3) provision which is equivalent to the provisions contained in or made under Part I, subject to such modifications as he thinks fit and specifies in the order;

(b) make as regards any investigation falling within subsection (4) provision which is equivalent to the provisions contained in or made under Part II, subject to such modifications as he thinks fit and specifies in the order.

(3) The proceedings falling within this subsection are—

(a) proceedings before a court martial constituted under the Army Act 1955;

(b) proceedings before a court martial constituted under the Air Force Act 1955;

(c) proceedings before a court martial constituted under the Naval Discipline Act 1957;

(d) proceedings before a Standing Civilian Court.

(4) An investigation falls within this subsection if it is conducted with a view to it being ascertained whether a person should be charged with an offence under any of the Acts mentioned in subsection (3) or whether a person charged with such an offence is guilty of it.

(5) An order under this section may make provision in such way as the Secretary of State thinks fit, and may in particular apply any of the provisions concerned subject to such modifications as he thinks fit and specifies in the order.

(6) Without prejudice to the generality of section 77(3), an order under this section may include provision—

(a) repealing section 11 of the Criminal Justice Act 1967 (alibi) as it applies to proceedings before courts martial;

(b) amending or repealing any provision of section 12 of that Act or of section 74 above.

79. Extent

(1) This Act does not extend to Scotland, with the exception of—

(a) sections 37, 38, 41, 42, 59, 60, 61(3), 63, 72, 73, 74(2) and (3) and 78, this section and section 81;

(b) paragraphs 6 and 7 of Schedule 3, and paragraph 8 of that Schedule so far as it relates to paragraphs 6 and 7;

(c) paragraph 5 of Schedule 5;

(d) paragraph 12 of Schedule 5 so far as it relates to provisions amending section 11 of the Criminal Justice Act 1987.

(2) Section 73 extends only to Scotland.

(3) Parts III and VI and sections 44, 47, 65, 67, 68 and 71 do not extend to Northern Ireland.

(4)   In its application to Northern Ireland, this Act has effect subject to the modifications set out in Schedule 4.

(5)   Section 74(2) and (3) extend to any place where proceedings before courts martial may be held.

(6)   Section 78 extends as follows—

(a)   so far as it relates to proceedings, it extends to any place where such proceedings may be held;

(b)   so far as it relates to investigations, it extends to any place where such investigations may be conducted.

80.   Repeals

The provisions mentioned in Schedule 5 are repealed (or revoked) to the extent specified in column 3, but subject to any provision of that Schedule.

81.   Citation

This Act may be cited as the Criminal Procedure and Investigations Act 1996.

SCHEDULES

Section 47   SCHEDULE 1
COMMITTAL PROCEEDINGS

PART I
MAGISTRATES' COURTS ACT 1980

Introduction

1.   The Magistrates' Courts Act 1980 shall be amended as mentioned in this Part of this Schedule.

Amendments

2.—(1)   Section 4 (general nature of committal proceedings) shall be amended as follows.

(2)   The following subsection shall be substituted for subsection (3)—

'(3)   Subject to subsection (4) below, evidence tendered before examining justices shall be tendered in the presence of the accused.'

(3)   In subsection (4) for the word 'given' (in each place) there shall be substituted 'tendered'.

3.   The following sections shall be inserted after section 5—

'5A.   Evidence which is admissible

(1)   Evidence falling within subsection (2) below, and only that evidence, shall be admissible by a magistrates' court inquiring into an offence as examining justices.

(2)   Evidence falls within this subsection if it—

(a)   is tendered by or on behalf of the prosecutor, and

(b)   falls within subsection (3) below.

(3)   The following evidence falls within this subsection—

(a)   written statements complying with section 5B below;

(b)   the documents or other exhibits (if any) referred to in such statements;

(c)   depositions complying with section 5C below;

(d)   the documents or other exhibits (if any) referred to in such depositions;

(e)   statements complying with section 5D below;

(f)   documents falling within section 5E below.

(4)   In this section 'document' means anything in which information of any description is recorded.

5B.   Written statements

(1)   For the purposes of section 5A above a written statement complies with this section if—

(a)   the conditions falling within subsection (2) below are met, and

(b)   such of the conditions falling within subsection (3) below as apply are met.

(2)   The conditions falling within this subsection are that—

(a)   the statement purports to be signed by the person who made it;

(b)   the statement contains a declaration by that person to the effect that it is true to the best of his knowledge and belief and that he made the statement knowing that, if it were tendered in evidence, he would be liable to prosecution if he wilfully stated in it anything which he knew to be false or did not believe to be true;

(c)   before the statement is tendered in evidence a copy of the statement is given, by or on behalf of the prosecutor, to each of the other parties to the proceedings.

(3)   The conditions falling within this subsection are that—

(a)   if the statement is made by a person under 18 years old, it gives his age;

(b)   if it is made by a person who cannot read it, it is read to him before he signs it and is accompanied by a declaration by the person who so read the statement to the effect that it was so read;

(c)   if it refers to any other document as an exhibit, the copy given to any other party to the proceedings under subsection (2)(c) above is accompanied by a copy of that document or by such information as may be necessary to enable the party to whom it is given to inspect that document or a copy of it.

(4)   So much of any statement as is admitted in evidence by virtue of this section shall, unless the court commits the accused for trial by virtue of section 6(2) below or the court otherwise directs, be read aloud at the hearing; and where the court so directs an account shall be given orally of so much of any statement as is not read aloud.

(5)   Any document or other object referred to as an exhibit and identified in a statement admitted in evidence by virtue of this section shall be treated as if it had been produced as an exhibit and identified in court by the maker of the statement.

(6)   In this section 'document' means anything in which information of any description is recorded.

5C.   Depositions

(1)   For the purposes of section 5A above a deposition complies with this section if—

(a)   a copy of it is sent to the prosecutor under section 97A(9) below,

(b)   the condition falling within subsection (2) below is met, and

(c)   the condition falling within subsection (3) below is met, in a case where it applies.

(2)   The condition falling within this subsection is that before the magistrates' court begins to inquire into the offence concerned as examining justices a copy of

the deposition is given, by or on behalf of the prosecutor, to each of the other parties to the proceedings.

(3)   The condition falling within this subsection is that, if the deposition refers to any other document as an exhibit, the copy given to any other party to the proceedings under subsection (2) above is accompanied by a copy of that document or by such information as may be necessary to enable the party to whom it is given to inspect that document or a copy of it.

(4)   So much of any deposition as is admitted in evidence by virtue of this section shall, unless the court commits the accused for trial by virtue of section 6(2) below or the court otherwise directs, be read aloud at the hearing; and where the court so directs an account shall be given orally of so much of any deposition as is not read aloud.

(5)   Any document or other object referred to as an exhibit and identified in a deposition admitted in evidence by virtue of this section shall be treated as if it had been produced as an exhibit and identified in court by the person whose evidence is taken as the deposition.

(6)   In this section ''document'' means anything in which information of any description is recorded.

5D.   Statements

(1)   For the purposes of section 5A above a statement complies with this section if the conditions falling within subsections (2) to (4) below are met.

(2)   The condition falling within this subsection is that, before the committal proceedings begin, the prosecutor notifies the magistrates' court and each of the other parties to the proceedings that he believes—

(a)   that the statement might by virtue of section 23 or 24 of the Criminal Justice Act 1988 (statements in certain documents) be admissible as evidence if the case came to trial, and

(b)   that the statement would not be admissible as evidence otherwise than by virtue of section 23 or 24 of that Act if the case came to trial.

(3)   The condition falling within this subsection is that—

(a)   the prosecutor's belief is based on information available to him at the time he makes the notification,

(b)   he has reasonable grounds for his belief, and

(c)   he gives the reasons for his belief when he makes the notification.

(4)   The condition falling within this subsection is that when the court or a party is notified as mentioned in subsection (2) above a copy of the statement is given, by or on behalf of the prosecutor, to the court or the party concerned.

(5)   So much of any statement as is in writing and is admitted in evidence by virtue of this section shall, unless the court commits the accused for trial by virtue of section 6(2) below or the court otherwise directs, be read aloud at the hearing; and where the court so directs an account shall be given orally of so much of any statement as is not read aloud.

5E.   Other documents

(1)   The following documents fall within this section—

(a)   any document which by virtue of any enactment is evidence in proceedings before a magistrates' court inquiring into an offence as examining justices;

(b)   any document which by virtue of any enactment is admissible, or may be used, or is to be admitted or received, in or as evidence in such proceedings;

(c)   any document which by virtue of any enactment may be considered in such proceedings;

(d)   any document whose production constitutes proof in such proceedings by virtue of any enactment;

(e)   any document by the production of which evidence may be given in such proceedings by virtue of any enactment.

(2)   In subsection (1) above—

(a)   references to evidence include references to prima facie evidence;

(b)   references to any enactment include references to any provision of this Act.

(3)   So much of any document as is admitted in evidence by virtue of this section shall, unless the court commits the accused for trial by virtue of section 6(2) below or the court otherwise directs, be read aloud at the hearing; and where the court so directs an account shall be given orally of so much of any document as is not read aloud.

(4)   In this section 'document' means anything in which information of any description is recorded.

5F.   Proof by production of copy

(1)   Where a statement, deposition or document is admissible in evidence by virtue of section 5B, 5C, 5D or 5E above it may be proved by the production of—

(a)   the statement, deposition or document, or

(b)   a copy of it or the material part of it.

(2)   Subsection (1)(b) above applies whether or not the statement, deposition or document is still in existence.

(3)   It is immaterial for the purposes of this section how many removes there are between a copy and the original.

(4)   In this section 'copy', in relation to a statement, deposition or document, means anything onto which information recorded in the statement, deposition or document has been copied, by whatever means and whether directly or indirectly.'

4.   In section 6 (discharge or committal for trial) the following subsections shall be substituted for subsections (1) and (2)—

'(1)   A magistrates' court inquiring into an offence as examining justices shall on consideration of the evidence—

(a)   commit the accused for trial if it is of opinion that there is sufficient evidence to put him on trial by jury for any indictable offence;

(b)   discharge him if it is not of that opinion and he is in custody for no other cause than the offence under inquiry;

but the preceding provisions of this subsection have effect subject to the provisions of this and any other Act relating to the summary trial of indictable offences.

(2)   If a magistrates' court inquiring into an offence as examining justices is satisfied that all the evidence tendered by or on behalf of the prosecutor falls within section 5A(3) above, it may commit the accused for trial for the offence without consideration of the contents of any statements, depositions or other documents, and without consideration of any exhibits which are not documents, unless—

(a)   the accused or one of the accused has no legal representative acting for him in the case, or

(b)   a legal representative for the accused or one of the accused, as the case may be, has requested the court to consider a submission that there is insufficient evidence to put that accused on trial by jury for the offence;
and subsection (1) above shall not apply to a committal for trial under this subsection.'

5.—(1)   Section 25 (change from summary trial to committal proceedings) shall be amended as follows.

(2)   In subsections (2) and (6) for the words 'may adjourn the hearing without remanding the accused' there shall be substituted 'shall adjourn the hearing.'

(3)   The following subsection shall be inserted after subsection (7)—
    '(8)   If the court adjourns the hearing under subsection (2) or (6) above it may (if it thinks fit) do so without remanding the accused.'

6.   Section 28 (using in summary trial evidence given in committal proceedings) shall be omitted.

7.   In section 97 (summons to witness and warrant for his arrest) in subsection (1)—
    (a)   the words 'at an inquiry into an indictable offence by a magistrates' court for that commission area or' shall be omitted;
    (b)   for the words 'such a court' there shall be substituted 'a magistrates' court for that commission area'.

8.   The following section shall be inserted after section 97—

'97A.   Summons or warrant as to committal proceedings
    (1)   Subsection (2) below applies where a justice of the peace for any commission area is satisfied that—
    (a)   any person in England or Wales is likely to be able to make on behalf of the prosecutor a written statement containing material evidence, or produce on behalf of the prosecutor a document or other exhibit likely to be material evidence, for the purposes of proceedings before a magistrates' court inquiring into an offence as examining justices,
    (b)   the person will not voluntarily make the statement or produce the document or other exhibit, and
    (c)   the magistrates' court mentioned in paragraph (a) above is a court for the commission area concerned.
    (2)   In such a case the justice shall issue a summons directed to that person requiring him to attend before a justice at the time and place appointed in the summons to have his evidence taken as a deposition or to produce the document or other exhibit.
    (3)   If a justice of the peace is satisfied by evidence on oath of the matters mentioned in subsection (1) above, and also that it is probable that a summons under subsection (2) above would not procure the result required by it, the justice may instead of issuing a summons issue a warrant to arrest the person concerned and bring him before a justice at the time and place specified in the warrant.
    (4)   A summons may also be issued under subsection (2) above if the justice is satisfied that the person concerned is outside the British Islands, but no warrant may be issued under subsection (3) above unless the justice is satisfied by evidence on oath that the person concerned is in England or Wales.
    (5)   If—

(a)   a person fails to attend before a justice in answer to a summons under this section,

(b)   the justice is satisfied by evidence on oath that he is likely to be able to make a statement or produce a document or other exhibit as mentioned in subsection (1)(a) above,

(c)   it is proved on oath, or in such other manner as may be prescribed, that he has been duly served with the summons and that a reasonable sum has been paid or tendered to him for costs and expenses, and

(d)   it appears to the justice that there is no just excuse for the failure, the justice may issue a warrant to arrest him and bring him before a justice at a time and place specified in the warrant.

(6)   Where—

(a)   a summons is issued under subsection (2) above or a warrant is issued under subsection (3) or (5) above, and

(b)   the summons or warrant is issued with a view to securing that a person has his evidence taken as a deposition,

the time appointed in the summons or specified in the warrant shall be such as to enable the evidence to be taken as a deposition before a magistrates' court begins to inquire into the offence concerned as examining justices.

(7)   If any person attending or brought before a justice in pursuance of this section refuses without just excuse to have his evidence taken as a deposition, or to produce the document or other exhibit, the justice may do one or both of the following—

(a)   commit him to custody until the expiration of such period not exceeding one month as may be specified in the summons or warrant or until he sooner has his evidence taken as a deposition or produces the document or other exhibit;

(b)   impose on him a fine not exceeding £2,500.

(8)   A fine imposed under subsection (7) above shall be deemed, for the purposes of any enactment, to be a sum adjudged to be paid by a conviction.

(9)   If in pursuance of this section a person has his evidence taken as a deposition, the clerk of the justice concerned shall as soon as is reasonably practicable send a copy of the deposition to the prosecutor.

(10)   If in pursuance of this section a person produces an exhibit which is a document, the clerk of the justice concerned shall as soon as is reasonably practicable send a copy of the document to the prosecutor.

(11)   If in pursuance of this section a person produces an exhibit which is not a document, the clerk of the justice concerned shall as soon as is reasonably practicable inform the prosecutor of the fact and of the nature of the exhibit.'

9.   Section 102 (written statements before examining justices) shall be omitted.

10.—(1)   Section 103 (evidence of children in certain committal proceedings) shall be amended as follows.

(2)   The following subsection shall be substituted for subsection (1)—

'(1)   In any proceedings before a magistrates' court inquiring as examining justices into an offence to which this section applies, a statement made in writing by or taken in writing from a child shall be admissible in evidence of any matter.'

(3)   Subsections (3) and (4) (exclusion of subsection (1) and of section 28) shall be omitted.

11.   Section 105 (deposition of person dangerously ill may be given in evidence before examining justices) shall be omitted.

12.   In section 106 (false written statements tendered in evidence) in subsection (1) for 'tendered' there shall be substituted 'admitted' and for 'section 102' there shall be substituted 'section 5B'.

13.   In Schedule 3 the following shall be substituted for paragraph 2(a) (representative may make statement on behalf of corporation before examining justices)—

'(a)   make before examining justices such representations as could be made by an accused who is not a corporation;'.

PART II
OTHER PROVISIONS

Criminal Law Amendment Act 1867

14.   Sections 6 and 7 of the Criminal Law Amendment Act 1867 (statements taken under section 105 of the Magistrates' Courts Act 1980) shall be omitted.

Bankers' Books Evidence Act 1879

15.   The following shall be inserted at the end of section 4 of the Bankers' Books Evidence Act 1879—

'Where the proceedings concerned are proceedings before a magistrates' court inquiring into an offence as examining justices, this section shall have effect with the omission of the words ''orally or''.'

16.   The following shall be inserted at the end of section 5 of the Bankers' Books Evidence Act 1879—

'Where the proceedings concerned are proceedings before a magistrates' court inquiring into an offence as examining justices, this section shall have effect with the omission of the words ''either orally or''.'

Administration of Justice (Miscellaneous Provisions) Act 1933

17.   In section 2 of the Administration of Justice (Miscellaneous Provisions) Act 1933 (procedure for indictment of offenders) in proviso (i) to subsection (2) for the words 'in any examination or deposition taken before a justice in his presence' there shall be substituted 'to the magistrates' court inquiring into that offence as examining justices'.

Criminal Justice Act 1948

18.   In section 41 of the Criminal Justice Act 1948 (evidence by certificate) the following subsection shall be inserted after subsection (5)—

'(5A)   Where the proceedings mentioned in subsection (1) above are proceedings before a magistrates' court inquiring into an offence as examining justices this section shall have effect with the omission of—

(a)   subsection (4), and

(b)   in subsection (5), paragraph (b) and the word ''or'' immediately preceding it.'

Theft Act 1968

19.   In section 27 of the Theft Act 1968 (evidence on charge of theft or handling stolen goods) the following subsection shall be inserted after subsection (4)—

'(4A) Where the proceedings mentioned in subsection (4) above are proceedings before a magistrates' court inquiring into an offence as examining justices that subsection shall have effect with the omission of the words from "subject to the following conditions" to the end of the subsection.'

20. In section 28 of the Theft Act 1968 (orders for restitution) in subsection (4) for the words from 'the depositions' to the end of the subsection there shall be substituted 'and such written statements, depositions and other documents as were tendered by or on behalf of the prosecutor at any committal proceedings'.

Children and Young Persons Act 1969

21. In Schedule 5 to the Children and Young Persons Act 1969, in paragraph 55 for the words 'section 102' there shall be substituted 'section 5B'.

Criminal Justice Act 1972

22.—(1) Section 46 of the Criminal Justice Act 1972 (written statements made outside England and Wales) shall be amended as follows.

(2) In subsection (1) the following words shall be omitted—
   (a) 'Section 102 of the Magistrates' Courts Act 1980 and';
   (b) 'which respectively allow';
   (c) 'committal proceedings and in other';
   (d) 'and section 106 of the said Act of 1980';
   (e) 'which punish the making of';
   (f) '102 or';
   (g) ', as the case may be'.

(3) The following subsections shall be inserted after subsection (1)—
   '(1A) The following provisions, namely—
   (a) so much of section 5A of the Magistrates' Courts Act 1980 as relates to written statements and to documents or other exhibits referred to in them,
   (b) section 5B of that Act, and
   (c) section 106 of that Act,
shall apply where written statements are made in Scotland or Northern Ireland as well as where written statements are made in England and Wales.

   (1B) The following provisions, namely—
   (a) so much of section 5A of the Magistrates' Courts Act 1980 as relates to written statements and to documents or other exhibits referred to in them, and
   (b) section 5B of that Act,
shall (subject to subsection (1C) below) apply where written statements are made outside the United Kingdom.

   (1C) Where written statements are made outside the United Kingdom—
   (a) section 5B of the Magistrates' Courts Act 1980 shall apply with the omission of subsections (2)(b) and (3A);
   (b) paragraph 1 of Schedule 2 to the Criminal Procedure and Investigations Act 1996 (use of written statements at trial) shall not apply.'

(4) Subsection (2) shall be omitted.

Sexual Offences (Amendment) Act 1976

23.—(1) Section 3 of the Sexual Offences (Amendment) Act 1976 (application of restrictions on evidence at certain trials to committal proceedings etc.) shall be amended as follows.

(2)   The following subsection shall be substituted for subsection (1)—

'(1)   Where a magistrates' court inquires into a rape offence as examining justices, then, except with the consent of the court, no restricted matter shall be raised; and for this purpose a restricted matter is a matter as regards which evidence could not be adduced and a question could not be asked without leave in pursuance of section 2 of this Act if—

(a)   the inquiry were a trial at which a person is charged as mentioned in section 2(1) of this Act, and

(b)   each of the accused at the inquiry were charged at the trial with the offence or offences of which he is accused at the inquiry.'

(3)   In subsection (2) for the words 'evidence or question' (in each place) there shall be substituted 'matter'.

Police and Criminal Evidence Act 1984

24.   The following shall be inserted at the end of section 71 of the Police and Criminal Evidence Act 1984 (microfilm copies)—

'Where the proceedings concerned are proceedings before a magistrates' court inquiring into an offence as examining justices this section shall have effect with the omission of the words 'authenticated in such manner as the court may approve.'

25.   In section 76 of the Police and Criminal Evidence Act 1984 (confessions) the following subsection shall be inserted after subsection (8)—

'(9)   Where the proceedings mentioned in subsection (1) above are proceedings before a magistrates' court inquiring into an offence as examining justices this section shall have effect with the omission of—

(a)   in subsection (1) the words "and is not excluded by the court in pursuance of this section", and

(b)   subsections (2) to (6) and (8).'

26.   In section 78 of the Police and Criminal Evidence Act 1984 (exclusion of unfair evidence) the following subsection shall be inserted after subsection (2)—

'(3)   This section shall not apply in the case of proceedings before a magistrates' court inquiring into an offence as examining justices.'

27.   In Schedule 3 to the Police and Criminal Evidence Act 1984 (computer records) at the end of paragraph 9 there shall be inserted the words '; but the preceding provisions of this paragraph shall not apply where the court is a magistrates' court inquiring into an offence as examining justices.'

Criminal Justice Act 1988

28.   In section 23 of the Criminal Justice Act 1988 (first-hand hearsay) the following subsection shall be inserted after subsection (4)—

'(5)   This section shall not apply to proceedings before a magistrates' court inquiring into an offence as examining justices.'

29.   In section 24 of the Criminal Justice Act 1988 (business etc. documents) the following subsection shall be inserted after subsection (4)—

'(5)   This section shall not apply to proceedings before a magistrates' court inquiring into an offence as examining justices.'

30.   The following shall be inserted at the end of section 26 of the Criminal Justice Act 1988 (statements in certain documents)—

'This section shall not apply to proceedings before a magistrates' court inquiring into an offence as examining justices.'

31.   The following shall be inserted at the end of section 27 of the Criminal Justice Act 1988 (proof of statements contained in documents)—
'This section shall not apply to proceedings before a magistrates' court inquiring into an offence as examining justices.'

32.   In section 30 of the Criminal Justice Act 1988 (expert reports) the following subsection shall be inserted after subsection (4)—
'(4A)   Where the proceedings mentioned in subsection (1) above are proceedings before a magistrates' court inquiring into an offence as examining justices this section shall have effect with the omission of—
        (a)   in subsection (1) the words "whether or not the person making it attends to give oral evidence in those proceedings", and
        (b)   subsections (2) to (4).'

33.   In section 32A(10) of the Criminal Justice Act 1988 (video recordings) the words 'notwithstanding that the child witness is not called at the committal proceedings' shall be omitted.

34.   In section 40 of the Criminal Justice Act 1988 (power to join in indictment count for common assault etc.) in subsection (1) for the words from 'in an examination' to the end of the subsection there shall be substituted 'to a magistrates' court inquiring into the offence as examining justices'.

Road Traffic Offenders Act 1988

35.   In section 11 of the Road Traffic Offenders Act 1988 (evidence by certificate as to driver, user or owner) the following subsection shall be inserted after subsection (3)—
'(3A)   Where the proceedings mentioned in subsection (1) above are proceedings before a magistrates' court inquiring into an offence as examining justices this section shall have effect with the omission of—
        (a)   subsection (2), and
        (b)   in subsection (3), paragraph (b) and the word "or" immediately preceding it.'

36.   In section 13 of the Road Traffic Offenders Act 1988 (admissibility of records as evidence) the following subsection shall be inserted after subsection (6)—
'(7)   Where the proceedings mentioned in subsection (2) above are proceedings before a magistrates' court inquiring into an offence as examining justices this section shall have effect as if—
        (a)   in subsection (2) the words "to the same extent as oral evidence of that fact is admissible in those proceedings" were omitted;
        (b)   in subsection (4) the word "and" were inserted at the end of paragraph (a);
        (c)   in subsection (4), paragraphs (c) and (d) and the words "as if the accused had appeared and admitted it" were omitted.'

37.   In section 16 of the Road Traffic Offenders Act 1988 (specimens) the following subsection shall be inserted after subsection (6)—
'(6A)   Where the proceedings mentioned in section 15(1) of this Act are proceedings before a magistrates' court inquiring into an offence as examining justices this section shall have effect with the omission of subsection (4).'

38.   In section 20 of the Road Traffic Offenders Act 1988 (speeding etc.) the following subsection shall be inserted after subsection (8)—

'(8A)   Where the proceedings for an offence to which this section applies are proceedings before a magistrates' court inquiring into an offence as examining justices this section shall have effect as if in subsection (8) the words from ''and nothing'' to the end of the subsection were omitted.'

PART III
COMMENCEMENT

39.   Parts I and II of this Schedule shall have effect in accordance with provision made by the Secretary of State by order.

Section 68   SCHEDULE 2
                        STATEMENTS AND DEPOSITIONS

Statements

1.—(1)   Sub-paragraph (2) applies if—
    (a)   a written statement has been admitted in evidence in proceedings before a magistrates' court inquiring into an offence as examining justices,
    (b)   in those proceedings a person has been committed for trial,
    (c)   for the purposes of section 5A of the Magistrates' Courts Act 1980 the statement complied with section 5B of that Act prior to the committal for trial,
    (d)   the statement purports to be signed by a justice of the peace, and
    (e)   sub-paragraph (3) does not prevent sub-paragraph (2) applying.
    (2)   Where this sub-paragraph applies the statement may without further proof be read as evidence on the trial of the accused, whether for the offence for which he was committed for trial or for any other offence arising out of the same transaction or set of circumstances.
    (3)   Sub-paragraph (2) does not apply if—
    (a)   it is proved that the statement was not signed by the justice by whom it purports to have been signed,
    (b)   the court of trial at its discretion orders that sub-paragraph (2) shall not apply, or
    (c)   a party to the proceedings objects to sub-paragraph (2) applying.
    (4)   If a party to the proceedings objects to sub-paragraph (2) applying the court of trial may order that the objection shall have no effect if the court considers it to be in the interests of justice so to order.

Depositions

2.—(1)   Sub-paragraph (2) applies if—
    (a)   in pursuance of section 97A of the Magistrates' Courts Act 1980 (summons or warrant to have evidence taken as a deposition etc.) a person has had his evidence taken as a deposition for the purposes of proceedings before a magistrates' court inquiring into an offence as examining justices,
    (b)   the deposition has been admitted in evidence in those proceedings,
    (c)   in those proceedings a person has been committed for trial,
    (d)   for the purposes of section 5A of the Magistrates' Courts Act 1980 the deposition complied with section 5C of that Act prior to the committal for trial,

(e)   the deposition purports to be signed by the justice before whom it purports to have been taken, and

(f)   sub-paragraph (3) does not prevent sub-paragraph (2) applying.

(2)   Where this sub-paragraph applies the deposition may without further proof be read as evidence on the trial of the accused, whether for the offence for which he was committed for trial or for any other offence arising out of the same transaction or set of circumstances.

(3)   Sub-paragraph (2) does not apply if—

(a)   it is proved that the deposition was not signed by the justice by whom it purports to have been signed,

(b)   the court of trial at its discretion orders that sub-paragraph (2) shall not apply, or

(c)   a party to the proceedings objects to sub-paragraph (2) applying.

(4)   If a party to the proceedings objects to sub-paragraph (2) applying the court of trial may order that the objection shall have no effect if the court considers it to be in the interests of justice so to order.

Signatures

3.—(1)   A justice who signs a certificate authenticating one or more relevant statements or depositions shall be treated for the purposes of paragraphs 1 and 2 as signing the statement or deposition or (as the case may be) each of them.

(2)   For this purpose—

(a)   a relevant statement is a written statement made by a person for the purposes of proceedings before a magistrates' court inquiring into an offence as examining justices;

(b)   a relevant deposition is a deposition made in pursuance of section 97A of the Magistrates' Courts Act 1980 for the purposes of such proceedings.

Time limit for objection

4.   Without prejudice to section 84 of the Supreme Court Act 1981 (rules of court) the power to make rules under that section includes power to make provision—

(a)   requiring an objection under paragraph 1(3)(c) or 2(3)(c) to be made within a period prescribed in the rules;

(b)   allowing the court of trial at its discretion to permit such an objection to be made outside any such period.

Retrial

5.   In Schedule 2 to the Criminal Appeal Act 1968 (procedural and other provisions applicable on order for retrial) in paragraph 1 for the words from 'section 13(3)' to 'before the original trial' there shall be substituted 'paragraphs 1 and 2 of Schedule 2 to the Criminal Procedure and Investigations Act 1996 (use of written statements and depositions) shall not apply to any written statement or deposition read as evidence at the original trial'.

Repeals

6.—(1)   Section 13(3) of the Criminal Justice Act 1925 (which relates to depositions taken before examining justices and is superseded by paragraph 2 above) shall be omitted.

(2)   Section 7 of the Criminal Justice Act 1967 (which is superseded by paragraph 3 above) shall be omitted.

Commencement

7.   This Schedule shall have effect in accordance with provision made by the Secretary of State by order.

Section 72   SCHEDULE 3
                                            FRAUD

Introduction

1.   The Criminal Justice Act 1987 shall be amended as provided by this Schedule.

Preparatory hearings

2.   In section 7 (power to order preparatory hearing) subsections (3) to (5) (power to make order that could be made at the hearing) shall be omitted.

3.—(1)   Section 9 (the preparatory hearing) shall be amended as follows.

(2)   In subsection (7) (warning of possible consequence under section 10(1)) the word '(1)' shall be omitted.

(3)   In subsection (10) for the words 'at or for the purposes of a preparatory hearing' there shall be substituted 'under this section'.

4.   The following section shall be inserted after section 9—

'9A.   Orders before preparatory hearing

(1)   Subsection (2) below applies where—

(a)   a judge orders a preparatory hearing, and

(b)   he decides that any order which could be made under section 9(4) or (5) above at the hearing should be made before the hearing.

(2)   In such a case—

(a)   he may make any such order before the hearing (or at the hearing), and

(b)   subsections (4) to (10) of section 9 above shall apply accordingly.'

5.   The following section shall be substituted for section 10 (later stages of trial)—

'10.   Later stages of trial

(1)   Any party may depart from the case he disclosed in pursuance of a requirement imposed under section 9 above.

(2)   Where—

(a)   a party departs from the case he disclosed in pursuance of a requirement imposed under section 9 above, or

(b)   a party fails to comply with such a requirement,

the judge or, with the leave of the judge, any other party may make such comment as appears to the judge or the other party (as the case may be) to be appropriate and the jury may draw such inference as appears proper.

(3)   In deciding whether to give leave the judge shall have regard—

(a)   to the extent of the departure or failure, and

(b)   to whether there is any justification for it.

(4)   Except as provided by this section no part—

(a)   of a statement given under section 9(5) above, or

(b)   of any other information relating to the case for the accused or, if there is more than one, the case for any of them, which was given in pursuance of a requirement imposed under section 9 above,
may be disclosed at a stage in the trial after the jury have been sworn without the consent of the accused concerned.'

Reporting restrictions

6.   The following sections shall be substituted for section 11 (reporting restrictions)—

'11.   Restrictions on reporting
(1)   Except as provided by this section—
(a)   no written report of proceedings falling within subsection (2) below shall be published in Great Britain;
(b)   no report of proceedings falling within subsection (2) below shall be included in a relevant programme for reception in Great Britain.
(2)   The following proceedings fall within this subsection—
(a)   an application under section 6(1) above;
(b)   a preparatory hearing;
(c)   an application for leave to appeal in relation to such a hearing;
(d)   an appeal in relation to such a hearing.
(3)   The judge dealing with an application under section 6(1) above may order that subsection (1) above shall not apply, or shall not apply to a specified extent, to a report of the application.
(4)   The judge dealing with a preparatory hearing may order that subsection (1) above shall not apply, or shall not apply to a specified extent, to a report of—
(a)   the preparatory hearing, or
(b)   an application to the judge for leave to appeal to the Court of Appeal under section 9(11) above in relation to the preparatory hearing.
(5)   The Court of Appeal may order that subsection (1) above shall not apply, or shall not apply to a specified extent, to a report of—
(a)   an appeal to the Court of Appeal under section 9(11) above in relation to a preparatory hearing,
(b)   an application to that Court for leave to appeal to it under section 9(11) above in relation to a preparatory hearing, or
(c)   an application to that Court for leave to appeal to the House of Lords under Part II of the Criminal Appeal Act 1968 in relation to a preparatory hearing.
(6)   The House of Lords may order that subsection (1) above shall not apply, or shall not apply to a specified extent, to a report of—
(a)   an appeal to that House under Part II of the Criminal Appeal Act 1968 in relation to a preparatory hearing, or
(b)   an application to that House for leave to appeal to it under Part II of the Criminal Appeal Act 1968 in relation to a preparatory hearing.
(7)   Where there is only one accused and he objects to the making of an order under subsection (3), (4), (5) or (6) above the judge or the Court of Appeal or the House of Lords shall make the order if (and only if) satisfied after hearing the representations of the accused that it is in the interests of justice to do so; and if the order is made it shall not apply to the extent that a report deals with any such objection or representations.

(8)   Where there are two or more accused and one or more of them objects to the making of an order under subsection (3), (4), (5) or (6) above the judge or the Court of Appeal or the House of Lords shall make the order if (and only if) satisfied after hearing the representations of each of the accused that it is in the interests of justice to do so; and if the order is made it shall not apply to the extent that a report deals with any such objection or representations.

(9)   Subsection (1) above does not apply to—

(a)   the publication of a report of an application under section 6(1) above, or

(b)   the inclusion in a relevant programme of a report of an application under section 6(1) above,

where the application is successful.

(10)   Where—

(a)   two or more persons are jointly charged, and

(b)   applications under section 6(1) above are made by more than one of them,

subsection (9) above shall have effect as if for the words "the application is" there were substituted "all the applications are".

(11)   Subsection (1) above does not apply to—

(a)   the publication of a report of an unsuccessful application made under section 6(1) above,

(b)   the publication of a report of a preparatory hearing,

(c)   the publication of a report of an appeal in relation to a preparatory hearing or of an application for leave to appeal in relation to such a hearing,

(d)   the inclusion in a relevant programme of a report of an unsuccessful application made under section 6(1) above,

(e)   the inclusion in a relevant programme of a report of a preparatory hearing, or

(f)   the inclusion in a relevant programme of a report of an appeal in relation to a preparatory hearing or of an application for leave to appeal in relation to such a hearing,

at the conclusion of the trial of the accused or of the last of the accused to be tried.

(12)   Subsection (1) above does not apply to a report which contains only one or more of the following matters—

(a)   the identity of the court and the name of the judge;

(b)   the names, ages, home addresses and occupations of the accused and witnesses;

(c)   any relevant business information;

(d)   the offence or offences, or a summary of them, with which the accused is or are charged;

(e)   the names of counsel and solicitors in the proceedings;

(f)   where the proceedings are adjourned, the date and place to which they are adjourned;

(g)   any arrangements as to bail;

(h)   whether legal aid was granted to the accused or any of the accused.

(13)   The addresses that may be published or included in a relevant programme under subsection (12) above are addresses—

(a)   at any relevant time, and

(b)   at the time of their publication or inclusion in a relevant programme;

and "relevant time" here means a time when events giving rise to the charges to which the proceedings relate occurred.

(14)   The following is relevant business information for the purposes of subsection (12) above—

(a)   any address used by the accused for carrying on a business on his own account;

(b)   the name of any business which he was carrying on on his own account at any relevant time;

(c)   the name of any firm in which he was a partner at any relevant time or by which he was engaged at any such time;

(d)   the address of any such firm;

(e)   the name of any company of which he was a director at any relevant time or by which he was otherwise engaged at any such time;

(f)   the address of the registered or principal office of any such company;

(g)   any working address of the accused in his capacity as a person engaged by any such company;

and here "engaged" means engaged under a contract of service or a contract for services, and "relevant time" has the same meaning as in subsection (13) above.

(15) Nothing in this section affects any prohibition or restriction imposed by virtue of any other enactment on a publication or on matter included in a programme.

(16) In this section—

(a)   'publish', in relation to a report, means publish the report, either by itself or as part of a newspaper or periodical, for distribution to the public;

(b)   expressions cognate with "publish" shall be construed accordingly;

(c)   "relevant programme" means a programme included in a programme service, within the meaning of the Broadcasting Act 1990.

11A.   Offences in connection with reporting

(1)   If a report is published or included in a relevant programme in contravention of section 11 above each of the following persons is guilty of an offence—

(a)   in the case of a publication of a written report as part of a newspaper or periodical, any proprietor, editor or publisher of the newspaper or periodical;

(b)   in the case of a publication of a written report otherwise than as part of a newspaper or periodical, the person who publishes it;

(c)   in the case of the inclusion of a report in a relevant programme, any body corporate which is engaged in providing the service in which the programme is included and any person having functions in relation to the programme corresponding to those of an editor of a newspaper.

(2)   A person guilty of an offence under this section is liable on summary conviction to a fine of an amount not exceeding level 5 on the standard scale.

(3)   Proceedings for an offence under this section shall not be instituted in England and Wales otherwise than by or with the consent of the Attorney General.

(4)   Subsection (16) of section 11 above applies for the purposes of this section as it applies for the purposes of that.'

7.   In the list in section 17(2) (provisions extending to Scotland) after the entry relating to section 11 there shall be inserted 'section 11A;'.

General

8.—(1)   This Schedule applies in relation to an offence if—

(a) on or after the appointed day the accused is committed for trial for the offence,

(b) proceedings for the trial on the charge concerned are transferred to the Crown Court on or after the appointed day, or

(c) a bill of indictment relating to the offence is preferred on or after the appointed day under the authority of section 2(2)(b) of the Administration of Justice (Miscellaneous Provisions) Act 1933 (bill preferred by direction of Court of Appeal, or by direction or with consent of a judge).

(2) References in this paragraph to the appointed day are to such day as is appointed for the purposes of this Schedule by the Secretary of State by order.

Section 79   SCHEDULE 4
              MODIFICATIONS FOR NORTHERN IRELAND

General

1. In their application to Northern Ireland the provisions of this Act mentioned in the following paragraphs of this Schedule shall have effect subject to the modifications set out in those paragraphs.

2. Where a provision of this Act which extends to Northern Ireland confers power on the Secretary of State to prepare a code of practice, that power may be so exercised as to prepare a code of practice having effect only in Northern Ireland and containing provisions different to those contained in any code of practice prepared under that provision and having effect in England and Wales.

3. In any provision of this Act which extends to Northern Ireland—

(a) reference to an enactment includes reference to an enactment comprised in Northern Ireland legislation;

(b) reference to a police officer is a reference to a member of the Royal Ulster Constabulary or of the Royal Ulster Constabulary Reserve.

Part I of this Act

4. In section 1 for subsections (1) and (2) substitute—

'(1) This Part applies where a person is charged with an offence, the court proceeds to deal summarily with the charge and that person pleads not guilty.

(2) This Part also applies where—

(a) a person is charged with an indictable offence and he is committed for trial for the offence concerned,

(b) a person is charged with an indictable offence and proceedings for the trial of the person on the charge concerned are transferred to the Crown Court by virtue of a notice of transfer given under Article 3 of the Criminal Justice (Serious Fraud) (Northern Ireland) Order 1988 (serious or complex fraud),

(c) a person is charged with an indictable offence and proceedings for the trial of the person on the charge concerned are transferred to the Crown Court by virtue of a notice of transfer given under Article 4 of the Children's Evidence (Northern Ireland) Order 1995 (certain cases involving children),

(d) a count charging a person with a summary offence is included in an indictment under the authority of Article 193A of the Road Traffic (Northern Ireland) Order 1981 (offences relating to drink or drugs), or

(e) an indictment charging a person with an indictable offence is presented under the authority of section 2(2)(c), (d), (e) or (f) of the Grand Jury (Abolition) Act (Northern Ireland) 1969.

(2A) In subsection (2)—

"indictable offence" means an offence which is triable on indictment, whether it is exclusively so triable or not;

"summary offence" has the same meaning as in Article 193A of the Road Traffic (Northern Ireland) Order 1981.'

5.—(1) In section 5(2) for 'section 5(9) of the Criminal Justice Act 1987' substitute 'Article 4(7) of the Criminal Justice (Serious Fraud) (Northern Ireland) Order 1988'.

(2) In section 5(3) for 'paragraph 4 of Schedule 6 to the Criminal Justice Act 1991' substitute 'paragraph 3 of Schedule 1 to the Children's Evidence (Northern Ireland) Order 1995'.

6. In section 13(1) for 'the bill of indictment is preferred' substitute 'the indictment is presented'.

7. After section 14 there shall be inserted—

'14A. Public interest: review for scheduled offences

(1) This section applies where this Part applies by virtue of section 1(2) and the offence charged is a scheduled offence within the meaning of section 1 of the Northern Ireland (Emergency Provisions) Act 1996.

(2) At any time—

(a) after a court makes an order under section 3(6), 7(5), 8(5) or 9(8), and

(b) before the accused is acquitted or convicted or the prosecutor decides not to proceed with the case concerned,

the accused may apply to the court for a review of the question whether it is still not in the public interest to disclose material affected by its order.

(3) In such a case the court must review that question, and if it concludes that it is in the public interest to disclose material to any extent—

(a) it shall so order; and

(b) it shall take such steps as are reasonable to inform the prosecutor of its order.

(4) Where the prosecutor is informed of an order made under subsection (3) he must act accordingly having regard to the provisions of this Part (unless he decides not to proceed with the case concerned).'

8. In section 15(1) at the end add 'and section 14A does not apply'.

9. In section 16 after '14(2)' insert ', 14A(2)' and after '14(3)' insert ', 14A(3)'.

10. In section 17(1)(a) after '14' insert ', 14A'.

11. In section 18 at the end add—

'(11) In section 13 (legal aid) of the Contempt of Court Act 1981 (as set out in Schedule 4 to that Act) in subsection (1)(a) after sub-paragraph (ii) there shall be inserted—

"(iia) by a magistrates' court or the Crown Court under section 18 of the Criminal Procedure and Investigations Act 1996; or".'

12.—(1) In section 19(1) for the words from the beginning to 'includes' substitute—

'Without prejudice to the generality of—

(a) Article 13 of the Magistrates' Courts (Northern Ireland) Order 1981 (magistrates' courts rules), and

(b) section 52 of the Judicature (Northern Ireland) Act 1978 (Crown Court rules),

the power to make rules under each of those provisions includes'.

(2) In section 19(2)(b) after '14(2)' insert ', 14A(2)'.

(3) In section 19(2)(d) after '14(3)' insert ', 14A(3)'.

(4) In section 19 omit subsection (3).

13.—(1) In section 20(2) for 'section 9 of the Criminal Justice Act 1987 or section 31 of this Act' substitute 'Article 8 of the Criminal Justice (Serious Fraud) (Northern Ireland) Order 1988'.

(2) In section 20(3) for the words from the beginning to 'that section' substitute 'Without prejudice to the generality of Article 13 of the Magistrates' Courts (Northern Ireland) Order 1981 (magistrates' courts rules) the power to make rules under that Article'.

(3) In section 20(5) for paragraph (b) substitute—

'(b) "enactment" includes a statutory instrument within the meaning of section 1(d) of the Interpretation Act (Northern Ireland) 1954.'

14. In section 21(3) for paragraph (e) substitute—

'(e) the indictment is presented (where this Part applies by virtue of section 1(2)(e))'.

Part IV of this Act

15. In section 39 for subsections (2) and (3) substitute—

'(2) For the purposes of this Part a hearing is also a pre-trial hearing if—

(a) it relates to a trial on indictment to be held in pursuance of an indictment presented under the authority of section 2(2)(c), (d), (e) or (f) of the Grand Jury (Abolition) Act (Northern Ireland) 1969, and

(b) it takes place after the indictment has been presented and before the start of the trial.

(3) For the purposes of this section the start of a trial on indictment occurs—

(a) in the case of a trial to which section 11 of the Northern Ireland (Emergency Provisions) Act 1996 applies (trial by court without a jury), at the opening of the case for the prosecution or, if the court accepts a plea of guilty before that time, when that plea is accepted,

(b) in any other case, when a jury is sworn to consider the issue of guilt or fitness to be tried or, if the court accepts a plea of guilty before a jury is sworn, when that plea is accepted,

but this is subject to Article 7 of the Criminal Justice (Serious Fraud) (Northern Ireland) Order 1988.'

16. In section 41(1) for 'Great Britain' where it twice occurs substitute 'Northern Ireland'.

17. In section 42(3) omit 'in England and Wales', and after 'Attorney General' insert 'for Northern Ireland'.

Part V of this Act

18. In section 45 for subsections (1) to (8) substitute—

'(1)   Article 4 of the Criminal Justice (Serious Fraud)(Northern Ireland) Order 1988 (notices of transfer in cases of serious or complex fraud) shall be amended as mentioned in subsections (2) and (3).

(2)   In paragraph (7)(a) (regulations) for the words 'a statement of the evidence' there shall be substituted 'copies of the documents containing the evidence (including oral evidence)'.

(3)   The following paragraph shall be inserted after paragraph (7)—

'(7A)   Regulations under paragraph (7)(a) may provide that there shall be no requirement for copies of documents to accompany the copy of the notice of transfer if they are referred to, in documents sent with the notice of transfer, as having already been supplied.'

(4)   In Schedule 1 to the Children's Evidence (Northern Ireland) Order 1995 (notices of transfer in certain cases involving children) paragraph 3 (regulations) shall be amended as mentioned in subsections (5) and (6).

(5)   In sub-paragraph (1)(a) for the words 'a statement of the evidence' there shall be substituted 'copies of the documents containing the evidence (including oral evidence)'.

(6)   The following sub-paragraph shall be inserted after sub-paragraph (1)—

'(1A)   Regulations under sub-paragraph (1)(a) may provide that there shall be no requirement for copies of documents to accompany the copy of the notice of transfer if they are referred to, in documents sent with the notice of transfer, as having already been supplied.'

(7)   In paragraph 5 of Schedule 1 to the 1995 Order (reporting restrictions) in sub-paragraph (8) for the words 'sub-paragraphs (5) and (6)' there shall be substituted 'sub-paragraphs (5) and (7)'.

(8)   This section applies where a notice of transfer is given under Article 3 of the 1988 Order or Article 4 of the 1995 Order (as the case may be) on or after the appointed day'.

19.   In section 46 for subsections (1) and (2) substitute—

'(1)   Part II of the Schedule to the War Crimes Act 1991 and section 1(4) of that Act so far as relating thereto (transfer procedure in Northern Ireland in cases of war crimes) shall cease to have effect.

(2)   In Article 29(2) of the Legal Aid, Advice and Assistance (Northern Ireland) Order 1981 (free legal aid in Crown Court) sub-paragraph (d) (which relates to a notice of transfer under Part II of the Schedule to the War Crimes Act 1991) shall cease to have effect.'

Part VII of this Act

20.   In section 54(6) omit paragraph (b) and in paragraph (c) for 'section 1 of the Perjury Act 1911' substitute 'Article 3 of the Perjury (Northern Ireland) Order 1979'.

21.   In section 56(2) for paragraphs (a) to (c) substitute—

'(a)   section 5 of the Criminal Law Amendment Act 1885 (no prosecution for offence under that section more than 12 months after the commission of the offence);

(b)   Article 19(1)(a) of the Magistrates' Courts (Northern Ireland) Order 1981 (magistrates' court not to hear and determine certain complaints unless made within 6 months of time when offence committed);

(c)   an enactment that imposes a time limit only in certain circumstances (as where proceedings are not instituted by or with the consent of the Director of Public Prosecutions for Northern Ireland).'

22.   In section 57 omit subsection (1).

23.—(1)   In section 58(1) omit paragraph (b) and the word 'or' immediately before it.

(2)   In section 58(9) omit paragraph (b).

24.   In section 59(1) for 'Great Britain' where it twice occurs substitute 'Northern Ireland'.

25.   In section 62 for subsections (1) and (2) substitute—

'(1)   In Article 81 of the Police and Criminal Evidence (Northern Ireland) Order 1989 (evidence through television links) the following paragraphs shall be inserted after paragraph (3)—

"(3A)   Where the court gives leave under paragraph (2) for a witness falling within paragraph (1)(b)(ii) to give evidence through a live television link, then, subject to paragraph (3B), the witness concerned may not give evidence otherwise than through a live television link.

(3B)   In a case falling within paragraph (3A) the court may give permission for the witness to give evidence otherwise than through a live television link if it appears to the court to be in the interests of justice to give such permission.

(3C)   Permission may be given under paragraph (3B)—
(a)   on an application by a party to the case, or
(b)   of the court's own motion;
but no application may be made under sub-paragraph (a) unless there has been a material change of circumstances since the leave was given under paragraph (2)."

(2)   In Article 81A of the Police and Criminal Evidence (Northern Ireland) Order 1989 (video recordings of testimony from child witnesses) the following paragraphs shall be inserted after paragraph (6)—

"(6A)   Where the court gives leave under paragraph (2) the child witness shall not give relevant evidence (within the meaning given by paragraph (6D)) otherwise than by means of the video recording; but this is subject to paragraph (6B).

(6B)   In a case falling within paragraph (6A) the court may give permission for the child witness to give relevant evidence (within the meaning given by paragraph (6D)) otherwise than by means of the video recording if it appears to the court to be in the interests of justice to give such permission.

(6C)   Permission may be given under paragraph (6B)—
(a)   on an application by a party to the case, or
(b)   of the court's own motion;
but no application may be made under sub-paragraph (a) unless there has been a material change of circumstances since the leave was given under paragraph (2).

(6D)   For the purposes of paragraphs (6A) and (6B) evidence is relevant evidence if—
(a)   it is evidence in chief on behalf of the party who tendered the video recording, and

(b)   it relates to matter which, in the opinion of the court, is dealt with in the recording and which the court has not directed to be excluded under paragraph (3).''.'

26.   For section 63 substitute—

'63.   Road traffic: provision of specimens

(1)   In Article 18(4) of the Road Traffic (Northern Ireland) Order 1995 (provision of blood or urine in course of investigating whether certain road traffic offences have been committed) after sub-paragraph (b) there shall be inserted—

''(bb)   a device of the type mentioned in paragraph (1)(a) has been used in the circumstances described in paragraph (2) but the constable who required the specimens of breath has reasonable cause to believe that the device has not produced a reliable indication of the proportion of alcohol in the breath of the person concerned, or''.

(2)   This section applies where it is proposed to make a requirement mentioned in Article 18(4) of the 1995 Order after the appointed day.

(3)   The reference in subsection (2) to the appointed day is to such day as is appointed for the purposes of this section by the Department of the Environment for Northern Ireland by order.

(4)   The power of the Department of the Environment for Northern Ireland to make an order under subsection (3) shall be exercisable by statutory rule for the purposes of the Statutory Rules (Northern Ireland) Order 1979.'

27.   In section 64 for subsection (1) substitute—

'(1)   In Article 63A of the Police and Criminal Evidence (Northern Ireland) Order 1989 the following paragraphs shall be substituted for paragraph (1) (checks against fingerprints etc. where a person has been arrested on suspicion of being involved in a recordable offence)—

''(1)   Where a person has been arrested on suspicion of being involved in a recordable offence or has been charged with such an offence or has been informed that he will be reported for such an offence, fingerprints or samples or the information derived from samples taken under any power conferred by this Part from the person may be checked against—

(a)   other fingerprints or samples to which the person seeking to check has access and which are held by or on behalf of a police force (or police forces) falling within paragraph (1A) or are held in connection with or as the result of an investigation of an offence;

(b)   information derived from other samples if the information is contained in records to which the person seeking to check has access and which are held as mentioned in sub-paragraph (a).

(1A)   Each of the following police forces falls within this paragraph—

(a)   the Royal Ulster Constabulary and the Royal Ulster Constabulary Reserve;

(b)   a police force within the meaning given by section 62 of the Police Act 1964;

(c)   a police force within the meaning given by section 50 of the Police (Scotland) Act 1967;

(d)   the States of Jersey Police Force;

(e)   the salaried police force of the Island of Guernsey;

(f)   the Isle of Man Constabulary.''.'

28.   For section 66 substitute—

'66.—(1)   After section 51 of the Judicature (Northern Ireland) Act 1978 there shall be inserted—

"51A.   Issue of witness summons on application to Crown Court

(1)   This section applies where the Crown Court is satisfied that—

(a)   a person is likely to be able to give evidence likely to be material evidence, or produce any document or thing likely to be material evidence, for the purpose of any criminal proceedings before the Crown Court, and

(b)   the person will not voluntarily attend as a witness or will not voluntarily produce the document or thing.

(2)   In such a case the Crown Court shall, subject to the following provisions of this section, issue a summons (a witness summons) directed to the person concerned and requiring him to—

(a)   attend before the Crown Court at the time and place stated in the summons, and

(b)   give the evidence or produce the document or thing.

(3)   A witness summons may only be issued under this section on an application; and the Crown Court may refuse to issue the summons if any requirement relating to the application is not fulfilled.

(4)   Where a person has been committed for trial for any offence to which the proceedings concerned relate, an application must be made as soon as is reasonably practicable after the committal.

(5)   Where the proceedings concerned have been transferred to the Crown Court, an application must be made as soon as is reasonably practicable after the transfer.

(6)   Where the proceedings concerned relate to an offence in relation to which an indictment has been presented under the authority of section 2(2)(c), (d), (e) or (f) of the Grand Jury (Abolition) Act (Northern Ireland) 1969, an application must be made as soon as is reasonably practicable after the indictment is presented.

(7)   An application must be made in accordance with Crown Court rules; and different provision may be made for different cases or descriptions of case.

(8)   Crown Court rules—

(a)   may, in such cases as the rules may specify, require an application to be made by a party to the case;

(b)   may, in such cases as the rules may specify, require the service of notice of an application on the person to whom the witness summons is proposed to be directed;

(c)   may, in such cases as the rules may specify, require an application to be supported by an affidavit containing such matters as the rules may stipulate;

(d)   may, in such cases as the rules may specify, make provision for enabling the person to whom the witness summons is proposed to be directed to be present or represented at the hearing of the application for the witness summons.

(9)   Provision contained in Crown Court rules by virtue of subsection (8)(c) may in particular require an affidavit to—

(a)   set out any charge on which the proceedings concerned are based;

(b)   specify any stipulated evidence, document or thing in such a way as to enable the directed person to identify it;

(c)   specify grounds for believing that the directed person is likely to be able to give any stipulated evidence or produce any stipulated document or thing;

(d)   specify grounds for believing that any stipulated evidence is likely to be material evidence;

(e)   specify grounds for believing that any stipulated document or thing is likely to be material evidence.

(10)   In subsection (9)—

(a)   references to any stipulated evidence, document or thing are to any evidence, document or thing whose giving or production is proposed to be required by the witness summons;

(b)   references to the directed person are to the person to whom the witness summons is proposed to be directed.

51B.   Power to require advance production

A witness summons which is issued under section 51A and which requires a person to produce a document or thing as mentioned in section 51A(2) may also require him to produce the document or thing—

(a)   at a place stated in the summons, and

(b)   at a time which is so stated and precedes that stated under section 51A(2),

for inspection by the person applying for the summons.

51C.   Summons no longer needed

(1)   If—   `

(a)   a document or thing is produced in pursuance of a requirement imposed by a witness summons under section 51B,

(b)   the person applying for the summons concludes that a requirement imposed by the summons under section 51A(2) is no longer needed, and

(c)   he accordingly applies to the Crown Court for a direction that the summons shall be of no further effect,

the court may direct accordingly.

(2)   An application under this section must be made in accordance with Crown Court rules; and different provision may be made for different cases or descriptions of case.

(3)   Crown Court rules may, in such cases as the rules may specify, require the effect of a direction under this section to be notified to the person to whom the summons is directed.

51D.   Application to make summons ineffective

(1)   If a witness summons issued under section 51A is directed to a person who—

(a)   applies to the Crown Court,

(b)   satisfies the court that he was not served with notice of the application to issue the summons and that he was neither present nor represented at the hearing of the application, and

(c)   satisfies the court that he cannot give any evidence likely to be material evidence or, as the case may be, produce any document or thing likely to be material evidence,
the court may direct that the summons shall be of no effect.

(2)   For the purposes of subsection (1) it is immaterial—

(a)   whether or not Crown Court rules require the person to be served with notice of the application to issue the summons;

(b)   whether or not Crown Court rules enable the person to be present or represented at the hearing of the application.

(3)   In subsection (1)(b) "served" means—

(a)   served in accordance with Crown Court rules, in a case where such rules require the person to be served with notice of the application to issue the summons;

(b)   served in such way as appears reasonable to the Crown Court, in any other case.

(4)   The Crown Court may refuse to make a direction under this section if any requirement relating to the application under this section is not fulfilled.

(5)   An application under this section must be made in accordance with Crown Court rules; and different provision may be made for different cases or descriptions of case.

(6)   Crown Court rules may, in such cases as the rules may specify, require the service of notice of an application under this section on the person on whose application the witness summons was issued.

(7)   Crown Court rules may, in such cases as the rules may specify, require that where—

(a)   a person applying under this section can produce a particular document or thing, but

(b)   he seeks to satisfy the court that the document or thing is not likely to be material evidence,
he must arrange for the document or thing to be available at the hearing of the application.

(8)   Where a direction is made under this section that a witness summons shall be of no effect, the person on whose application the summons was issued may be ordered to pay the whole or any part of the costs of the application under this section.

(9)   Any costs payable under an order made under subsection (8) shall be taxed by the Master (Taxing Office), and payment of those costs shall be enforceable in the same manner as an order for payment of costs made by the High Court in a civil case or as a sum adjudged summarily to be paid as a civil debt.

51E.   Issue of witness summons of Crown Court's own motion

For the purpose of any criminal proceedings before it, the Crown Court may of its own motion issue a summons (a witness summons) directed to a person and requiring him to—

(a)   attend before the court at the time and place stated in the summons; and

(b)   give evidence or produce any document or thing specified in the summons.

51F. Application to make summons ineffective

(1)   If a witness summons issued under section 51E is directed to a person who—

(a)   applies to the Crown Court, and

(b)   satisfies the court that he cannot give any evidence likely to be material evidence or, as the case may be, produce any document or thing likely to be material evidence, the court may direct that the summons shall be of no effect.

(2)   The Crown Court may refuse to make a direction under this section if any requirement relating to the application under this section is not fulfilled.

(3)   An application under this section must be made in accordance with Crown Court rules; and different provision may be made for different cases or descriptions of case.

(4)   Crown Court rules may, in such cases as the rules may specify, require that where—

(a)   a person applying under this section can produce a particular document or thing, but

(b)   he seeks to satisfy the court that the document or thing is not likely to be material evidence,

he must arrange for the document or thing to be available at the hearing of the application.

51G.   Punishment for disobedience to witness summons

(1)   Any person who without just excuse—

(a)   disobeys a witness summons requiring him to attend before the Crown Court; or

(b)   disobeys a requirement made by the Crown Court under section 51B,

shall be guilty of contempt of that court and may be punished summarily by that court as if his contempt were in the face of the court.

(2)   A person shall not be committed to prison by reason of any disobedience mentioned in subsection (1) for a period exceeding three months.

51H.   Further process to secure attendance of witnesses

(1)   If the Crown Court is satisfied by evidence on oath that—

(a)   a witness in respect of whom a witness summons is in force is unlikely to comply with the summons; and

(b)   the witness is likely to be able to give evidence likely to be material evidence or produce any document or thing likely to be material evidence in the proceedings,

the Crown Court may issue a warrant to arrest the witness and bring him before the court.

(2)   Where a witness who is required to attend before the Crown Court by virtue of a witness summons fails to attend in compliance with the summons, the Crown Court may—

(a)   in any case, cause to be served on him a notice requiring him to attend the court forthwith or at such time as may be specified in the notice;

(b)   if the court is satisfied that there are reasonable grounds for believing that he has failed to attend without just excuse, or if he has failed to comply with a notice under paragraph (a), issue a warrant to arrest him and bring him before the court.

(3) A witness brought before the Crown Court in pursuance of a warrant under this section may be remanded by that court in custody or on bail (with or without sureties) until such time as the court may appoint for receiving his evidence or dealing with him under section 51G.

(4) Where a witness attends the Crown Court in pursuance of a notice under this section, the court may direct that the notice shall have effect as if it required him to attend at any later time appointed by the court for receiving his evidence or dealing with him under section 51G.'

(2) No subpoena ad testificandum or subpoena duces tecum shall issue after the appointed day in respect of any criminal proceedings for the purposes of which—

(a) a witness summons may be issued under section 51A of the Judicature (Northern Ireland) Act 1978; or

(b) a summons may be issued under Article 118 of the Magistrates' Courts (Northern Ireland) Order 1981 (process for attendance of witnesses in magistrates' courts).

(3) In section 47(4) of the Judicature (Northern Ireland) Act 1978 after the words "Subject to" there shall be inserted the words "section 66(2) of the Criminal Procedure and Investigations Act 1996 (subpoenas not to issue in certain criminal cases) and to".

(4) This section applies in relation to any proceedings for the purposes of which no summons requiring the attendance of a witness has been issued before the appointed day.

(5) The references in subsections (2) and (4) to the appointed day are to such day as is appointed for the purposes of this section by the Secretary of State by order.'

29. In section 69(1) for 'section 9 of the Criminal Justice Act 1967' substitute 'section 1 of the Criminal Justice (Miscellaneous Provisions) Act (Northern Ireland) 1968' and for 'subsection (3)(a)' substitute 'subsection (4)(a)'.

30. In section 70 for subsection (1) substitute—

'(1) In Article 10 of the Magistrates' Courts (Northern Ireland) Order 1981—

(a) in paragraph (1) (power of Lord Chancellor to defray expenses in connection with proceedings) after the words "justice or clerk" (where they first occur) there shall be inserted "in relation to any matter other than a criminal matter", and

(b) after paragraph (1) there shall be inserted—

"(1A) The Lord Chancellor shall defray any expenses reasonably incurred by a resident magistrate or other justice of the peace or by a clerk of petty sessions in, or in connection with, any proceedings or claim brought as a result of the execution, or purported execution, of the office of that magistrate, justice or clerk in relation to any criminal matter, unless it is proved, in respect of the matters giving rise to the proceedings or claim, that he acted in bad faith.".'

31.—(1) In section 74 for subsection (1) substitute—

'(1) The Evidence of Alibi Act (Northern Ireland) 1972 shall cease to have effect.'

(2) In section 74 omit subsections (2) and (3).

(3)   In section 74 for subsection (4) substitute—

'(4)   In Article 8(6) of the Criminal Justice (Serious Fraud) (Northern Ireland) Order 1988 (disclosure in cases involving fraud) in sub-paragraph (a) for the words "section 1 of the Evidence of Alibi Act (Northern Ireland) 1972" there shall be substituted the words "section 5(7) of the Criminal Procedure and Investigations Act 1996".'

32.   In section 75(1) for 'sections 52(3) and 54(7)' substitute 'section 54(7)'.

33.   For section 76 substitute—

'76.   Power of magistrates' courts
Anything authorised or required by this Act to be done by, to or before the magistrates' court by, to or before which any other thing was done, or is to be done, may be done by, to or before any magistrates' court acting for the same county court division as that court.'

34.   In section 80 omit '(or revoked)'.

35.   For Schedule 3 substitute—

'SCHEDULE 3
FRAUD

Introduction

1.   The Criminal Justice (Serious Fraud) (Northern Ireland) Order 1988 shall be amended as provided by this Schedule.

Notice of transfer

2.   In Article 3 (transfer of certain fraud cases to the Crown Court) in paragraph (1)(b)(ii) for the words "seriousness and complexity" there shall be substituted the words "seriousness or complexity".

Preparatory hearings

3.—(1)   Article 6 (power to order preparatory hearing) shall be amended as follows.

(2)   In paragraph (1) for the words "seriousness and complexity" there shall be substituted the words "seriousness or complexity".

(3)   Paragraphs (3) to (5) (power to make order that could be made at the hearing) shall be omitted.

4.—(1)   Article 8 (the preparatory hearing) shall be amended as follows.

(2)   In paragraph (7) (warning of possible consequence under Article 9(1)) the word "(1)" shall be omitted.

(3)   In paragraph (10) for the words "at or for the purposes of a preparatory hearing" there shall be substituted "under this Article".

5.   The following Article shall be inserted after Article 8—

"Orders before preparatory hearing

8A.—(1)   Paragraph (2) applies where—
    (a)   a judge orders a preparatory hearing, and
    (b)   he decides that any order which could be made under Article 8(4) or (5) at the hearing should be made before the hearing.
    (2)   In such a case—

(a) he may make any such order before the hearing (or at the hearing), and

(b) paragraphs (4) to (10) of Article 8 shall apply accordingly.''

6. The following Article shall be substituted for Article 9 (later stages of trial)—

"Later stages of trial

9.—(1) Any party may depart from the case he disclosed in pursuance of a requirement imposed under Article 8.

(2) Where—

(a) a party departs from the case he disclosed in pursuance of a requirement imposed under Article 8, or

(b) a party fails to comply with such a requirement, the judge or, with the leave of the judge, any other party may make such comment as appears to the judge or the other party (as the case may be) to be appropriate and the jury may draw such inference as appears proper.

(3) In deciding whether to give leave the judge shall have regard—

(a) to the extent of the departure or failure, and

(b) to whether there is any justification for it.

(4) Except as provided by this Article no part—

(a) of a statement given under Article 8(5), or

(b) of any other information relating to the case for the accused or, if there is more than one, the case for any of them, which was given in pursuance of a requirement imposed under Article 8,

may be disclosed at a stage in the trial after the jury have been sworn without the consent of the accused concerned.''

Reporting restrictions

7. The following Articles shall be substituted for Article 10 (reporting restrictions)—

"Restrictions on reporting

10.—(1) Except as provided by this Article—

(a) no written report of proceedings falling within paragraph (2) shall be published in Northern Ireland;

(b) no report of proceedings falling within paragraph (2) shall be included in a relevant programme for reception in Northern Ireland.

(2) The following proceedings fall within this paragraph—

(a) an application under Article 5(1);

(b) a preparatory hearing;

(c) an application for leave to appeal in relation to such a hearing;

(d) an appeal in relation to such a hearing.

(3) The judge dealing with an application under Article 5(1) may order that paragraph (1) shall not apply, or shall not apply to a specified extent, to a report of the application.

(4) The judge dealing with a preparatory hearing may order that paragraph (1) shall not apply, or shall not apply to a specified extent, to a report of—

(a) the preparatory hearing, or

(b) an application to the judge for leave to appeal to the Court of Appeal under Article 8(11) in relation to the preparatory hearing.

(5)   The Court of Appeal may order that paragraph (1) shall not apply, or shall not apply to a specified extent, to a report of—

(a)   an appeal to the Court of Appeal under Article 8(11) in relation to a preparatory hearing,

(b)   an application to that Court for leave to appeal to it under Article 8(11) in relation to a preparatory hearing, or

(c)   an application to that Court for leave to appeal to the House of Lords under Part II of the Criminal Appeal (Northern Ireland) Act 1980 in relation to a preparatory hearing.

(6)   The House of Lords may order that paragraph (1) shall not apply, or shall not apply to a specified extent, to a report of—

(a)   an appeal to that House under Part II of the Criminal Appeal (Northern Ireland) Act 1980 in relation to a preparatory hearing, or

(b)   an application to that House for leave to appeal to it under Part II of the Criminal Appeal (Northern Ireland) Act 1980 in relation to a preparatory hearing.

(7)   Where there is only one accused and he objects to the making of an order under paragraph (3), (4), (5) or (6) the judge or the Court of Appeal or the House of Lords shall make the order if (and only if) satisfied after hearing the representations of the accused that it is in the interests of justice to do so; and if the order is made it shall not apply to the extent that a report deals with any such objection or representations.

(8)   Where there are two or more accused and one or more of them objects to the making of an order under paragraph (3), (4), (5) or (6) the judge or the Court of Appeal or the House of Lords shall make the order if (and only if) satisfied after hearing the representations of each of the accused that it is in the interests of justice to do so; and if the order is made it shall not apply to the extent that a report deals with any such objection or representations.

(9)   Paragraph (1) does not apply to—

(a)   the publication of a report of an application under Article 5(1), or

(b)   the inclusion in a relevant programme of a report of an application under Article 5(1),

where the application is successful.

(10)   Where—

(a)   two or more persons are jointly charged, and

(b)   applications under Article 5(1) are made by more than one of them,

paragraph (9) shall have effect as if for the words ''the application is'' there were substituted ''all the applications are''.

(11)   Paragraph (1) does not apply to—

(a)   the publication of a report of an unsuccessful application made under Article 5(1),

(b)   the publication of a report of a preparatory hearing,

(c)   the publication of a report of an appeal in relation to a preparatory hearing or of an application for leave to appeal in relation to such a hearing,

(d)   the inclusion in a relevant programme of a report of an unsuccessful application made under Article 5(1),

(e)   the inclusion in a relevant programme of a report of a preparatory hearing, or

(f)   the inclusion in a relevant programme of a report of an appeal in relation to a preparatory hearing or of an application for leave to appeal in relation to such a hearing,
at the conclusion of the trial of the accused or of the last of the accused to be tried.

(12)   Paragraph (1) does not apply to a report which contains only one or more of the following matters—

(a)   the identity of the court and the name of the judge;

(b)   the names, ages, home addresses and occupations of the accused and witnesses;

(c)   any relevant business information;

(d)   the offence or offences, or a summary of them, with which the accused is or are charged;

(e)   the names of counsel and solicitors in the proceedings;

(f)   where the proceedings are adjourned, the date and place to which they are adjourned;

(g)   any arrangements as to bail;

(h)   whether legal aid was granted to the accused or any of the accused.

(13)   The addresses that may be published or included in a relevant programme under paragraph (12) are addresses—

(a)   at any relevant time, and

(b)   at the time of their publication or inclusion in a relevant programme; and "relevant time" here means a time when events giving rise to the charges to which the proceedings relate occurred.

(14)   The following is relevant business information for the purposes of paragraph (12)—

(a)   any address used by the accused for carrying on a business on his own account;

(b)   the name of any business which he was carrying on on his own account at any relevant time;

(c)   the name of any firm in which he was a partner at any relevant time or by which he was engaged at any such time;

(d)   the address of any such firm;

(e)   the name of any company of which he was a director at any relevant time or by which he was otherwise engaged at any such time;

(f)   the address of the registered or principal office of any such company;

(g)   any working address of the accused in his capacity as a person engaged by any such company;
and here "engaged" means engaged under a contract of service or a contract for services, and "relevant time" has the same meaning as in paragraph (13).

(15)   Nothing in this Article affects any prohibition or restriction imposed by virtue of any other enactment on a publication or on matter included in a programme.

(16)   In this Article—

(a)   "publish", in relation to a report, means publish the report, either by itself or as part of a newspaper or periodical, for distribution to the public;

(b)   expressions cognate with "publish" shall be construed accordingly;

(c)   "relevant programme" means a programme included in a programme service, within the meaning of the Broadcasting Act 1990.

Offences in connection with reporting

10A.—(1)   If a report is published or included in a relevant programme in contravention of Article 10 each of the following persons is guilty of an offence—

(a)   in the case of a publication of a written report as part of a newspaper or periodical, any proprietor, editor or publisher of the newspaper or periodical;

(b)   in the case of a publication of a written report otherwise than as part of a newspaper or periodical, the person who publishes it;

(c)   in the case of the inclusion of a report in a relevant programme, any body corporate which is engaged in providing the service in which the programme is included and any person having functions in relation to the programme corresponding to those of an editor of a newspaper.

(2)   A person guilty of an offence under this Article is liable on summary conviction to a fine of an amount not exceeding level 5 on the standard scale.

(3)   Proceedings for an offence under this Article shall not be instituted otherwise than by or with the consent of the Attorney General for Northern Ireland.

(4)   Paragraph (16) of Article 10 applies for the purposes of this Article as it applies for the purposes of that.''

General

8.—(1)   This Schedule applies in relation to an offence if—

(a)   the accused is committed for trial on the charge concerned, or proceedings for the trial on the charge concerned are transferred to the Crown Court, on or after the appointed day, or

(b)   an indictment relating to the offence is presented on or after the appointed day under the authority of section 2(2)(c), (e) or (f) of the Grand Jury (Abolition) Act (Northern Ireland) 1969.

(2)   References in this paragraph to the appointed day are to such day as is appointed for the purposes of this Schedule by the Secretary of State by order.'

36.   For Schedule 5 substitute—

'SCHEDULE 5
REPEALS

1.   WAR CRIMES

Chapter or Number	Short title	Extent of repeal
1981 NI 18.	The Legal Aid, Advice and Assistance (Northern Ireland) Order 1981.	In Article 29(2), sub-paragraph (d) and the word ''or'' immediately before it.
1991 c. 13.	The War Crimes Act 1991.	Section 1(4), so far as relating to Part II of the Schedule. Section 3(3). Part II of the Schedule.

2.   SUMMONSES TO WITNESSES

Chapter	Short title	Extent of repeal
1831 c. 44.	The Tumultuous Risings (Ireland) Act 1831.	Section 8.

This repeal has effect in accordance with section 66 of this Act.

3.   ALIBI

Chapter or Number	Short title	Extent of repeal
1972, c. 6 (N.I.).	The Evidence of Alibi Act (Northern Ireland) 1972.	The whole Act.
1980 NI 6.	The Criminal Justice (Northern Ireland) Order 1980.	In Schedule 1, paragraph 61.
1988 NI 16.	The Criminal Justice (Serious Fraud) (Northern Ireland) Order 1988.	In the Schedule, paragraph 3.
1995 NI 3.	The Children's Evidence (Northern Ireland) Order 1995.	In Schedule 2, paragraph 6.

These repeals have effect in accordance with section 74 of this Act.

4.   FRAUD

Chapter or Number	Short title	Extent of repeal
1988 NI 16.	The Criminal Justice (Serious Fraud) (Northern Ireland) Order 1988.	Article 6(3) to (5). In Article 8(7) the word "(1)".
1990 c. 42.	The Broadcasting Act 1990.	In Schedule 20, paragraph 50.

These repeals have effect in accordance with Schedule 3 to this Act.'

Section 80   SCHEDULE 5
                                  REPEALS

1.   REINSTATEMENT OF CERTAIN PROVISIONS

Chapter	Short title	Extent of repeal
1994 c. 33.	Criminal Justice and Public Order Act 1994.	Section 34(7). Section 36(8). Section 37(7). Section 44. Schedule 4. In Schedule 11, the entries mentioned in note 1 below.

1.   The entries in Schedule 11 to the 1994 Act are those relating to the following—
    (a)   sections 13(3) and 49(2) of the Criminal Justice Act 1925;
    (b)   section 1 of the Criminal Procedure (Attendance of Witnesses) Act 1965;
    (c)   section 7 of the Criminal Justice Act 1967 and in section 36(1) of that Act the definition of 'committal proceedings';
    (d)   in paragraph 1 of Schedule 2 to the Criminal Appeal Act 1968 the words from 'section 13(3)' to 'but';
    (e)   in section 46(1) of the Criminal Justice Act 1972 the words 'Section 102 of the Magistrates' Courts Act 1980 and', 'which respectively allow', 'committal proceedings and in other', 'and section 106 of the said Act of 1980', 'which punish the making of', '102 or' and ', as the case may be', and section 46(2) of that Act;
    (f)   in section 32(1)(b) of the Powers of Criminal Courts Act 1973 the words 'tried or';
    (g)   in Schedule 1 to the Interpretation Act 1978, paragraph (a) of the definition of 'Committed for trial';
    (h)   in section 97(1) of the Magistrates' Courts Act 1980 the words from 'at an inquiry' to 'be) or', sections 102, 103, 105, 106 and 145(1)(e) of that Act, in section 150(1) of that Act the definition of 'committal proceedings', and paragraph 2 of Schedule 5 to that Act;
    (i)   in section 2(2)(g) of the Criminal Attempts Act 1981 the words 'or committed for trial';
    (j)   in section 1(2) of the Criminal Justice Act 1982 the words 'trial or';
    (k)   paragraphs 10 and 11 of Schedule 2 to the Criminal Justice Act 1987;
    (l)   in section 20(4)(a) of the Legal Aid Act 1988 the words 'trial or', and section 20(4)(bb) and (5) of that Act;
    (m)   in section 1(4) of the War Crimes Act 1991 the words 'England, Wales or', and Part I of the Schedule to that Act.
    2.   The repeals under this paragraph (reinstatement of certain provisions) have effect in accordance with section 44 of this Act.

2. WAR CRIMES

Chapter	Short title	Extent of repeal
1988 c. 34.	Legal Aid Act 1988.	Section 20(4)(bb).
1991c. 13.	War Crimes Act 1991.	In section 1(4) the words 'England, Wales or'. Section 3(2). Part I of the Schedule.

3. EITHER WAY OFFENCES

Chapter	Short title	Extent of repeal
1980 c. 43.	Magistrates' Courts Act 1980.	Section 19(2)(a).

This repeal has effect in accordance with section 49 of this Act.

4. REMAND

Chapter	Short title	Extent of repeal
1980 c. 43.	Magistrates' Courts Act 1980.	In section 128, subsections (1A)(c) and (3A)(c). In section 128A(1) the words 'who has attained the age of 17'.

These repeals have effect in accordance with section 52 of this Act.

5. SPECIMENS

Chapter	Short title	Extent of repeal
1992 c. 42.	Transport and Works Act 1992.	In section 31(4) the word 'or' at the end of paragraph (b).

This repeal has effect in accordance with section 63 of this Act.

6.   WITNESS ORDERS

Chapter	Short title	Extent of repeal
1965 c. 69.	Criminal Procedure (Attendance of Witnesses) Act 1965.	Section 1 In section 3(1) the words 'witness order or'. In section 4(1) the words 'witness order or' and (where they next occur) 'order or'. In the proviso to section 4(1) the words from 'in the case' (where they first occur) to 'witness summons'. In section 4(2) the words 'a witness order or' and (where they next occur) 'order or'.
1971 c. 23.	Courts Act 1971	In Schedule 8, paragraph 45(1).
1980 c. 43.	Magistrates' Courts Act 1980.	Section 145(1)(e).

These repeals have effect in accordance with provision made by the Secretary of State by order under section 65 of this Act.

7.   SUMMONSES TO WITNESSES

Chapter	Short title	Extent of repeal
1965 c. 69.	Criminal Procedure (Attendance of Witnesses) Act 1965.	Schedule 1.
1971 c. 23.	Courts Act 1971.	In Schedule 8, paragraph 45(2) and (5).

These repeals have effect in accordance with section 66 of this Act.

8.   PRELIMINARY STAGES

Number	Short title	Extent of revocation
S.I. 1987/299	Prosecution of Offences (Custody Time Limits) Regulations 1987.	Regulation 5(7).

This revocation has effect in accordance with section 71 of this Act.

9. ALIBI

Chapter	Short title	Extent of repeal
1967 c. 80.	Criminal Justice Act 1967.	Section 11.
1980 c. 43.	Magistrates' Courts Act 1980.	In Schedule 7, paragraph 64.
1987 c. 38.	Criminal Justice Act 1987.	In Schedule 2, paragraph 2.
1994 c. 33.	Criminal Justice and Public Order Act 1994.	In Schedule 4, paragraph 15(3). In Schedule 9, paragraphs 6(2) and 7.

These repeals have effect in accordance with section 74 of this Act.

10. COMMITTAL PROCEEDINGS

Chapter	Short title	Extent of repeal
1867 c. 35.	Criminal Law Amendment Act 1867	Section 6. Section 7.
1972 c. 71.	Criminal Justice Act 1972.	In section 46(1) the following words— 'Section 102 of the Magistrates' Courts Act 1980 and'; 'which respectively allow'; 'committal proceedings and in other'; 'and section 106 of the said Act of 1980'; 'which punish the making of'; '102 or'; ', as the case may be'. Section 46(2).
1980 c. 43.	Magistrates' Courts Act 1980.	Section 28. In section 97(1) the words 'at an inquiry into an indictable offence by a magistrates' court for that commission area or'. Section 102. Section 103(3) and (4). Section 105. In Schedule 7, paragraph 2.

Index